INVITATION TO ECONOMICS

INVITATION TO ECONOMICS

Understanding Argument and Policy

Thomas Mayer

A John Wiley & Sons, Ltd., Publication

This edition first published 2009
© 2009 Thomas Mayer

Blackwell Publishing was acquired by John Wiley & Sons in February 2007. Blackwell's publishing program has been merged with Wiley's global Scientific, Technical, and Medical business to form Wiley-Blackwell.

Registered Office
John Wiley & Sons Ltd, The Atrium, Southern Gate, Chichester, West Sussex, PO19 8SQ, United Kingdom

Editorial Offices
350 Main Street, Malden, MA 02148-5020, USA
9600 Garsington Road, Oxford, OX4 2DQ, UK
The Atrium, Southern Gate, Chichester, West Sussex, PO19 8SQ, UK

For details of our global editorial offices, for customer services, and for information about how to apply for permission to reuse the copyright material in this book please see our website at www.wiley.com/wiley-blackwell.

The right of Thomas Mayer to be identified as the author of this work has been asserted in accordance with the Copyright, Designs and Patents Act 1988.

Wiley also publishes its books in a variety of electronic formats. Some content that appears in print may not be available in electronic books.

Designations used by companies to distinguish their products are often claimed as trademarks. All brand names and product names used in this book are trade names, service marks, trademarks or registered trademarks of their respective owners. The publisher is not associated with any product or vendor mentioned in this book. This publication is designed to provide accurate and authoritative information in regard to the subject matter covered. It is sold on the understanding that the publisher is not engaged in rendering professional services. If professional advice or other expert assistance is required, the services of a competent professional should be sought.

Library of Congress Cataloging-in-Publication Data

Mayer, Thomas, 1927–
    Invitation to economics : understanding argument and policy / Thomas Mayer.
        p. cm.
    Includes bibliographical references and indexes.
    ISBN 978-1-4051-8358-1 (hardcover : alk. paper)—ISBN 978-1-4051-8393-2 (pbk. : alk. paper) 1. Economics. 2. Economists. 3. Economic policy.
4. Reasoning. 5. Critical thinking. I. Title.
    HB171.M4613 2009
    330—dc22

                                                                    2008030366

A catalogue record for this book is available from the British Library.

Set in 10.5/13pt Times by Graphicraft Limited, Hong Kong
Printed in Singapore by Ho Printing Pte Ltd

1   2009

To Dorothy

WARNING:
Reading this book may make you
a nuisance to your friends

Contents

Boxes

Preface

We live in an era of information flooding. Our problem is less how to acquire additional information than to distinguish genuine and useful information from its counterfeit. Accordingly, this book aims to make you a better consumer of information about economic issues by sharpening your capacity to distinguish the genuine from the counterfeit, or to put it less politely, to hone your BS detectors.

Standard introductory economics courses and textbooks try to teach economics by teaching concepts and theories which they then illustrate by concrete examples taken from everyday life, which are intended to illustrate and legitimize the theory. Some other books, such as Steven Levitt's and Stephen Dubner's *Freakanomics* uses less familiar examples, such as the behavior of Sumo wrestlers and the tendency of drug dealers to live with their mothers, to show how economics can explain all sorts of behavior that on the surface seems puzzling, thus demonstrating the power and reach of economic analysis.

This book follows a different tack. It emphasizes concrete problems relating to economic policies, many of them taken from newspapers, because its purpose is not to provide readers with an imposing theoretical structure and with refined technical tools, or to elicit a gee-wiz response, but to help them to think critically about the policy proposals that they will come across, and to locate deficiencies in arguments made for or against them. Such an ability to evaluate what one hears or reads *could* be inculcated by teaching a heavy dose of theory, but it can also be inculcated by teaching relatively little theory, and instead by developing the reader's intuition and common sense, and by instilling in him or her the habit of applying this common sense in a critical manner, and not to accept an argument merely because its conclusion is emotionally satisfying, or to reject it because its conclusions are unwelcome. It is amazing how far common sense, accompanied by a critical attitude and a willingness to think about a problem instead of jumping at an emotionally satisfying conclusion, can carry you in economics.

Such skill in locating weaknesses in arguments will come in useful in debating with those on the other side of economic issues. But I hope it will do more than this: that it will also make you aware of faults in some of the arguments offered by your own side, and hence more willing to grant that those on the other side are not necessarily in the grip of dogma, ideology, moral obtuseness, self-interest, or plain old stupidity. Many, perhaps most, of the economic issues being debated are not ones in which one side is obviously right, and the other obviously wrong, particularly if you make due allowance for the non-economic considerations that rightly influence our evaluations of economic policies. Hence, although some readers may become irate at my criticizing some favorite position of theirs, I hope that the book will help to calm down the prevailing furor of political rhetoric, and in a small way help to bring us together. In particular, I try to show that much of the disagreement on various economic policies is not due to a difference in values, with one side favoring what will help the poor and the other side favoring what will help the rich, but is a disagreement on the factual issue of what effect the policy would have.

I hope that this book will encourage you to be critical when presented with information and arguments not simply in economics, but also in other fields: for example, when confronted with yet another report stating that you should exercise, since a study has shown that people who exercise are healthier, you should ask which is cause and which is effect. Similarly, when reading one more breast-beating complaint that Americans, unlike others, have an irrational unwillingness to use public transportation, you might ask whether this unwillingness is in large part rational, given that the low density of American housing makes efficient public transportation less feasible in the United States than in other countries. Such skepticism does not require any specialized knowledge of physiology or traffic engineering, but merely a willingness to draw on the knowledge you already have. There is a field in philosophy called applied logic, and though confined to economics, this book is an attempt to contribute to it. Economics provides a convenient way of teaching applied logic because so many of the arguments on economics that one finds in the media are easy to knock down.

I am deeply indebted to George Lobell for excellent editorial guidance, many valuable suggestions, and detailed comments. I am also indebted for valuable comments on the manuscript, or on parts of it, to Facundo Albornoz-Crespio, David Colander, Brandon Dupont, Bonni Stakowiak, Peter Lindert, and Sherman Shapiro. But my greatest indebtedness is to my colleagues, alive and deceased, whose ideas I have shamelessly stolen. If there is any originality in this book it is in matters of presentation and emphasis, and not in the underlying economic analysis. Finally, I am dis-indebted to the brilliant folk at Microsoft without whose over-engineered Word program this book would have been finished sooner.

1

Introduction

There is no lack of information about economics. If you seek comprehensive discussions, there are textbooks, and if you prefer more specialized and scholarly analyses there are monographs and journal papers galore. If you seek information about the latest developments, there are numerous stories in the media, while TV programs, magazines, and books slake the thirst of those seeking advice on how to invest. And if you are after headier fare, and want to set your blood boiling, many editorials and magazine articles offer you harrowing tales about the stupidity and venality of the other side, and the wisdom and virtue of those who share your ideology.

1.1   What This Book Provides

This book tries to satisfy a different need: to enable you to keep your head above water in this sea of valid and invalid information by empowering you to spot naive and spurious economic arguments, that is, to become a critical instead of a passive consumer of economic arguments. Accordingly, it gives many examples of spurious arguments, and explains why they are wrong. (Box 1.1 illustrates how easy it sometimes is to spot inadequacies in a popular argument, if one just takes the trouble to think about it.) Its theme is that in much, though by no means all, of economics, a little serious thinking can go a long way. Although it focuses on only one subject, economics, its emphasis on thinking things through means that it could also be described as a book on applied logic.[1]

However, this book is not just an exercise in negation. It does present some economic theory, because that is needed to spot spurious economic arguments. But the theory it presents is not the structured and carefully explicated version

Box 1.1: Federal Funding for Stem Cell Research

When President Bush vetoed a bill to provide federal funding for stem cell research many people complained that this would obstruct the discovery of cures for many serious diseases. One may certainly disagree with the President's decision (as I do), but it is wrong to treat it, as much of the popular discussion does, as a fatal or near-fatal blow to such research. One reason is that firms hoping to gain lucrative patent rights could finance some of it, and so could charitable institutions and state governments, as California is already doing. But a more important reason is that the United States is not the only country in the world. Other countries, such as Britain and Singapore, are eager to subsidize stem cell research to gain a strong position in a promising high-tech industry. This does not mean that President Bush's decision not to fund stem cell research will have no effect. It will slow it down, since most of the scientists engaged in this research are currently in the United States. But, assuming that his decision is not overturned after the 2008 election, the main effect of President Bush's action will be that the United States will lose much of a new high-tech industry to other countries.

The reader may believe that all this is pretty obvious, and does not require any special knowledge of economics. But that is precisely my point. The pressure of media deadlines, the eagerness to score partisan points, and ideological blinkers hide many things that become obvious when one takes the time to think about them. And this book is intended to help you do so.

found in standard textbooks. It is a much less formal one, which tries to provide an intuitive "feel" for economics, something that economics courses often fail to do because of their strong emphasis on the technical apparatus of economics. Even those who have taken some economics courses will therefore find new things here.

In order to do that in the space of this average-length book, and to do it as painlessly as possible, I have avoided, where feasible – and that is in most places – theoretical concepts that would require elaborate explanations, and I have introduced as few technical terms as possible. You will not learn the lingo of economics here. For example, supply and demand curves show up only in an appendix that can be skipped without losing continuity. Introductory textbooks need an abundance of diagrams because these courses are intended to provide not only a general education in economics for non-majors, but also to provide the foundations that economics majors need for their more advanced courses. By contrast, I assume that readers of this book are not planning to take more advanced economics courses. And why put up a five-story scaffold to build a one-story house? Instead, I concentrate on basic economic logic. But making this logic part of someone's mental reflexes requires more than simply stating it in a persuasive way. I have therefore provided numerous examples. Proofs prove, but examples explain and convince.

Moreover, unlike writers of textbooks, I have felt no need to be comprehensive. Thus, except for a few passing comments, I have omitted macroeconomics (the part of economics that deals with recessions and unemployment, expansions, economic growth, and inflation), even though my own work has been primarily in macroeconomics, because macroeconomics requires technical apparatus, and provides fewer easy ways of demonstrating the theme of this book. Two additional reasons are the currently unsettled state of macroeconomics, and a wish to keep this book relatively short.

The research that economists, particularly academic economists, do is usually complex and mathematical. But much – though certainly not all – of what economics has to contribute to the outside world, its exports, so to speak, are ideas that are simple and intuitive, and do not require the mathematical sophistication that academic economists look for in each others' work. Even those with math phobia can read and enjoy the most renowned book on economics ever written, Adam Smith's *The Wealth of Nations*. The only mathematical background I assume, is that readers know how to add, subtract, multiply, and divide, and can look at a chart. Box 10.1 provides the only other bits of mathematics needed, except for the equation for a straight line, which is explained in chapter 13. And even these are needed only in very few places, which can be readily skipped. If Brian Greene could write a book on modern physics that has virtually no mathematics in the text it should be possible to do the same with economics.[2] This is not to deny that mathematics is immensely helpful in economics, but much of economics can be understood on an intuitive level without it. Similarly, I do not assume any prior knowledge of economics other than what you find in a newspaper.

Moreover, I realize that for most people, though not for me, the feeling of satisfaction one gets from understanding a subject is less for economics than for physics. And, being an economist, I know that if you offer something of lesser value you have to do so at a lower cost. The main cost of reading a book is the time and effort required. I have, therefore, made this book much easier going than the popular books on physics that I buy, try to read, and in good part don't understand. It is intended for the coffee break, not the coffee table. Such a book should be of interest to humanists because it deals, not with ways of making a killing on the stock market, but with the way human beings spend much of their time, and, in that respect, economics is a humanity.

1.2   Looking around Corners

What the book does require is a willingness to look beyond readily apparent surface effects for indirect effects, and at long-run as well as immediate effects; or putting it another way, a readiness to "look around corners," and to watch for the operation of the law of unintended consequences. That means recognizing that if the government adopts a new policy, not only will the target of this policy be affected, but so will some other conditions, perhaps in highly undesirable ways. For example, suppose the government requires airlines to install a costly new safety device that will on average save three lives per year. If your ethics tell you that saving even one life is more important than corporate profits you might be tempted to approve. But, when faced with greater expenses, airlines will raise fares. This will induce some people to drive instead of flying. And since driving is more dangerous than flying, the net result of requiring the safety device could well be more fatalities. Or, to take a more complex example: as explained in chapter 8, it turns out that a law giving artists a share in the capital gains obtained when their work is resold makes artists *worse* off. People often ignore such indirect effects and act like an inexperienced chess player who moves up a pawn to capture his opponent's knight, and does not consider that he will simply move the knight. Chapters 8 and 9 provide many such examples of how the law of unintended consequences frustrates good intentions.

Related to the pervasiveness of indirect effects is the pervasiveness of trade-offs. If you want more of one thing you generally have to accept less of something else; if you eat your cake now you won't have it tomorrow. Economists call this "opportunity cost." For example, watching network TV is not free; its opportunity cost is not spending the time doing something else, as well as letting ads induce you to spend your money inefficiently. One major function of economics is to point out these sometimes hidden opportunity costs – if we restrict imports we save the jobs of some American workers, but also reduce exports, and thus sacrifice the jobs of some other American workers.[a] This book will provide many examples of such opportunity costs.

Both opportunity costs and the law of unintended consequences are frequently ignored, and that is not surprising. People feel a tension between what

---

[a]   As we reduce imports American importers pay fewer dollars to foreign exporters. This reduces the supply of dollars on the foreign exchange market, and thereby causes the dollar to rise relative to foreign currencies. As a result, American goods now cost more in foreign countries, and foreigners buy fewer of them.

both their conscience and their self-image as decent people demand of them, and what their self-interest urges them to do. One way to reduce this uncomfortable tension is to follow the call of self-interest in one's own daily activities, and at the same time to support policies that promise to improve the welfare of the poor, or to curb the spread of sexual immorality, etc.[b] But for that to work one must believe that these policies will do more good than harm. And it is easier to convince oneself of that if one looks only at their intended effects and avoids searching for their unintended consequences.

1.3   Ideological Stance

This book differs not only from textbooks, but also from "advocacy books," that is, those books that try to persuade you of a certain political line. At their best such books can provide much insight, but they generally present only one side of the issue, and when not at their best they tend to insist either that a market economy is a virtually faultless generator of human happiness; or else, that the world would be a wonderful place if it were not for corporate greed. What I do advocate, is treating economic issues as grist for serious thinking, rather than as an opportunity to strike an emotionally satisfying posture. To be sure, a large share of the arguments that I question come from the liberal side.[c] But that is not meant to imply that conservatives are on the whole smarter than liberals; it is due to liberals advocating more policy changes than conservatives do, and therefore facing more often the temptation to jump from a desired outcome to the advocacy of some policy, without adequately considering its unintended consequences. And it is such jumps, whether by liberals or conservatives, that are the target of this book. My disagreements with liberals are primarily not with their goals but with the means by which they hope to attain them. For what it's worth, I have voted

---

[b]   No, this is not a matter of hypocrisy. Hypocrites lay claim to virtues that they know they do not possess. The people I am talking about do not realize that they are advocating certain policies primarily to make themselves feel good.

[c]   The terms "liberal" and "conservative" are slippery. They are not synonyms with Democratic and Republican or with pro-business and anti-business. Thomas Sowell (*A Conflict of Visions*, New York, Basic Books, 2007) provides much deeper definitions; liberals believe in the perfectibility of man and his capacity to reason, and want to change institutions to improve man, while conservatives don't. But since this is a book on economics my use of these terms focuses primarily on one aspect of this distinction: liberals are more inclined to favor government intervention in the market than are conservatives. On this definition, those who advocate favorable tax treatment for certain industries are liberals, not conservatives.

Democratic in most presidential elections. Within limits I am not opposed to helping the poor, but only to inefficient and counter-productive attempts to do so.

Here is an example. As I am writing this (July 2008) the sub-prime mortgage crisis has caused undeserved suffering for many people. I feel sorry for them. Yet I strongly oppose some policies that would largely alleviate their problem, such as Senator Clinton's proposal to freeze for five years interest rates which are set to rise on variable rate sub-prime loans. Such a freeze would send a message to potential mortgage lenders that making variable rate loans, or for that matter any, mortgage loans, has become riskier since in the future they may again not be allowed to receive the interest rate set in the contract. They will respond by charging higher interest rates on mortgage loans when they do make them. Another possible indirect effect of forcing lenders to freeze mortgage rates might be a significant fall in the value of the dollar as foreign investors come to believe that property rights in the United States are no longer sacrosanct, and therefore reduce their holdings of US securities and sell the proceeds in the foreign exchange market. Still another indirect effect, this one favorable, is that limiting the number of foreclosures would ameliorate the fall in house prices, and thus avoid or ameliorate what could become a serious recession. On the other hand, the losses lenders would suffer if mortgages are renegotiated would limit the credit they make available to other potential borrowers. A further effect is that bailing out borrowers would create expectations of future bailouts, and hence tempt people to take out mortgages on terms they cannot afford. And there is also the question of whether the government has the right to confiscate some of the lenders' property, because that is what reducing the interest rate to which they are contractually entitled surely amounts to.

Here is another example. In 2007 the Bush administration tried to reduce greenhouse gas emissions and oil imports (and thus oil prices) by requiring greater use of gasahol. In doing so it ignored two indirect effects. First, the production of gasahol generates more greenhouse gases than its use saves. Second, using more corn to produce fuel leaves less corn available as food, and thus drives up food prices. Poor people in Mexico, for whom corn is a major component of their diet, have been particularly hard hit, but a rise in corn prices increases other food prices too, as consumers substitute away from corn towards other foods.

Thus, the Clinton proposal, the Bush gasahol initiative, and similar proposals, have many indirect effects, and I cannot be certain whether their net effects are favorable or unfavorable. But what I am certain about is that one should consider such indirect effects before deciding whether to support or oppose these proposals. Fostering such a mindset is a much more crucial objective of this book than is the teaching of technical concepts, such as oligopoly, comparative costs, and regression coefficients.

Along these lines some readers, both liberals and conservatives, will find something disconcerting in this book. This is an admission of uncertainty and of the limitations of our knowledge. (The bumper sticker on my car says "Don't believe everything you think.") Since the 1990s, political partisanship has sharpened and we now live in an era of bad feeling. This book is a plea for open-mindedness and a greater willingness to see both sides of an issue. It tries to show liberals that free markets, by which I mean markets operating with only narrowly circumscribed government intervention (i.e., protection of property rights and prohibition of fraud, and perhaps of certain types of monopoly), are generally an extraordinarily efficient tool for enhancing productivity and incomes. And it tries to show conservatives that there are some situations in which government intervention enhances efficiency, and that, in any case, economic efficiency is not the only criterion by which to judge a policy.

All the same, regardless of whether you are a liberal or a conservative you can read this book without fear that it will sap your deeply held commitment on broad issues of economic and social policy, because these commitments usually involve much more than the considerations of economic efficiency that are the primary subject of this book. For example, you may discover here that a free market is much more efficient than you thought, but still believe that considerations of justice or of social cohesion – topics not discussed here – justify extensive government intervention. Or conversely, the criticisms of free markets discussed here may convince you that free markets are not all that efficient, and yet you may continue to be a stalwart supporter of free markets, because you believe that government intervention is even less efficient, or that it is an unacceptable interference with economic freedom.

1.4 Economics Embedded in Philosophy and Sociology

Since the nineteenth century, economists have striven to make economics more akin to natural science or mathematics This has led them to isolate the economic aspects of a problem from its usually less tractable ethical and sociological aspects. For economists, this shedding of non-economic aspects of problems has been a fruitful and convenient research strategy. But it does make things harder for general readers, whose interest in economic problems is part and parcel of their interest in the broader social and ethical problems in which the economic problems are embedded. And what makes this worse, much worse, is that economists usually do not tell them what philosophical and sociological aspects of the problem need to be melded with the economic aspect that they have studied. To avoid leaving the reader in this position I do pay attention to some controversial issues that are outside of economics. But since I can claim no expertise on them, and since there is usually no generally accepted answer, I merely raise these issues without pretending to resolve them.

1.5   My Own Biases

At this point I should confess my own ideological preconceptions, so that you can be on guard against my biases. I am a conservative in the sense that I accept the tragic vision of life, as set out, for example, by Thomas Sowell, a vision that quakes at the difficulties and dangers that arise in trying to improve the world. If you classify people into those who believe that every problem has a solution, and those who believe that every solution has a problem, put me into the latter group. I see most policy choices as requiring trade-offs, often painful ones, rather than as requiring only that one take an enlightened and morally correct stance.

More specifically, I believe in a free-market economy, but I do not *believe* in it. I recognize that it has some serious faults, and also that the case for it requires value judgments on which people may readily differ. My belief in a free-market economy is based less on a sunny view about how it works than on pessimism about the alternative, and on a belief that the best is the enemy of the good. Through the profit motive, a market economy provides a way, though admittedly an imperfect one, of communicating the wishes of consumers to producers, while communicating to consumers the admittedly imperfectly measured costs of providing various goods. For the political process to improve on it, would, in most cases, require much more knowledge than we possess, and also much less self-interested behavior on the part of those making the decisions.

Many eons ago some organic chemicals combined into living cells. Why should one expect that their descendents have learned to govern themselves efficiently? And if we cannot govern ourselves efficiently, shouldn't we limit the role of government? (This raises an interesting question about the culture war: shouldn't one expect Darwinians to reject the optimistic view of man, and therefore to settle for a market economy, and that believers in intelligent design and therefore in the perfectibility of man, should favor government intervention?) My conservative ideology is consistent with concern about the plight of the poor and with a wish to help them, but it is inconsistent with supporting policies merely because they are *intended* to help the poor.

Since one of the functions of this book is to interpret economics to non-economists I should also admit my biases with respect to economics. Most economists are what they themselves call "mainstream economists," rather than "heterodox economists," such as Marxists. And since I am in the mainstream tradition that is the type of economics I serve up. But I am critical of the formalist turn it has taken in the last few decades, usually associated with the much greater use of mathematics, and prefer a more intuitive approach that aims more for insight than for rigor. This will show up not only in specific comments I make, but also in what topics I discuss. Although, by and large, this book aims to present the common viewpoint of mainstream economists I have not tried all that hard to suppress my own idiosyncrasies.

1.6   What Is to Come?

Here is a brief description of what is to follow: The next two chapters (2 and 3) describe the field of economics. They discuss topics such as what economists do, the tools and techniques they use, and what economics can and cannot accomplish. This may help you to decide how much credence to give to the subsequent chapters, and whether to invest more time in reading economics, as well as what biases to watch out for.

Much of the prevailing confusion in discussions about economics and economic policy results from the use of vague or emotion-laden terms, and from the failure to distinguish between seemingly similar concepts, as well as from the misapplication of some concepts. Chapter 4, therefore, looks at some terms that are used in popular as well as in professional discussions of economics and politics, and shows how they can mislead, while chapter 5 discusses the often sharp difference between certain concepts that in many discussions are treated as though they were identical.

Another source of confusion is the failure to understand the principles that determine how resources are allocated, and how the prices of goods are determined. Chapter 6, therefore, discusses the price mechanism. The success of an economy depends in substantial part on providing the right incentives for work and risk taking. Everyone knows in a general way that these are important, But God is in the details, and these details are not so well known; hence chapter 7 discusses them.

With this background we are finally in a position to evaluate many debates about microeconomic policies. And, as chapters 8 and 9 illustrate, one can get far in doing so simply by using common sense to look for the indirect effects of some policies instead of jumping to *seemingly* obvious conclusions. Some of the issues discussed in these chapters are important policy problems, but some others are minor, chosen only because they provide a convenient way of showing how to apply economic reasoning. A reader who works through the discussion of these issues should be in a position to deal with many other economic issues as they arise – and that is the purpose of this book.

Contrary to the impression one gets from introductory economics courses, economics is not just "a bunch of theory." Most economists spend much the major part of their working time doing empirical economics. And although the category of empirical economics includes purely verbal discussions of historical events, the bulk of this empirical work involves numbers, and hence statistics. The economic arguments found in the news media, too, frequently rely on statistics. Hence, if you want to learn how to protect yourself from spurious economic arguments you have to know something about statistics. Neither blind faith in numbers, nor the mantra "figures don't lie, but liars figure" will do. Just like purely verbal claims, claims based on numbers need critical appraisal. And this is true also in other fields, such as medicine. It is, therefore, no wonder that *New York Times* columnist David Brooks advised students bound for Harvard to read Reinhold Niebuhr and Plato's *Gorgius*, to "take a course on ancient Greece . . . [and] learn a foreign language . . . spend a year abroad . . . take a course in neuroscience . . . [and] *take statistics*."[3]

This may seem strange to those whose interests are primarily humanistic. But it shouldn't, because what you have to learn about statistics differs sharply from what is taught in the formula-laden, math-dominated statistics course you may have been forced to take in college. These courses have to be almost entirely mathematical because their primary task is to teach you how to calculate various statistical measures such as standard deviations and regression coefficients. Here, the purpose is to get you to understand what these measures mean, what their limitations are, and above all how to differentiate between valid and invalid claims based on them. Focusing in these aspects of statistics, rather than on the how-to aspect, brings out the humanistic aspect of statistics. One important humanistic theme is the need to combine extensive and mottled knowledge and observations into a succinct and comprehensible theme, and another is how to draw conclusions as best we can from the incomplete information that we have. Behind its cobweb curtain of equations and mathematical proofs this is what statistics is about: inference under conditions of incomplete quantitative information.

And for that you need numeracy. Numeracy is not mathematics, you can be exceedingly good at it without knowing much math – and you can know much math without being numerate.[d] It consists of the knack of spotting when an argument based on data is spurious, and also the knack of drawing the sometimes hidden message out of sets of data – it was said about one economist, Nobel laureate Simon Kuznets, who was especially good at this, that he could "make the data sing." Former Federal Reserve Chairman Alan Greenspan was also a master at this. A third aspect of numeracy is knowing the approximate magnitudes of economic variables, such as GDP or the federal deficit. This book does not deal with the latter, if you want to know the GDP or the deficit, then look them up. Nor does it pay much attention to drawing subtle messages out of data, doing that requires experience as well as aptitude. But it does train you in spotting errors dressed in the garb of statistics.

Accordingly, this book has five chapters – albeit two of them short ones – on empirical economics and statistics. The first of these three chapters (10) is about reading – yes, plain old reading, but reading critically. Its two appendices show you several limitations of some sets of data that many readers accept as though they were unchallengeable "facts." The American public would be shocked if it knew how questionable are some of the data that provide the bases for certain important polices. It would probably be even more shocked if it realized that even with the best will in the world not much can be done about this.

The following short chapter (11) takes up two seemingly simple subjects, the meaning of percentages, and how to read graphs, and shows that they are not all that simple after all.

Just about all our economic data are samples, and samples can be deceptive. They may be too small, and they may be intentionally or unintentionally biased. So the next, short chapter (12) deals with these problems, particularly with biases in selecting the sample. The penultimate chapter (13) takes up regression analysis, the primary statistical tool used in economics and many other fields to connect causes and effects. This is inherently precarious because all that the data can show is the existence or absence of co-movements among

---

[d] Here is an example: to reduce their risks, financial institutions look for a set of assets whose values have in the past moved in different directions, so that their risks washed out. To do that, someone who is better at math than at numeracy will use a sophisticated mathematical model to calculate the correlation in the values of assets and stop there. Someone who is numerate may or may not use such a model, but will also eyeball the data to see if the negative correlation holds up in periods of financial stress when excessive risk may lead to bankruptcy, and is not just the product of the normal periods, which predominate in the data.

certain variables along with the nature of any co-movements, and the leap from co-movement to causation is dangerous.

At this point, some readers may feel like throwing up their hands and concluding that the potential pitfalls of statistical analysis are so great that it cannot be used to make an even half-way convincing case for anything. To show that such pessimism is unwarranted, the last chapter gives some examples of the successful application of regression analysis. The book concludes with a brief epilogue suggesting further reading.

One final point: like many authors, I think that everyone should read every word I have ever written, but I realize that this is a distinctly minority opinion. Accordingly, the book has a loose enough structure that readers can skip some chapters, and go on to read subsequent ones – except for chapter 13, which is based on chapter 12. I have also used several appendices and many boxes, so that it is easy to skip many topics.

NOTES

1   For a well-written introduction to that field see Jamie Whyte, *Crimes against Logic*, New York, McGraw-Hill, 2005.
2   Brian Greene, *The Elegant Universe*, New York, W.W. Norton, 2004.
3   David Brooks, "Harvard Bound? Chin Up," *New York Times*, March 2, 2006, p. A 29 (italic added).

PART I

THE SUBJECT OF ECONOMICS

2

What Economists Do

This chapter focuses on what economists try to do, on how they try to do it, and on some related characteristics of economics. The next chapter then evaluates how well they perform their tasks.

2.1   What Economics Encompasses

The most common definition of economics is the study of the allocation of scarce means and resources among our competing ends. But this definition is overly broad; for example, it includes a lot of what engineers do. Yet it does bring out that economic theory is a way of thinking that is useful in many different areas. Thus economists study not just the economy as usually defined, but also a wide range of other topics, such as the Neolithic revolution, which introduced agriculture, the optimal punishment for crime, the behavior of political parties, marriage and divorce, the time devoted to sleep, competition among various religions, etc. Moreover, both political science and sociology, particularly the former, have been strongly influenced by economic theory. Under the name "rational actor theory" they have imported the basic paradigm of economics. Economists have also made important contributions to history, showing for example, that the introduction of railroads had much less of an impact on the American economy than historians had taught us. Political philosophy, too, has imported ideas from economics.

And, in the natural sciences, economic theory has made major contributions to sociobiology and ecology, and has in turn been influenced by these subjects. Indeed, Alexander Rosenberg a philosopher who specializes in the philosophies of both economics and biology, believes that formal economic theory is of more use in biology than it is in understanding the economy.[1] Admittedly, that is due, in part, to his belief – a belief I do *not* share – that economic theory does not tell us much about how the economy functions, that it is better described as a branch of mathematics than as an empirical science.

A substantial proportion of economists work for businesses and governments. A glance at the professional journals of economists may seem to contradict this, because nearly all the articles are written by academic economists. This is because economists in government and business often work on topics that are of interest only to their employers, some of whom may treat their findings as proprietary information, and also because they have much less incentive to publish than do academic economists. As a result, economics has an academic stamp, with all the advantages and disadvantages that this implies. Introductory economics courses and textbooks, too, give a misleading impression of what most economists do, because their job is to teach the basic, underlying theory, and they lack the time to take up the empirical evidence that backs up what they teach. Nearly all business and government economists work on applying this theory, or more advanced versions of it, to practical problems, rather than working on the fundamental theory itself. And academic economists, too, spend much of their time testing various extensions of the theory. While the professional journals carry some purely theoretical and some purely empirical papers, the typical paper is one that presents some extension of the basic theory and then proceeds to test it. Economics is much less "theoretical" than most people think.

There is considerable diversity in economics. The largest group of economists consists of those concerned with using statistical techniques specially adapted to economics, called "econometrics," to test hypotheses and theories (two terms that I will treat as synonyms throughout this book), and to quantify them, or to forecast the course of the economy or the effect of certain policies. But there are also pure theorists, using the latest developments in mathematics to formalize some components of economic theory as abstract theorems. And there are Marxist economists studying the distribution of economic power among classes, feminist economists studying how the gender of economists affects the results of their research, financial economists trying to predict stock prices, and economic historians explaining particular historical events. In their professional tastes, economists range from those who delight in formal mathematical proofs of theorems to those who, like engineers, just want to get the job done, and if it can be done only in a rough and ready fashion, so be it. (See box 2.1.)

The two broad areas into which economics is divided are microeconomics, which deals with the behavior of individual firms and households, and

Box 2.1: Mathematicians and Engineers

A leading mathematical economist, Nobel laureate Gerard Debreu wrote in 1991:[1]

> In the past two decades, economic theory has been carried away further by a seemingly irresistible current that can be explained only partially by the intellectual successes of its mathematization. Essential to an attempt at a fuller explanation are the values imprinted on an economist by his study of mathematics. When a theorist who has been so typed judges his scholarly work, those values do not play a silent role; they may play a decisive role. The very choice of the questions to which he tries to find answers is influenced by his mathematical background. Thus the danger is ever present that the part of economics will become secondary, if not marginal to that judgment.

By contrast, here is an engineer, Warren Gibson, describing how to calculate the result of car crashes:

> Engineers like to linearize equations whenever possible because linear equation solutions are so much simpler and cheaper than nonlinear. But car crashes are highly nonlinear events and must be analyzed as such. With nonlinearity in the picture, the theorems . . . [that we use in the linear case] go out the window, as does any assurance of a unique solution. How can we continue in the face of such calamities? We just press on. If over time, certain practices lead to stable and verifiable results, we learn from experience and adopt those practices. Such attitudes give mathematicians heartburn, but engineers just shrug. Never mind the theorems; we have a job to do.[2]

While many economists lean more towards Debreu's position, others (including myself) prefer Gibson's.

---

[1] Gerard Debreu, "The Mathematization of Economic Theory," *American Economic Review*, vol. 81, March 1991, p. 5.
[2] Warren Gibson, "The Mathematical Romance: An Engineer's View of Mathematical Economics," *Economic Journal Watch* vol. 2, no. 1, 2005, p. 153.

macroeconomics which looks at the behavior of the economy as a whole, and deals with topics such as the rate of economic growth, inflation, and unemployment. But economists, like other scientists, are highly specialized; don't ask an economic theorist to predict next year's GDP, or a labor economist about taxes.

2.2   How Economists Work

Let us now look at various methods by which economists ply their trade, except for surveys, which I defer until chapter 10. Starting in the second half of the nineteenth century the main tool used by economists has been neo-classical theory. (It is called "neo-classical" to distinguish it from the "classical" economics inaugurated by Adam Smith.) This theory has focused on deducing the logical implications of a few "stylized facts" – that is, a few broad, more or less approximate, observations, such as that people try to maximize their incomes – plus a dash of introspection. This theory is at the heart of introductory economics and of much of the core course requirements in both the BA and Ph.D. programs. It is the theory that most economists reach for almost instinctively. Given the obstacles that economists face in making observations (see chapters 10 and 13) that is hardly surprising. It is also not surprising that as more data and new econometric techniques have become available, along with a vast increase in computing power, economists have become more interesting in measurement and in testing theories against the data. Similarly, as economic theory developed, and more and more of the implications of the few stylized facts had already been drawn, many economists have turned to psychology and sociology for additional observations that can be used to advance economic theory, and have also adopted the experimental techniques of psychology.

2.2.1   Neo-classical theory

Let's, therefore, look at the traditional and strong version of neo-classical theory. While some economists advocate this version, some others combine traditional neo-classical theory with the findings of behavioral economics and experimental economics discussed below.

Maximizing behavior: an overview

Neo-classical theory starts from the proposition that people try to maximize *something* (just what, we'll take up later) for now let's just call it *y*. Economists usually call it "utility" by which they essentially mean the feeling of pleasure you receive from a good or from some action, but if you like to think of it as happiness, or whatever else people value, you can substitute that for y. People are idiosyncratic, and like Jack Spratt and his wife, prefer different things. But that does not concern economists. Unlike psychology and sociology neo-classical theory generally does not ask why you enjoy one good more than another, and indeed usually deals as little as possible with utility in some absolute sense, focusing instead on people's preferences for one good relative to another.

And it does not classify these preferences and their underlying utilities as rational or irrational. If you spend every spare moment memorizing the name of every street in Chicago, because knowing that is the pride and joy of your life, most people will consider you crazy. Crazy you may be, but to an economist you are not *irrational*, as long as you have weighed the costs and benefits of various ways of memorizing these street names, and memorize them in the most efficient way available to you. How hard do you have to try to weigh them? Up to the point where the benefit of spending more time that way is no greater than the costs of spending this time.

The next step is to assume that people are rational in the sense that they can figure out which actions will maximize y, and that they then proceed to take these actions. Since an economist can also figure out which actions maximize y, then if she knows what the y is that people are trying to maximize, she can predict what they will do. To illustrate with an example from outside economics: suppose a hiker becomes lost and the other members of his party try to find him. They ask themselves, what is the rational thing for him to do, given the constraint that he does not have a compass and map (usually it is to remain where he is when he first realizes that he is lost, and to wait to be found), and assume that this is what he will do. Similarly, given a consumer's preferences among goods (that is, knowing her y), and the constraints (her income and the costs of various goods) we can determine what she should – and, therefore, will – buy. Once one knows a person's preferences and constraints, predicting her behavior just requires the application of logic, sometimes – but fortunately not always – in a complex and subtle chain of reasoning. Box 2.2 gives an example of how neo-classical theory, if used carefully, can explain what otherwise would seem the surprising behavior of a firm.

When applying this type of theory to specific cases we must be careful to make – when needed – allowance for special, local conditions, the same way as a physicist takes the existence of air pressure into account when she scurries away if a heavy block of lead is about to fall on her head, but not if a piece of paper is. An important part of the skill of an economist consists

Box 2.2: An Example of the Need for Care in Applying Standard Theory

It seems obvious that when competitors charging a lower price enter an industry the dominant firm in that industry is likely to lower its own price, and surely will not raise it. But sometimes what seems obvious at first glance, looks a lot less obvious at a second glance. Suppose that a patent held by a pharmaceutical company, Cure-it Inc., expires, and drug stores now stock low-priced generic versions. What happens to the price of the previously patent-protected drug? Suppose that there are now many firms producing a generic version, so that competition among them drives the price down to the point where it just covers the cost of production plus a normal profit, and also assume that the cost of production of the new companies is the same as that of Cure-it. Assume further, that although the generic versions are just as good as Cure-it's, some customers still prefer Cure-it, because they are not certain that the generic versions are really as good as Cur-it's. Since there is now no special profit to be earned by selling the drug at the same price as the generics, Cure-it has no incentive to hold on to a large share of the market. It is better off selling the drug at a higher price to those customers willing to pay more. As a result, it loses its price-sensitive customers. Since its remaining customers are people whose demand is not price-sensitive, it could, in principle, even pay the company to raise its price. Whether it does so or not depends, in part, on how price sensitive its remaining customers are.

of the ability to adjust general theories and models to deal with specific circumstances. Unfortunately, all too often we find out that we have to adjust our theories only after it turns out that our predictions have gone astray.

Just what are we maximizing?

For neo-classical theory to be useful we must be able to say just what the *y* is that people are maximizing – and it must be something specific enough that we can use it to draw meaningful conclusions. Just to say that they try to maximize "utility" and let it go at that, does not suffice, because, by itself, utility is so vaporous a concept that often we cannot tell what actions will maximize it. Economists, therefore, specify that a person's utility is a function of only a few variables; of just how many depends on the problem at hand. For many problems, one can take utility as depending only on the household's real income, because the other variables that determine utility can be assumed to remain constant, and hence are not relevant. For others, such as determining how taxes affect people's willingness to work, one must take into account that utility also depends (negatively) on how many hours they work. And when analyzing people's investment decisions one must consider their aversion to bearing risk. But how about the other variables that determine a person's utility, such as her health and her relations with relatives and friends? Usually these obviously major determinants of utility are unaffected by the particular economic activity being considered, such as buying good A rather than good B and, and in most cases economists can, therefore, ignore them.

What about the welfare of others? The story told so far, features a person who cares only about his or her own welfare. The most obvious objection to that can be dealt with easily, by thinking of the utility-maximizing unit as the family rather than as an individual. But we observe altruism also towards those outside the family; people do make charitable contributions. A sensible response is to broaden the concept of utility to allow A's utility to depend also on B's utility; in other words, to replace the assumption of selfish behavior with the assumption of *self-interested* behavior. The self-interested person is someone who has certain goals and wants to maximize the flow of resources towards the achievement of these goals. These goals can include a high income for oneself, but can also include higher incomes for the poor, greater accessibility to art for the general public, etc. But even when it is not a matter of their own consumption, everyone wants to be the one who decides where resources go. I know an economist who was prepared to become rather nasty when a trade association tried to renege on paying for a report it had commissioned from him. But when he finally got his fee he gave it all to a charity.

While substituting self-interestedness for selfishness makes economics look less cynical (but see box 2.3), and more importantly makes it more consistent with observed behavior, it does so at the cost of limiting what economists can predict. For example, if two equally convenient stores offer the same product at different prices, we want to be able to predict that the consumer will buy it at the cheaper store. But we cannot do that if we allow him to feel sympathy for the owner of the more expensive store because it is a local business. Economists generally finesse this problem. In principle, they do not deny the existence of altruism, but, in practice, unless the problem they are dealing with clearly calls for assuming not selfish but self-interested behavior, they assume selfish behavior because that simplifies the analysis. Given the small percentage of their incomes that most people contribute to charity, this is not entirely unreasonable, but also not entirely satisfactory.

Box 2.3: Is Self-interested Behavior a Vice or a Virtue?

We admire the saintly person who treats other people's welfare as just as important as her own. But do we want everyone to be like that? Perhaps; but perhaps not. Economies that have offered much scope not just for self-interest, but also for outright selfishness have done well, and a rising tide lifts all, well almost all, boats. Besides, all too often concern about the welfare of others carries with it an urge to tell them how they should – and, therefore, *must* – live. Moreover, a system of self-interest is not bereft of all moral standards. It requires the bourgeois virtues of industry, thrift, sobriety, and moderation. Thus, de Tocqueville described what he called "properly understood" self-interest, what is sometimes called "enlightened self-interest" as:[1]

> [A] doctrine not very lofty but clear and sure. It does not work to attain great objects, but it attains all those it aims for without too much effort . . . [It] does not produce great devotion; but it suggests little sacrifices each day; by itself it cannot make a man virtuous, but it forms a multitude of citizens who are regulated, temperate, moderate, farsighted, masters of themselves; and if it does not lead directly to virtue through the will, it brings them near to it insensibly through habits . . . [It] perhaps prevents some men from mounting far above the ordinary level of humanity, but many others who were falling below do attain it and are kept there. Consider some individuals, they are lowered. View the species it is elevated.

---

[1]   Cited in Gertrude Himmelfarb, *The Road to Modernity*, New York, Knopf, 2005, pp. 231–2.

For firms, it is much easier to specify what they maximize. They exist to earn a profit, so we normally take their profits as the y that they try to maximize, and we assume that – within reason – they are concerned only with their own welfare, i.e. profits, and not with other people's welfare. There is, however, the nasty problem (see chapter 7) that the incentives of a firm's managers are not perfectly aligned with its profitability, so that the firm may not always act in a way that maximizes its profits.

Governments present a messier problem. Despite the air of cynicism that numerous people put on, many people see the government as motivated by public interest. For a long time, economists did the same. But in the second half of the twentieth century a rival view developed that sees the government as maximizing the interests of its "owners," that is, of the bureaucrats, politicians, and special interests that control it. These two views of the government are not exclusive. Certain decisions, such as whether to adopt a restrictive monetary policy, may be – indeed I think they are – dominated by concern for the public welfare, while others, such as whether to build a particular bridge, may be motivated by the self-interest of politicians and bureaucrats, and still other decisions (a substantial majority?) may have both motivations.

Rational behavior

To base economics on the assumption that people behave entirely rationally, as neo-classical theory does, may give the impression that economists are building a Mcmansion on quicksand, that they are indulging in an "irrational passion for dispassionate rationality." If people are swayed only by rational considerations most advertisers and many politicians would be out of business. How then can neo-classical economists make such a silly assumption?

At one time, many economists argued that they had no choice: that they had to assume rational behavior, because, otherwise, how would they know which one of the vast number of potential irrational behaviors to assume instead? However, this defense has been greatly weakened by the rise of behavioral economics described below.

One remaining possibility is to argue that the assumption of rational behavior is not as unrealistic as it seems at first glance. Remember that, as already explained, in economics, rationality refers only to the means used to attain certain ends, not to the ends themselves. Second, reliance on habits and rules of thumb does not necessarily contradict the assumption of rational behavior. Indeed, it is often rational because it saves effort. Third, although in many spheres people do not behave rationally, they are more likely to do so in their economic behavior. In deciding how to vote people can easily afford to be irrational, because their individual vote is most unlikely to make a difference to what happens to them. But that is not so for their decision how to invest. Fourth, for many economic decisions you get relatively quick and reliable feedback – think of going to a new restaurant and not liking it – and that helps you to make the right decisions. Hence, even though not *all* economic behavior is rational, much of it is at least approximately so.

Fifth, one can argue, along Darwinian lines, that even if only a few people act rationally, they are the ones who will have greater economic success and, therefore, end up managing most of the economy's resources, so that for the most important economic decisions rational behavior is an appropriate assumption. There are, however, several problems with this argument. Yes, really stupid behavior will eventually put you out of business, but "eventually" may be a long time. Someone who bought stock in 1995 because little green men told him to, was richly rewarded for the next five years. Moreover, you can make money for a very long time even if your decisions are merely good, though not fully rational. And, as we all know, if not from personal experience then at least from observation, people can survive even if they make some really silly decisions. The same is true of governments, and – in the short run – also for firms that are wealthy enough to cushion losses or to live with profits that are lower than they could be. This does not mean that the Darwinian argument has no traction at all, but only that, though it is more than a weak reed, it is not a mighty oak.

A quite different, more subtle, and also much more general way of justifying the rationality assumption is to point out that for most (though judging by their practice, not for all) economists, rationality is not really a hard and fast *assumption*, but only a tentative conjecture. They try it first, and if it does not work: for example, if it leads to wrong results, they modify it by introducing some particular irrationality, such that, up to some point, people prefer to consume more today at the cost of consuming less tomorrow. Looked at this way the "assumption" of rational behavior (as well as the assumption of self-interested or selfish behavior) are not "assumptions" that anyone believes to be true. They are idealizations that purposely distort reality to some extent for the sake of tractability, a standard scientific procedure. And when dealing with actual problems they are often relaxed. Much of the work of economists in recent years – and much of the progress that has been made – has consisted of relaxing these restrictive assumptions. Those who criticize economics for being "theoretical" and using unrealistic assumptions so that it is disconnected from the "real world," are in most part unfamiliar with modern economics, and perhaps unduly influenced by the watered down version of economics that they were taught probably many years ago.[2]

Along these lines, many economists have adopted a much bolder and more general defense of the rationality assumption and of unrealistic assumptions in general. This is to deny that the realism of assumptions matters, and to argue that good theories can be built on the sand of unrealistic assumptions. Even though people make irrational choices, let's *assume* that they do not, and see if the resulting theory predicts correctly. If it does, the theory is useful, never mind its assumptions. At first glance that seems bizarre; we can be certain of the result of a syllogism only if both its premises are correct. But on second glance there is more to it – see appendix 2.1 to this chapter. However, if you do argue that it is the accuracy of your theory's prediction, and not the realism of its assumptions that matters, then you have to show *convincingly* that it does in fact predict well. Showing that its logical chain is valid and elegant does not suffice. Sometimes economists are too cavalier about that.

Thick versus thin theory

All in all, the neo-classical *theorist* – and we have been looking so far only at theory – works with a "thin" theory, and does not aim to describe, as someone with a "thick" theory would, the multitudinous feelings and mental processes that determine a person's economic decisions.[a] That she leaves to psychologists, sociologists, and to applied economists. Thus, an economic historian might discuss how the Protestant reformation affected mores in a way that facilitated economic growth, while an international trade economist might describe how changing attitudes towards globalization affect international trade. Neo-classical theory guides and facilitates work in applied economics, but does not restrict it dogmatically to rational behavior and given ends.

Such a division of labor may seem reasonable, but there is a problem. Mores and attitudes, such as moral constraints on "unfair" behavior, e.g., price gouging and cutting wages, as well as cognitive biases, e.g., inability to calculate probabilities correctly, could induce people and firms to act in ways that differ from what the assumptions of rational self-interested behavior predict. Here is where behavioral economics comes in.

2.2.2   Behavioral economics

Behavioral economists amend neo-classical theory in two ways. First, as already mentioned, one of the justifications offered for the rationality assumption is to argue that there is no feasible alternative to it. But, behavioral economists say, that although this was true at one time, it is no longer so. In recent decades cognitive psychologists and behavioral economists have shown that at least some observed irrational and seemingly unpredictable behavior is predictable after all, because it is systematic. For example, there is loss aversion – people are more likely to sell stock on which they have made a paper profit

---

[a]   Mathematics is the exemplar of a thin theory. It allows you to work with algebraic terms that may denote anything or nothing. History is an exemplar of a thick theory. It abounds in rich detail about specific people and events. For a strong criticism of economic theory as being too thin, see Daniel Hausman, *The Inexact and Separate Science of Economics*, Cambridge, Cambridge University Press, 1992.

than stock on which they have made a paper loss, even though selling losers would reduce their tax liability. Furthermore, though the old maxim "it's no use crying over spilled milk" tells us to ignore sunk costs, people often do not do that, and throw good money after bad. For example, they may continue to read a book that bores them because they spent good money for it. (*Note*: This is not a hint!) When a correct choice requires calculation involving probabilities, even well educated people frequently make naive errors. Moreover, people overestimate the future enjoyment they will obtain from material goods and underestimate the future benefits of social interaction, which suggests that they probably work too hard. And, as discussed below, laboratory experiments have provided many other examples of irrational, but systematic behavior. Box 2.4 provides a summary of the more important biases that behavioral economics stresses.

At times, instead of people's thinking governing their decisions, their decisions govern their thinking; if you are offered a risky, high-paying job you may take it, and then convince yourself that it isn't all that risky, so that you did the right thing. More generally, recent work in neuroscience has shown that our decisions are governed to a much greater extent than we used to believe by feelings, and not by rational thought. When making decisions the part of the brain that specializes in emotions and not in logical thinking is often the one where the probes light up.

Moreover, the human mind does not have the unlimited computing power that neo-classical theory sometimes attributes to it. We should think of people as acting with bounded rather than with unlimited rationality. Like chess players they cannot consider all possible consequences of all possible moves, but must rely to a large extent on rules of thumb and on their trained intuition, so that their decisions will frequently be sub-optimal. They do not maximize, but "satisfice," that is, make decisions that are adequate rather than perfect.

Many behavioral economists also argue that people's goals, and hence their y's, are not fixed, for example, that their aspiration levels change as their circumstances change. In particular, that people's happiness depends more on their incomes relative to that of their peers than, as neo-classical economics implies, on their absolute incomes. (More on that in chapter 3.)

Behavioral economists have also studied the effect of some social norms, such as the avoidance of price gouging. Surveys show that people deeply resent a store taking advantage of a special situation, for example, raising its mark-up on snow shovels after a blizzard. Such customer resentment, along with the merchant's own sense of fairness, may affect at least some prices. Perhaps this explains why there is considerable evidence that when suppliers

Box 2.4: Widespread Mental Quirks

Diane Coyle classifies the major quirks that behavioral economists have emphasized into the following six categories:[1]

1   *The law of small numbers*: People fail to make sufficient allowance for randomness and, therefore, tend to jump to unwarranted conclusions from a small number of cases. (More on this in chapter 10.)
2   *Confirmatory bias*: After forming a firm belief, people tend to ignore contradictory evidence, or even to misinterpret it as confirming evidence. (Academic economists are hardly exempt from this!)
3   *Anchoring*: When estimating some quantity we often tend to pick some number that is readily at hand, even if it is totally unrelated. One experiment asked students, who had just seen the spin of a wheel of fortune, to guess how many member countries the UN has. The spin of the wheel influenced their choice.
4   *Hindsight bias*: We tend to exaggerate the extent to which we predicted correctly what would happen.
5   *Bias in memory*: People overemphasize the relevance and importance of memorable and vivid experiences. We all know that traffic accidents occur, but we drive more carefully after just having seen one.
6   *Overconfidence*: Many more than half of us think we are above-average drivers. People overestimate the role of ability and underestimate the role of luck in accounting for their success.

And adding one to Coyle's list:

7   *Loss aversion*: We attach more importance to avoiding losses than to obtaining equally large gains – one study suggests a 2:1 ratio. This is so even for small gains and losses.

---

[1]   Diane Coyle, *The Soulful Science*, Princeton, Princeton University Press, 2007, pp. 130–1.

run short they frequently stock out rather than sell their limited supplies to the highest bidders.

While some adherents to traditional neo-classical theory treat the anomalies that behavioral economists have cited as special, unimportant cases that future research will show to be consistent with traditional neo-classical theory, or else, as a good place to deploy the fudge factor, behavioral economists take them seriously, and try to incorporate them into economics. In doing so, they break down the barriers isolating economics from psychology and sociology, and mine the rich lode of knowledge that these fields have produced.

But neo-classical economists can respond that they do so at the cost of introducing too much complexity. And further, since it is often hard to gauge just how important irrational behavior is in specific cases, behavioral economists also introduce vagueness and uncertainty, and thus limit the answers that economics can give. Moreover, some neo-classical economists have challenged the evidence that behavior economists have provided, for example, by demonstrating that some irrational behavior that behavioral economists cite does not show up among those who have substantial experience in that particular market, and are, therefore, the influential players in it.

To illustrate the debate between hard-line neo-classical economists and behavioral economists, appendix 2.1 discusses the behavior of the stock market. Can its fluctuations be explained almost entirely by rational behavior, or is it often driven by "psychology," so that we need to call on behavioral economics to explain it? And if so, shouldn't we use behavioral economics also in analyzing other markets?

Behavioral economics has important implications for policy. For example, on the one hand, by showing that people's decisions are sometimes irrational and contrary to their own interests, it weakens the case for relying on markets instead of on government controls. But on the other hand, behavioral economics also suggests that governments, too, act irrationally. Hence, in deciding, for example, whether to impose a new type of regulation on consumer borrowing, one factor we need to consider is whether it will reduce the damage due to the inefficient behavior of borrowers by more than it will increase the damage it will cause due to the irrational behavior of the regulatory agency.

2.2.3   Experimental economics

Experimental economics – that is, the study of economic behavior in a laboratory setting by presenting various choices to a set of subjects (usually students) – is not synonymous with behavioral economics. Behavioral economists have also looked at how people function in real-world markets, such as the stock market. And some economists who have used experimental methods have found results that confirm traditional neo-classical theory and not behavioral economics. But there is a substantial overlap; most of the evidence for behavioral economics comes from experimental economics, and most of the evidence from experimental economics supports behavioral economics.

A simple experiment might ask subjects to choose between receiving $10 outright or participating in a lottery that gives them a 10 percent chance of winning $101 and a 90 percent chance of winning nothing. If they don't care about risk they should choose the latter. And by varying the amount they can win in such a lottery we can see just how averse they are to risk. Much more complex choices between different types of lotteries have also been used. Other experiments have tested the consistency of preferences. The assumption of rational behavior embedded in neo-classical theory implies that if you prefer good A to good B, and good B to good C, you will also prefer good A to good C. But that does not always happen. Experiments have also provided much – though not necessarily conclusive – evidence for other instances of irrational behavior, such as an endowment effect, which is that the mere fact that you possess a certain good makes you value it more than you otherwise would. Moreover, experiments have shown that a person's preference for one good over another is influenced by what, in principle, should be irrelevant characteristics, such as how the choice was framed; for example, some people who prefer good A to good B will no longer do so when presented also with a third alternative, good C, that is inferior to B. Such a framing effect also showed up in experiments in which people were asked to quickly estimate the product of a set of numbers. Those given the numbers $8 \times 7 \times 6 \times 5 \times 4 \times 3 \times 2 \times 1$ came up with a higher estimate than those given the same series of numbers written as: $1 \times 2 \times 3 \times 4 \times 5 \times 6 \times 7 \times 8$, because they tended to calculate the first few products and then take a guess based on these products.

Experimental economics has not only questioned the rationality assumption of neo-classical theory, but has also raised questions about its maximizing assumption. In experiments called "ultimatum games" people are paired and offered a sum of money if they can agree on how to divide it between themselves, with one of them, the "proposer," making an offer to her partner, which he can accept or reject. If he rejects it, both get nothing. If they are rational utility maximizers, the proposer would offer only a trivial sum, say a dime, to her partner and he would accept it since a dime is better than nothing. Yet we find that proposers offer much more than a trivial share, though it is usually less than half the sum, and that their partners usually reject very small offers, thus implying that a feeling of fairness matters. Few readers are likely to find this so surprising, but it is not what neo-classical economics, at least in its simple version implies.

Testing, and when necessary, modifying, neo-classical economics is not the only use of experimental economics. It has also been employed to study how the market determines prices, and here it has generally supported the predictions of neo-classical theory. On a more practical level, it has been used to find the best way to organize auction markets, so that governments elicit the highest bids when they auction off Treasury bills or a radio spectrum.

But experimental economics is not without its problems. First, to keep costs down the stakes offered in such experiments are usually small, so that participants have little incentive to think things through. Perhaps if offered, say, $1 million, people would behave more rationally. But whether the size of stakes is or is not critical, is still a matter of dispute; there is some evidence that – at least within moderate bounds – it is not. A second problem arises from the Darwinian argument already discussed; that what may be true of the average participant in experiments need not be true of those who make most of the important economic decisions, so that the market as a whole behaves much more rationally than experimental economics suggests.

My description of both behavioral and experimental economics may have seemed somewhat disorganized, consisting of many individually reasonable propositions that do not cohere into a unified whole nearly as well as neo-classical theory does. And that is a major criticism of behavioral and experimental economics. They are primarily criticisms and qualifications of traditional neo-classical theory that have yet to be melded into a unified theory. Therefore, one cannot as of now reject the possibility that they will turn out to be mere fads.

Until recently, both behavioral economics and experimental economics were considered outside the mainstream of economics (which many economists, treat as a severe condemnation), but by now they have become highly respected. A recent survey of graduate students at elite universities found that almost a quarter considered reading in psychology and sociology to be "very important."[3] I doubt that, ten years earlier, as many as 10 percent would have said so, even though already in 1987 Herbert Simons had received the Nobel prize in economics for work in which bounded rationality played a large part. But when in 2002 Daniel Kahneman and Vernon Smith shared the Nobel prize in economics for their work in behavioral and experimental economics it was a signal that these subjects had arrived.

Although I am moderately enthusiastic about behavioral economics, there is little of it in this book. One reason is that, as I will try to demonstrate, applying the neo-classical maximizing model is often relatively easy and productive. Applying behavioral economics needs more specialized knowledge of when and how emotions, biases, and mental quirks affect behavior. Many problems can be solved without such knowledge, and those are the problems that this book focuses on. Yet I doubt that even fervent advocates of behavioral economics will find much here that they disagree with. The second reason is that while behavioral economics may be the wave of the future, I write in the present, not the future. It will take time before we have a mature behavioral theory of economics. At present, behavioral economics is – and perhaps always will be – a set of qualifications to neo-classical theory, rather than a comprehensive theory of its own.

One can tell a story in which economists first undertook the relatively simple task of developing a theory relying on rational self-interested behavior, which allowed them to answer, at least as first approximations, a surprisingly wide range of questions. Once that was done, they could switch their attention to extending that theory by introducing both irrational and altruistic behavior. But this is, as yet, very much work in progress. And, while it will probably supplement in important ways the material presented here, I am confident that it will not invalidate much of it.

2.2.4   Measurement

To say that science *is* measurement may be going too far, but surely emphasis on measurement is one of the main characteristics of science. If economics aspires to emulate the natural sciences, it must measure, both to test its theories and to quantify its findings. For example, saying that if x happens prices will rise, is usually not sufficient; it must say whether they will rise by much or by little, and, preferably, provide a narrow numerical range for the increase. Saying that cutting tax rates will raise tax receipts because it will induce people to work harder may sound great as a 15-second TV spot. But it will leave economists asking whether the tax revenue gained from people working harder will be large enough to offset all, and not just a small part of the revenue loss from cutting tax rates. If the term "theoretical" is used pejoratively to denote reliance on speculative thinking and a disconnect from the real world, then economists are much less "theoretical" than most other people when they talk about economic issues.

Measurement is a standard part of economics. Much of current work in economics consists of the application of econometric methods to economic data – chapter 14 will provide some examples. Ph.D. programs in economics require considerable training in econometrics, and most Ph.D. dissertations and papers in the professional journals of economics measure and do not simply theorize. Experimental economics is, by its very nature, about measurement, and behavioral economics is too, since behavioral economists have to show that they have found an empirical regularity that is inconsistent with neo-classical theory. The last five chapters of this book deal with measurement.

2.3   Some Characteristics of Economics

One justification for referring to a subject as a "discipline" is that there are certain presuppositions and characteristics, and yes, also biases, that most of its practitioners share and that shapes their work. Here are three characteristics of economics that I believe are easy to justify. The next chapter, which evaluates economics, takes up some more contentious ones.

2.3.1   Only individuals act

A basic presupposition of economics is its insistence on the obvious but easily forgotten fact that only individuals and not abstractions, such as classes, industries, or nations, can act, so that one must explain economic phenomena by the motivations and opportunities of individuals and not of groups. This explanatory strategy is not quite as obvious and trivial as it may seem at first glance, because people's motivation and opportunities depend to a considerable extent on those of the class or other groups they belong to. Sociologists sometimes, and Marxist economists usually, therefore, prefer the shortcut of looking at groups as though they were the ultimate actors. But they need to show – and may have difficulty doing so – that the group motives they talk about are somehow transmuted into the motives of the specific individuals who compose the group. This can happen for groups that share a common ideology or a sense of belonging. Feelings of belonging and loyalty are what matter here, because the sense of a common fate does not suffice. Suppose I believe that all economists will receive $1,000 if 90 percent of us contribute one dollar each to a lobbying fund. If I am selfish I will *not* contribute my dollar. Assuming that most others will contribute I can free-ride on their contribution. And if I am wrong and most economists do not contribute, I would be wasting my dollar. In game theory, which is much used in economics, this is known as the prisoner's dilemma. What is needed to mitigate such problems is a sense of cohesion, group loyalty, and fairness, so that the incentives of the group become the incentives of the individual members.

This distinction between individual motives and group motives is more than a theoretical nicety. Ignoring it can easily lead to confusion. For example, if a certain good is produced in only one country, say a certain type of coffee in Colombia, someone may complain that Colombia has a monopoly of this coffee. But Colombia itself does not produce it, some of its citizens do, and, if they all act on their own rather than collude, there is no monopoly. Similarly, though landlords as a group control all rental housing, unless they collude, they acquire no market power. More generally, whenever you hear that "they" do something, or "they don't want you to know" ask yourself who the mysterious "they" are, and whether the people who compose the "they," individually, have the incentive and the power to act as the story you are being told requires.

Moreover, since only individuals can feel pain or pleasure, most economists believe that it is only the well-being of individuals that matters. Although that seems trite not everyone seems to accept it. I just read an article expressing the hope that a certain primitive tribe in Brazil will continue to live its traditional life, and not succumb to civilization. I disagree. If – and admittedly that may not be the case – individual members of the tribe prefer living in cities, why object? Why subordinate their preference for a certain lifestyle to your preference for a greater diversity of lifestyles?

2.3.2   Models

All thinking involves a "model" in the sense that it implicitly or explicitly selects a limited number of factors to be considered, and then deals with their interactions. Even the simple act of seeing involves imposing a certain pattern, i.e., a model, on the electrical impulses the eyes send to the brain. In thinking about a complicated problem of any type, a common procedure is first to simplify it, solve for this simplified version, and then to stick the complications back in. Until this last stage, the process may look like an oversimplification. And if one forgets, as sometimes happens, to stick the right complications back in, it will be an oversimplification. When someone complains that a theory or model is unrealistic it usually is, or should be, failure at this last stage that she is complaining about.

Neo-classical economics – and most other economic theorizing – often, and in its advanced applications nearly always, involves an *explicit* model with a stated set of assumptions and more or less formal, usually largely mathematical, reasoning from these assumptions that culminates in carefully specified conclusions. Such models are like tinker-toy economies that are simple enough for our minds to manipulate, and yet contain all the elements of the real world that are relevant for the problem at hand. Their assumptions are set out at the beginning of the model (though, of course, not all assumptions can be set out – there are too many) and describe a hypothetical economy that has a limited number of components, such as consumers with known preferences for each good, and producers who beyond some point face rising unit costs as they increase output. The models then work out the consequences resulting from the rational interactions of these utility-maximizing consumers and producers. Box 2.5 shows a simple version of such a model.

Box 2.5: A Simple Model

Let's see how models are constructed by looking at a simple model of the price of a good. Since this price is determined by supply and demand, we can write the following simple expressions for supply and demand:

$$D = -aP + bX_D \qquad (1)$$

$$S = cP + dX_S \qquad (2)$$

where D denotes demand for the good, P its price, X_D all other factors that determine the demand for it; S the supply of the good and X_S all factors, other than the price, that determine how much its producers will supply, while a, b, c, and d are constants that, as will be explained in chapter 13, can be estimated from past data.[1] Next we rewrite (1) and (2) by shifting P to the left-hand side. and D and S to the right-hand side. This gives:[2]

$$P = -D/a + bX_{D/a} \qquad (1a)$$

$$P = S/c + dX_{S/c} \qquad (2a)$$

We now add the proposition that the market clears, that is, that the price settles at the point where demanders can buy as much as they want at that price, and sellers can sell as much as they want. At any higher price more would be supplied and less demanded, so that the price would fall again, and the converse holds for any lower price.

To put the model through its paces suppose that incomes rise, so that more is demanded. This means that X_d rises, so (1a) tells us that the price will rise. Or, suppose that production costs rise, so that X_S rises. Equation (2b) tells us that P will rise. All of this is of course obvious, but then this is a very simple model. To get results that are not so obvious we can estimate a, b, c, and d to see by how *much* prices will rise.

---

[1] If you don't like equations, here it is in words: demand depends negatively on the price of an item; that is, less is demanded if its price goes up, and it also depends on a set of other factors, such as the incomes of buyers. Supply depends positively on the price the seller can get for the good, and also on a set of other factors, for example, the cost of production of the good.

[2] To shift a term to the other side of the equals sign you just change its sign. And since in equation (1) P is multiplied by a we have to get rid of the a by dividing both sides of the equation by a. Similarly, in equation (2) we divide both sides by c.

These models distinguish between exogenous variables and endogenous variables. Exogenous variables are those variables whose values are determined by factors outside the model. We plug the values of these variables into the model to derive the values of the endogenous variables, that is, those variables whose values we want to find. For example, a model might take the income of the rest of the world to be exogenous, and then work out what will happen to the exports of China if it devalues its currency. There is nothing inherently exogenous or endogenous about any variable. It is the model builder who decides what to treat as exogenous. For example, a larger version of this model might include equations that allow for the effects of a Chinese devaluation on the incomes of the rest of the world, thereby turning this variable into an endogenous variable.

A benefit of explicit modeling is that someone who disagrees with the conclusions that a modeler has reached can see if her quarrel is with the assumptions or with the logical chain, and in the latter case can readily check who is right. A disadvantage is that an assumption that seems plausible when first stated might later be implicitly interpreted in a much stronger, and hence less plausible way. For example, the stated assumption might be that firms adjust their prices to equate supply and demand for their products. This seems reasonable, and hence the reader may accept it. But a few pages later it may have silently morphed into the assumption that firms *immediately* adjust their prices.

The toy economy of the model may look bizarre. For example, its consumers may have infinite lifespans. But if the modeler has included the relevant elements and abstracted only from the irrelevant ones (such as that consumers die and are replaced by their heirs), this model will work well; that is, it will mirror the behavior of the real-world economy with respect to the issue at hand, say, the effect of interest rates on saving, even though it would hardly be a good model for the purpose of estimating the demand for coffins. Arguing along the lines of appendix 2.1, the primary ways of finding out whether the model includes the relevant elements is to see whether it predicts (or post-dicts) well, or whether adding some omitted aspect of the real world significantly improves its predictions. If it helps us to make correct predictions or explains some interesting observed phenomena, then even a "weird" model, such as one with immortal consumers, is a useful tool. There is a saying "all models are wrong, but some are useful."

2.3.3   Consequentialism

Economists (qua, economists, never mind what they do in their personal lives) are consequentialists, judging policies not by the good or bad intentions of their advocates, but by their consequences. That seems like no big deal. Doesn't everyone evaluate policies by their consequences? Yes and no; just about everyone pays *some* attention to consequences, but many people, probably most, also take other considerations into account. For example, those who value sincerity and authenticity highly are willing to sacrifice some consequential good for the sake of sincerity and authenticity; for example, they might support a presidential candidate because they think he is sincere, even if they have some doubts about his policy.[b] And I suspect that nearly everyone abandons consequentialism at some point. Suppose, you are in a totalitarian country where someone who opposed the dictatorship is about to be shot by a firing squad, all of them excellent shots, so that each one is sure to fire a fatal bullet. But one member of the firing squad has failed to show up. So their commander, who is a stickler for correct procedures, offers you a deal. If you will participate and give your word to aim a potentially killing shot he will pay $5 to your favorite charity. Would you do it? After all, your shot does not have any bad consequences. (Saying you will just give the $5 on your own is not an adequate response because you could give those $5 in addition to the $5 from the firing squad.) Or, to take a more realistic example, wouldn't you be more upset to hear that a friend has been murdered than that he has been killed in a traffic accident?

In saying that economists are consequentialists I do not mean that no economist ever looks beyond consequences, but only that it is unusual. Nor do I mean that consequentialism is a theorem or an empirical finding of economics. It is a mindset, an underlying attitude, and an important one, since it induces economists to focus on the effects of actions rather than on motives. For example, economists (again, qua economists) are not greatly troubled by the fact that most of those who come to a devastated area, such as New Orleans, to rebuild it do so to make money, and not out of altruism. A nail pounded for the noblest of motives will hold up the roof no better than one pounded for financial motives. As George Stigler[4] put it:

> Why are . . . [motives] so important? Am I to admire the man who injures me in an awkward and mistaken attempt to protect me, and to despise the man who to earn a good income performs for me some great and lasting service? Oddly enough, I suspect that an answer is that motive makes a difference – that it is less objectionable to be injured by an incompetent benefactor than by a competent villain. But I leave with you the question: Are motives as important as effects?

---

[b]   Thomas Sowell (*A Conflict of Visions*, New York, Basic Books, 2007) provides an excellent discussion of the role that sincerity plays in two basic political ideologies.

This deemphasizing of motives is by no means beyond challenge. Someone might argue that paying attention to motives can make us morally worthier people, because it fosters a virtuous state of mind, and that is what we should aim for; or else they might say that virtue is its own reward.[5] Economists have an obvious bias against taking such arguments seriously since they diminish the value of understanding the economic consequences of actions, which is what economists have to offer. But even those who reject consequentialism as an underlying philosophy should pay attention to economics, because consequences, even if they are not the dominant consideration in every case, still matter.

APPENDIX 2.1

Unrealistic Assumptions Can a Good Theory Make

One way to justify the descriptively unrealistic assumption of rational behavior is to adhere to a school of philosophy of science called instrumentalism that defends the use of unrealistic assumptions. It treats scientific theories not as claims about what is true, but merely as instruments that help you to make correct predictions. And, if a certain unrealistic assumption allows you to make such predictions, then go ahead and use it.

One does not have to go all the way with the instrumentalists to argue that the validity of a theory does not depend primarily on the realisticness of its assumptions but of its predictions.[c] Take a trivial, everyday example: when taking a shower in an old-fashioned bathtub with separate hot and cold taps you have to adjust them so that the water has both the desired pressure and the right temperature. This requires solving two simultaneous equations. A designer of plumbing fixtures may be able to estimate with sufficient accuracy the wear and tear a shower head has to withstand by assuming that people actually solve such simultaneous equations, even though the assumption that everyone remembers their high school algebra is surely wrong.

We should, therefore, classify assumptions, not as being "realistic" or "unrealistic descriptions of reality," but as useful or as not useful. Theory is not

---

[c] I say "realisticness" instead of "realism" to distinguish this debate from the quite different debate about realism vs. nominalism in philosophy. With "prediction" I do not mean just detailed numerical predictions, such as, that GDP will rise by 2.25 percent next year, but also qualitative statements, such as, that if a country raises its interest rates its exports will be at least somewhat less than they otherwise would be.

intended to be a camera that records every detail, but more like a portrait that reveals the essence of the sitter. Reality is so multifaceted and fine-grained that no set of assumptions can be extensive and detailed enough to do it full justice. Once we think of assumptions in terms of their accuracy, rather than as being true or false in an absolute sense, we need to ask whether an assumption is sufficiently accurate for the purpose at hand. There is no way we can know this a priori. What we have to do is to see whether a theory based on it predicts and explains sufficiently well. In other words, instead of testing the theory by seeing whether its assumptions are realistic, we test the theory by seeing how well it predicts and explains, and infer from this whether its assumptions are useful. This implies that assumptions that work well for one theory, may not work well when used for a theory that tries to predict or explain something else. But that is not surprising; civil engineers can ignore relativity effects in their calculations, astronomers cannot; surgeons do not use kitchen knives and cooks do not use surgical scalpels. To be sure, the more widely applicable, and hence general, a theory is, the better. But all that means is that we need to judge theories by more than the single criterion of their being "right" in the sense of their providing the most accurate prediction.

This claim that we can confidently make assumptions that are false has led to much controversy, with critics claiming, for example, that it ignores the distinction between an assumption being merely an incomplete description of reality, and its being outright false. It is a fascinating debate, but this is not the place to review it.[6]

A somewhat different defense of the rationality and utility-maximizing assumptions is to treat them not as statements that purport to be about the real world, but instead as ways of organizing our thoughts and generating theories, that is, as the core of a research program that allows us to derive specific theories we can then test against the data. Regardless of whether people actually maximize in a rational way, as long as the research program of treating them as *if* they did, does generate more insightful theories that predict better than rival theories, then let's go ahead and assume that people behave that way. Deciding whether the resulting theories really are more insightful, accurate, general, convenient, and fruitful is, of course, a matter of judgment; but that is in the nature of theory choice, not only in economics, but also in the natural sciences.

One final point about assumptions: in economics many assumptions are just intended to be simplifying devices. For example, a paper on monetary policy may make the assumption that the United States is a closed economy with no foreign trade or international capital flows. This assumption is legitimized by an understanding between the author and the reader that, with regard to the particular problem being considered, adding foreign trade or international capital flows will not change the results, but would just make the algebra more tedious. Readers accept this assumption because their intuition tells them that it is harmless. This is an example of the type of tacit knowledge used in every field, which is not to say that it is always right.

APPENDIX 2.2

Is the Stock Market Efficient?

The stock market provides a natural arena for the clash between traditional neo-classical theory and behavioral economics. There has been much contention, long predating the rise of behavioral economics, between those who think that the market is dominated by the "fundamentals" of expected profits and interest rates, and those who think that "psychology" dominates it. Moreover, like the commodity markets, it is a market in which professional traders and sophisticated investors play a large role, and hence if rational behavior dominates anywhere it should be in these markets. Also, we have much better data on stock prices than on most other prices.

The story told by a straightforward version of neo-classical theory is that of a stock market in which investors are entirely rational income maximizers. Each stock sells at its appropriate value, which is equal to the discounted value (discounting will be explained in chapter 5), of its expected current plus future earnings. Rational speculators prevent its price from departing from this value, except momentarily, by quickly buying up any stock that sells for less, and dumping and selling short any stock that sells for more. (Selling short means selling stock you do not own in the expectation of buying it for less before the date you have to deliver it.) In such an "efficient market," as this is called, there are no bargains lying around for casual investors. Every stock sells at the price that is appropriate, given the available information. It would, therefore, be entirely reasonable for investors to select their stocks by throwing darts at the stock-market page of the newspaper. To be sure, some will make a big profit because they happen to be lucky, but lady luck taketh as well as giveth. Speculators, since they have to compete against each other, earn on average just the normal return on their effort and capital, while unusually prescient ones earn just a normal return for their acumen. Only those who happen to know something the rest of the market does not, or can guess better than others do, consistently make an abnormal profit, a profit that for extremely able investors can be extremely large. Other people, instead of buy-ing individual stocks or managed mutual funds with their high management fees, would be better off buying index funds. These are mutual funds that do not try to outguess the market, but hold all the stocks that are in a particu-lar stock market index, such as the S. & P. 500. Since they thereby avoid the cost of deciding which stocks to buy or sell, they charge a lower fee.

According to this "efficient market theory," apart from an upward trend, stock prices change only as new information about future earnings, or about the interest rate at which these earnings should be discounted, becomes avail-able. Old information, e.g., that yesterday a firm announced higher earnings, is stale information. By the time you tell your broker to buy this stock, the information has already driven up the price of the stock to its new, appro-priate level. That stock prices fluctuate only in accordance with new infor-mation, does not imply that they are fairly stable. Catastrophes, such as 9/11, major technological breakthroughs, major political changes, and newly reported earnings that exceed expected earnings can generate large sudden changes in stock prices, as can information pertaining to individual firms. But, according to efficient market theory, these changes will be no larger than what is justified by changing objective circumstances.

Is this how the stock market really behaves? To a substantial extent, yes. When new information becomes available, stock prices do change. But sometimes they fluctuate much more than can readily be explained by expected changes in earnings, or in the discount rate. On one day, October 19, 1987, a day on which there was no shocking news, stock prices fell by 22.6 percent. More recently, the dot.com boom of the late 1990s seems eas-ier to explain as the result of irrational exuberance and mob psychology than as the result of cool-headed, rational calculation. Moreover, looking beyond market averages we also find anomalies in the prices of individual stocks. A dramatic example is what happened when 3Com sold off part – but only part – of the stock it held in its subsidiary, Palm. The amount that investors paid for this Palm stock was so high that when the Palm stock that 3Com had retained is valued at that price, it exceeded the value of the outstanding stock of 3Com itself. At least at first glance this seems to suggest that the rest of 3Com had a *negative* value! Moreover, on average, during January, stocks of small companies rise more than stocks in large companies. Although this difference is less now than it used to be before this "January effect" became public knowledge, according to efficient-market theory it should have been virtually eliminated by now.

Traditional neo-classical economists can respond in two ways. One is to say that the behavior cited by their behaviorist critics is consistent with rational behavior. Thus 3Com may have been valued at less than the market value of its remaining Palm stock because, had 3Com tried to sell this stock, then its market price would have fallen substantially. And with sufficient ingenuity one can come up with some sort of explanation for the sudden falls in stock prices in 1987 and 2000. But whether these explanations are at all plausible is another matter.

Another, at least to me, and I suspect to most economists, more plausible explanation, is that the stock market is not the exemplar of a smoothly functioning market that enthusiastic believers in efficient-market theory claim. Many of those who hold a stock are reluctant to sell it when it becomes overvalued, either because they would be subject to capital gains tax, or because it would not be worth their while to keep up with the news that would let them know that it is overvalued. A smoothly and efficiently functioning market, therefore, requires speculators who can operate on a sufficiently large scale to make it worth their while to acquire such information, and they must have sufficient funds, so that when they buy a stock or sell it short, it drives the price all the way to its appropriate level. But there are often severe limits on speculators' purchases and short sales. To undertake large-scale purchases or short sales speculators might need to borrow substantial amounts, and may not be able to do that. And even if they can borrow enough, they run the risk that by the time the loan has to be repaid the price of the stock has not yet moved in the direction they anticipated, but has shifted in the opposite direction. Hence, even if they are right in the long run they face a substantial risk that to repay the loan they may have to take a loss. Aversion to such risk limits the role that speculators can play in "policing" the market, and keeping stock prices at the levels justified by fundamentals. That a certain strategy is bound to work if you just give it sufficient time provides little solace to those who do not have an infinite amount of time.

In addition, when a sophisticated investor sees naive investors bidding the price of a stock further and further up, way above the level justified by fundamentals, she may decide to buy it too, in the expectation that the naive investors will drive it even higher, thus allowing her to sell it to them later at a higher price. If sophisticated investors behave that way they are exacerbating, not reducing price fluctuations.

Traditional neo-classical economists can, therefore, respond to behavioral economists' criticism of efficient-market theory as applied to the stock market by conceding that the stock market is not always fully efficient, but, nonetheless, claiming that in *most* cases efficient-market theory does supply the correct answer. Thus, for most people, it is naive to try to beat the market: index funds are a more sensible investment for them than managed funds that generate high costs by extensive trading. Further, neo-classical economists can argue, certain inefficiencies in the stock market are due to the difficulties of selling short, and do not indicate a fundamental shortcoming in the basic rational, maximizing model of neo-classical economics. Moreover, while irrational exuberance and irrational pessimism may explain excessive volatility of the stock market, they are much less likely to show up in the markets for everyday goods.[7]

NOTES

1   Alexander Rosenberg, *Economics: Mathematical Politics or Science of Diminishing Returns?*, Chicago, University of Chicago Press, 1992.

2   For an excellent discussion of how economics has changed in that way see Diane Coyle, *The Soulful Science*, Princeton, Princeton University Press, 2007.

3   David Colander, "The Making of an Economist Redux," *Journal of Economic Perspectives*, vol. 19, winter 2005, p. 191.

4   George Stigler, *The Intellectual and the Marketplace*, Chicago, University of Chicago Press, 1984, p. 155.

5   Jean Anouilh's play, *Antigone* (*Five Plays*, New York, Hill and Wang, 1958) provides a stirring literary statement of the anti-consequentialist case.

6   For a brilliant exposition of this general approach (though only partially instrumentalist) that avoids the jargon and technicalities of philosophy of science, see Milton Friedman's *Essays in Positive Economics*, Chicago, University of Chicago Press, 1953, ch. 1. For a more recent discussion of this issue as it arises in economics see the papers in Uskali Mäki (ed.), *The Methodology of Positive Economics: Milton Friedman's Essay Fifty Years Later*, Cambridge, Cambridge University Press, forthcoming.

7   For informative and clear summaries of the debate about the rationality of the stock market see Burton Malkiel, "The Efficient Market Hypothesis and its Critics," *Journal of Economic Perspectives*, vol. 17, winter 2003, pp. 59–82; and Robert Shiller, "From Efficient Market Theory to Behavioral Finance," *Journal of Economic Perspectives*, vol. 17, winter 2003, pp. 83–104.

3

How Well Do They Do It?

What economics can do is straightforward; it can successfully explain and predict much of the behavior of the economy. In addition, even in some situations where economic theory does not predict well, it can still be useful as a normative theory, that is, as a theory that informs consumers and firms about what they *should* do to maximize utility and profits.

3.1 Forecasting

Critics of economics complain that: "economists cannot forecast." Is that true? No, it is not. And it isn't even false. It is meaningless. It is not even a grammatical sentence, because, although it has a noun and a verb clause, it has neither an explicit nor implicit object. What is it that economists cannot forecast? Is it whether the unemployment rate will be greater or less than 10 percent next month, or that unemployment in June 2020 will be between 5.53 and 5.58 percent? How far ahead must a forecast stretch, and how accurate must it be to be counted as a success?

3.1.1 Conditional versus unconditional forecasts

Two types of forecasts need to be distinguished: conditional forecasts and unconditional ones. The latter are straightforward statements that such and such will happen at a certain time. This is perhaps the most helpful type of forecast, and also the most difficult to make. Conditional forecasts, on the other hand, state that if x happens, then y will happen. That does not tell you whether y will occur unless you know whether or not x will. Unfortunately, economic theory allows you to make only conditional forecasts. For example, monetary theory tells you that if our central bank, the Federal Reserve, lowers interest rates substantially the inflation rate will eventually be higher than it otherwise would be. But to know whether the inflation rate will actually rise over the next two years, we need to supplement monetary theory with some theory that tells us whether the Fed will lower interest rates. And that theory, in turn, makes only conditional forecasts. For example, if, all of a sudden, there is a threat of massive bank failures the Fed is likely to adopt a new policy, one that the theory does not predict. This problem also exists in the natural sciences. If you heat a container of hydrogen, its pressure increases, but not if the container springs a leak.

The conditionality of a prediction is sometimes described by the Latin phrase "ceteris paribus" which means "other things being equal." Suppose my theory predicts that if the excise tax on beer is raised the price of hops will fall. The government now raises the excise tax, but, lo and behold, the price of hops rises instead of falling. Has my theory predicted badly? Not necessarily, because it is a ceteris paribus theory that tells us what will happen to the price of hops if the beer tax is raised, *and if nothing else that affects the price of hops changes*. But the price of hops may rise because a drought occurred. I can then defend my theory by arguing that, had it not been for the rise in the excise tax, the price of hops would have risen even more than it did.

Does the availability of this ceteris paribus defense mean that economic theories cannot be falsified because their ceteris paribus proviso gives them a ready escape hatch whenever the data refuse to confirm them? Not quite; for two reasons. First, to be considered useful a theory must be comprehensive enough that the disturbing factors that are held ceteris paribus are "outside" factors that the theory did not have to include. For example, suppose my theory predicts that a cut in the federal funds rate will lead to a permanent reduction in unemployment. But unemployment does not fall permanently. I cannot then wiggle out by saying that unemployment would have fallen permanently were it not for the fact that the inflation rate rose, because one of the known effects of a cut in the federal funds rate is to raise the inflation rate, and I should have made allowance for that in my theory.

Second, and more generally, if in many different cases the theory's predictions are falsified by subsequent events, and if all the ceteris paribus scapegoats that its proponents can muster provide only explanations that while not totally outlandish are implausible, then we should conclude that the theory cannot predict correctly, and should, therefore, be discarded. And even if the explanations are plausible, if they have to be invoked too often,

---

Box 3.1: A Warning about Ceteris Paribus

My breakfast cereal box proudly proclaims that: "research . . . shows that people who ate two bowls of Post Healthy Classics cereals each day, as part of a reduced caloric diet, *Lost 10lbs* . . ." (italics in original). Yes, they probably did, but perhaps so did people who took an extra sip of water each day "*as part of a reduced caloric diet.*"

Every empirical statement has an explicit or implicit ceteris paribus clause, so before accepting it ask whether the great exploit you are told about is that of the star who is given top billing, or of some poor extra imprisoned in ceteris paribus. How can you tell? By a mixture of common sense, tacit as well as explicit knowledge of the subject, and the application of a statistical technique discussed in chapter 13.

---

then the theory should be discarded, not because it is wrong – it may be correct – but because it is of little use. We want our theories to be not only true, but also useful in explaining and predicting observed events.

All the same, the ceteris paribus problem does significantly reduce the testability and also the utility of economic theory – as well as providing ill-intentioned people with a convenient tool (see box 3.1). But economics is not the only subject that has this disease. Even proud and majestic physics suffers from it and some of its hypotheses that work so well in the lab, where ceteris can be held paribus, do not work as well in the rough-and-tumble world outside the lab.[1] Admittedly, economics has it worse because economists are generally not able to state – and allow for – their ceteris paribus conditions nearly as well as physicists can.

3.1.2 Getting specific: forecasting macroeconomic variables

That many large firms subscribe to economic forecasting services suggests that economic forecasts, while far from being as good as we would like them to be, are also not useless. Moreover, even if forecasts of real GDP and the price level are no better than simply assuming that they will rise at the same rate next year as this year, this would not mean that economic theory is useless for prediction. Such forecasts are only a one type of prediction which economists make. Much of economics consists of microeconomics, and even within macroeconomics, much of the work of economists consists of predicting the effects of policies and of particular events, in other words, of conditional forecasts. More fundamentally, science is concerned not just with prediction, but also with explanation. Knowing why things happen is important, not simply for satisfying our curiosity, but also for practical purposes. To be sure, to validate explanations requires successful predictions, but a science is not required to be able to predict everything that we would like it to.

3.1.3   Forecasting asset prices

Economists are not good at predicting some variables like the stock market and asset prices in general, because, as discussed in appendix 2.2, efficient-market theory tells us that would require knowing something that the participants in these asset markets don't already know and have incorporated in asset prices. And since they can read what economists write, economists don't have much of an advantage over them. Just the opposite: professional traders have an advantage over most economists because they are specialists on a very narrow segment of the economy, certain speculative markets. So it is not surprising that most economists are not rich.

3.1.4   Predicting the effects of economic policies and of shocks

How about the effect of economic policies, or of a shock to the economy, such as a jump in oil prices? Can economists predict that? Again, the question is too loose. Is it asking whether economists can predict policy effects slightly better, or very substantially better than others can? Or is it asking whether economists can make completely reliable predictions? Moreover, what policies are we talking about? The effects of some policies are easy to predict, the effects of some others are not. And even if one could somehow refine the question in a way that resolves these problems, we still could not come up with a solid answer because, as already discussed, our *theories* make conditional, not unconditional, predictions. And if our unconditional forecasts go awry, the fault may lie with the assumptions about the behavior of exogenous variables that economists have to make to turn a conditional prediction into an unconditional one. All I can say is that the – admittedly casual – impressions I have gathered over many years have convinced me that economists usually – though certainly not always – predict the effects of economic policies better than others do. Obviously, I am biased, but perhaps not all that much, since I have spent considerable time criticizing some major tendencies in modern economics. I wish I could give a more satisfactory answer, but wishing does not make it so.

3.2 Choosing the Right Policies: The Problem of Value Judgments

Predicting the effects of economic policies is certainly useful, but the policy-maker who has to chose among policies needs to know more than just what effects each policy will have, that is, their *positive* aspects. She also needs to know which of these effects is more desirable; can economists help her in making the necessary normative judgments? If not, this would be painful for economists to accept, because they have been telling governments all along to adopt this policy and not that, and this, almost always, involves normative judgments. Essentially, all policies result in some redistribution of income, and the question whether one distribution of income is better than another is a matter of justice as well as of positive economics. And economists can claim no special expertise on what is just. Let's get more specific. An economist who stays entirely within her role as a positive scientist cannot advocate a policy that would raise per capita income by $1,000, if, in doing so, it would reduce the income of one person by $1. (See box 3.2.)

Economists have four main responses, none of which is fully satisfactory. One is to more or less dismiss the whole problem by saying that if we adopt all or most policies that raise per capita income, those who lose from one policy will gain from some other policy, so that, in the long run, distributional effects essentially wash out, while making all of us better off. That leaves me uneasy. Consider adopting a particular policy that increases average income by raising the aggregate incomes of billionaires by slightly more than it lowers the aggregate incomes of the poor, thus raising mean income. Would you really advocate this policy, or would you say that we should reject it, and just let the effects of the other policies we already have adopted, or will adopt in the future, take care of the averaging?

A second response is that those who benefit from the policy should pay compensation to those who lose from it. If what the winners gain is large enough so that they can compensate all the losers – and actually do so – and yet are still better off than before, then some people gain from the policy and nobody is made worse off. Such a policy is said to be a "Pareto improvement" after the Italian economist and sociologist Wilfredo Pareto (1848–1923). That works fine on the blackboard, but in practice, while one can often identify the major classes of gainers and losers, one cannot identify all the individuals who gain or lose, or find a feasible way of compelling the winners to compensate the losers.

Box 3.2: Justice

A leading political philosopher, the late John Rawls, told us:[1] "Justice is the first virtue of social institutions, as truth is of systems of thought . . . [L]aws and institutions no matter how efficient and well-arranged must be reformed or abolished if they are unjust."

I disagree. Suppose one person is unfairly derived of $1, but, as a result, everyone else's income goes up by $1,000. Would Rawls really have disapproved? Insistence that quantities should be entirely ignored when ordering states of the world by their desirability seems intuitively wrong to me, and I suspect to most people. We all agree that highway fatalities are a terrible thing, worse than *some* wasted time, but few would support a 3 mile an hour speed limit even if it would cut fatalities by over 90 percent.

Moreover, questions of justice are often difficult to settle even for disinterested persons, and it is sometimes extremely difficult if not impossible, to convince people that a decision is fair if they, themselves, stand to lose from it. (All I want from life are just two things: first, is that I am treated fairly, and, second, that I am the one who decides what is fair.) Moreover, questions of justice sometimes involve non-quantifiable matters, where one cannot just split the difference. Giving justice absolute priority, therefore, fosters strife, and surely harmony as well as justice is a desirable goal, and some trade-off is appropriate?

---

[1]   John Rawls, *A Theory of Justice*, Cambridge, MA, Harvard University Press, 1973, p. 3.

A third response is that a policy represents an improvement, even if no compensation is paid, as long as it raises the income of the gainers by more than it lowers the income of the losers. But that is just an evasion of the ethical issue; justice is swept aside.

A fourth response is to throw in the towel and accept that economics – by itself – cannot decide that one policy is superior to another. That still allows economists to tell policy-makers or the public that a certain policy raises per capita income by, say 5 percent, but imposes the following losses on the following groups, and then leave it to policy-makers or voters to make the required value judgment. Passing the buck to policy-makers seems reasonable. They, or those who appointed them, have been elected to make value judgments. In principle, that sounds sensible. But, in practice, there are problems. First, neither the policy-maker nor the economist will submit to this division of labor. Policy-makers may be too busy to articulate their normative judgments relating to all the numerous decisions that hit their desks, and may want their economic advisers to give them a simple "yes" or "no." Or, even if they have the time, they may be reluctant to make these value judgments, since they may not want to be aware of, and, hence, feel guilty about, hurting some people. They may, therefore, appoint economic advisers who, even if they cannot claim expertise in making normative judgments, make them anyway. Advisers are paid to make the lives of their bosses easier, not to present them with hard choices. At the same time, since economics is hardly accorded the same respect as physics, policy-makers are apt to substitute their own views of the economic consequences of various policies for those of their economists, either directly, or indirectly by appointing as their advisers, not the most proficient economists, but those who agree with them on positive as well as on normative issues.

Moreover, even if policy-makers were willing to make all the necessary value judgments, economists could not relinquish *all* value judgments to them. Some value judgments are inexorably bound tightly with positive judgment. For example, the economist's emphasis on the importance of the efficient allocation of resources, which surely contains a value judgment, is likely to influence his positive judgments, if only by directing his attention to certain problems and not to others: he is more likely to see and to stress the inefficiencies which a certain policy creates than any beneficial effects on justice or on social cohesion that it may have. Indeed, economists are likely to treat certain value judgments as so unproblematic that they will not even mention them to the policy-maker. One example of such a usually hidden value judgment is the consequentialism that is bred into the bones of economists. Another example is the premise that, other things being equal, making a person better off, as generally defined in economics – that is, as satisfying his preferences for more or different goods – is obviously a good thing. But that requires a value judgment that is far from trivial. If you doubt this, ask yourself whether you really want to satisfy the preferences of the sadist, the malevolent, the envious, the racist, the badly informed, the person who would like to impose his own lifestyle on his neighbors, or the temporary preferences of the addict. Some people might reply "yes," but many would not. Nor would everyone honor the preferences of a drunk who wants you to give him back his car key.[2]

More fundamentally, some religious and ethical leaders, e.g., Mahatma Gandhi, have built their systems on the renunciation of material wealth. One can argue that, ultimately, whether or not we want the economy to be governed by consumer preferences depends on the type of people we want our society to produce. To be sure, even a religious community or a warrior band wants to produce the goods it needs as efficiently as possible, but its economic arrangements may well be heavily influenced by its other perceived needs, such as keeping economic activity from becoming too important. The Spartans used iron money, not because they thought it efficient, but because its very clumsiness inhibited an emphasis on commercial wealth. I suspect that part of the reason why intellectuals tend to be critical of capitalism is because it caters to (they would probably say, "creates") tastes that they consider deplorable. There is, of course, nothing incoherent about believing that personally you should not put great emphasis on material possessions, but that the economic system should enable people who want to do just that, to go ahead and do it, while you and your friends pursue alternative goals. But this smacks of elitism and, hence, saying so, is unfashionable.

Even in our supposedly materialistic society we judge policies by more than their economic efficiency. For example, we do not allow destitute people to sell themselves into slavery, not only or even primarily, because it would make them worse off, but because we do not want to live in a society that degrades human beings that way. For similar reasons, rightly or wrongly, we prohibit the sale of human organs for transplants, a policy a number of economists have questioned because of its inefficiency and the resultant loss of human life. And we rightly hesitate to pass some laws that would enhance efficiency because these laws interfere with freedom, or ignore some people's rights, or are otherwise unjust (see box 3.3). Where to call a halt to the quest for economic efficiency and give primacy to other values is hard to say. For a long time, this question received little public attention, but now environmentalists have put it back on the agenda.

Fortunately, the problem created by hidden value judgments is not *quite* as bad as it seems. The reason why economic advisers should be forthright about the value judgments underlying their recommendations is that policy-makers may not share them, and may, therefore, want to reject their advisers' policy recommendations – which require that they know what these value judgments are. But many implicit value judgments, particularly some deeper ones, such as that it is desirable to make people materially better off, are value judgments that policy-makers share with their advisers. Hence, by combining these value judgments with their positive judgments their advisers are not inducing policy-makers to do something they would not do if they were aware of these value judgments.

One final point about value judgments. At least those of us who are not complete relativists read a person's value judgments as telling us something

---

Box 3.3: Efficiency versus Justice

After the unification of East and West Germany the Germans faced the problem that productivity and hence wages were much lower in the former East Germany than in the former West Germany. To maximize economic efficiency East German wages should initially have been kept near their lower level, so that East German firms would be competitive and West German and foreign firms would have an incentive to operate in East Germany. Eventually, the resulting increase in East German productivity would then have pulled wages up, but that might have taken a long time. In the meantime how do you justify paying an East German railroad engineer who drives a train from Dresden in East Germany to Hamburg in West Germany less than a West German engineer who drives it back to Dresden? The German response was to raise East German wages substantially, though not all the way, to West German standards. As a result East German unemployment has continued to be much higher than West German unemployment.

So, regardless of whether Germany made the right decision when it comes to choosing economic policy you should talk to philosophers as well as to economists. Treating economics as an isolated, more or less self-contained field is perhaps justifiable when doing positive economics, that is, describing the world as it is – but not when doing normative economics, that is, making judgments about what should be done.

---

about his or her moral standing. If someone tells you that he feels no guilt about driving an SUV because he is only concerned with his own welfare and not with the welfare of others, you are likely to consider him an immoral person. But if he tells you that he feels no guilt because he believes that global warming will do more good than harm, you may consider him totally mistaken, but not immoral. Positive judgments like this may tell you something about a person's knowledge or intelligence, but not about his decency.

3.3 Implementing Economic Policies

Suppose economic theory tells us unequivocally that a certain policy to which there is no ethical objection would raise income – if efficiently administered. That qualification could be enough to kill it. Here is an example: in the 1970s many savings and loans failed because they were legally restricted to making mainly long-term, fixed-rate mortgage loans, while their funds came primarily from short-term deposits. As interest rates rose in the 1960s and 1970s receipts from their loans made at the previous, lower interest rates did not keep up with the interest rate they now had to pay to depositors. We economists offered a solution: allow them to make all sorts of loans, including short-term loans, and variable-rate mortgage loans. That recommendation was accepted, and yes, it solved the problem. But in doing so it created another problem. Fly-by-night operators could buy a near-bankrupt savings and loans cheaply and, given the freedom to make all sorts of loans, use its funds to make fraudulent loans to corporations they controlled. Now it became fraud rather than rising interest rates that caused massive failures. If we economists considered this problem at all, and I suspect few of us did, we thought that the legal system could control such fraud. We were wrong (mea culpa). Here is another example: in the 1990s nearly all economists dealing with the issue were united in recommending to less developed countries that they open up their capital markets to foreign investors. Many did, and suffered a financial crisis. We had wrongly assumed that their governments could regulate their banks effectively. To be sure, this does not mean that all government policies or policies advocated by economists land up doing great harm, but sometimes it does happen, and it is worth watching out for.

The moral of this tale is something that should be obvious, but that economists tend to neglect: choosing the right economic policy frequently requires the skills of political scientists and lawyers and not just of economists. So, before accepting the policy recommendations of economists, ask yourself whether we can administer the policy efficiently.

Also ask yourself whether the policy will avoid the serious distortions in its operations that the political process is likely to generate. A government program may be cost-effective and desirable if, as originally intended, its benefits go primarily to the poor. But, once it is put into effect, there will be pressure from potential, but under the current law, ineligible, beneficiaries, and from the bureaucracy that administers it and wants to see it enlarged, from its congressional sponsors, and from enthusiasts among the public, to extend it to those who are not poor. Constituencies create programs, and programs, in turn, create bigger constituencies, and these then have the political muscle to enlarge the program, thus creating still bigger constituencies. Some slopes are slippery.

3.4　Biases

Are economists likely to give biased advice? Yes, of course, they are, and so are members of other professions. Part of this bias is due to self-selection.

Those who become economists are likely to have at least somewhat different values than do other people, and to let these value judgments influence their advice. Another part is due to the socialization into the culture of one's profession that is such a significant part of graduate training. These biases should be brought into the open. This section deals with ones that relate to economics as a whole; the following section deals with a few that are specific to some economists.

One obvious bias is that economists, like other specialists, overvalue what their profession has to offer, and hence devalue the contributions and interests of others.[a] Economists, therefore, seek an economic explanation for phenomena which others seek to explain as political, cultural, etc. Some examples of this are economic theories of marriage, crime, addiction, and time allocation. It is writ in the credo of neo-classical economists (though not of behavioral economists) that if something can possibly be explained as the product of economic factors, such as prices and incomes, and can also be explained by, say, sociological factors, the economic explanation is to be preferred. For example, my dentist reminds me to floss. Why does he do that since the more cavities I get, the more he earns? A sociological, or for that matter a commonsense, explanation is that he has been socialized into the belief that dental hygiene is important, and is fulfilling his professional obligation. An economist's explanation is that he is trying to maximize his income by enhancing my trust in him, and thus reduce the probability that I will switch dentists. Such a preference for economic explanations can be rationalized – though only to some extent – by the argument that economics is the most advanced of the social sciences, and hence offers the most trustworthy explanations. However, this is a weak argument because, while an economic explanation may, therefore, be more coherent and rigorous, the phenomenon itself does not know that, and may be grounded in sociological and not in economic factors.

Another bias is that economists look for explanations that allow them to show their virtuosity by employing the complex, usually mathematical, tools they have (sometimes painfully) acquired. If you have just been given a hammer, the entire world looks like nails. Economists also have some

---

[a] Rebecca Blank (in R. Blank and W. McGurn, *Is the Market Moral?*, Washington, DC, Brookings Institution, 2004, p. 91) tells the following delightful story of what happened when an economist-colleague casually asked her what she was working on: "In an unguarded moment . . . I replied, 'I am writing a series of essays on the interconnections between economics and Christian faith' . . . He physically backed away from me several steps, narrowed his eyes suspiciously, and demanded, 'Why would you want to do that?' "

(fortunately limited) tendency to give preference to theories that can be rigorously explicated, even if they do not perform all that well on statistical tests, over less rigorous theories that perform better on these tests. Given the weakness of the available statistical data and methods (see chapters 10–13) this is not entirely unreasonable. They have also felt strongly impelled to give economics the authority of a science, and thus to claim superiority over the large number of people who express strong opinions about economic issues which they have not studied *scientifically* (see box 3.4). A related bias is that economists tend to deemphasize short-run effects because economic theory is much better at explaining the long run rather than the short run. Thus, economists may argue that a firm's power to raise prices, if exercised, will soon disappear as other firms enter its market and, therefore, makes little difference on the whole. But practical people see things differently. If I can make lots of money for, say, two years, that's great, even if I earn just a normal profit after that. (A warning to the reader: many of my colleagues would strongly disagree with this paragraph, and treat such biases as unimportant.)

There may also be some ideological bias. Some on the left complain that economists have sold out to business, while some on the right complain that academic economists are a bunch of left radicals poisoning the minds of innocent students. A recent study found that 34.3 percent of academic

---

Box 3.4: Is Economics a Science?

Mainstream economists proudly proclaim economics to be a science, while many critics of mainstream economics (and this includes some heterodox economists) deny it scientific status. Who is right? It seems to me that, if one wants to be hard-nosed about it, neither one is: that one cannot say whether or not economics is a science, and that if one could, it would not matter what the answer is.

Deciding whether economics is a science would require a criterion for demarking science from other knowledge, and we don't have such a criterion. In the first half of the twentieth century we thought we had one: falsifiability by empirical evidence. But that idea fell apart. Currently, many philosophers believe that the search for a demarcation criterion is futile, that there is a continuum stretching from the way we decide questions of everyday life to the way physicists work, and that there is no convenient point at which to draw the line between science and non-science. Other languages, such as German, get along very well without it. Thus, the German term

"Wissenschaft," includes subjects like philosophy and art history along with the natural sciences. A separate term "Naturwissenschaften" then distinguishes the latter from the humanistic sciences, "Geisteswissenschaften" and from the social sciences, "Sozialwissenschaften."

But suppose we could somehow find a way of deciding whether economics is a science; what good would it do? It would not tell us how much credence to give to economics, because credibility is not all that closely related to scientific status. It is much more likely that next year I will read an article that will make me abandon my belief in the current scientific consensus that the universe is between ten and twenty billion years old, than that something will persuade me to abandon my belief that sadism is evil.

If one is less hard-nosed and settle for a relaxed standard of what is science, then economics is a science. As Diane Coyle explains:

> Economics is a science not because it mimics the same specific techniques or equations as natural scientists, nor because it consists of falsifiable statements, . . . but because it tries to model human behavior in general statements (or equations) with relatively few variables, and seeks to bring the model face to face with empirical evidence. Its scientific method is similar to the approach taken in other largely non-experimental sciences such as evolutionary biology or geology.[1]

Perhaps the best solution is to use the term "science" in its broader sense of systematized specialized knowledge, as in German and French (and in English into the nineteenth century), and, if so, economics is clearly a science. The energy saved by not debating whether economics is inherently a science in the narrower sense of the term, could then be used to see to what extent economists behave in accordance with the scientific ethos, that is, evaluate evidence in a disinterested way, be ready to abandon previously held convictions when the evidence requires it, and, in general, be more interested in establishing the truth than in building their reputations. But here, too, there are problems. Surely not all natural scientists live up to these high ideals, and while I *suspect* that economists do so less than do natural scientists, it is hard to determine to what extent, if any, that is so. And by how much the failure to live up to the scientific ideal reduces the validity of the results obtained is also hard to determine.

One final point: the use of mathematics is not an adequate criterion for distinguishing science from non-science – astrologers, too, use mathematics.

---

[1] Diane Coyle, *The Soulful Science*, Princeton, Princeton University Press, 2007, p. 237.

economists classified themselves as Democrats, 37.1 as independents and 28.6 percent as Republicans, which makes economists more moderate than most other academics.[3] The results of a survey shown in appendix 3.1 also suggest moderation. And so does a survey of economics graduate students at seven leading universities.[4] It found that 47 percent classified themselves as liberals, 24 percent as moderates, 16 percent as conservatives, 6 percent as radicals, with another 6 percent stating that politics was not important to them. Graduate study seems to have made these students more conservative; 10 percent of the first-year students called themselves conservative, while 23 percent of the fourth- and higher-year students did. One part, but only a part, of the explanation for this change might be that the training of economists, which centers on understanding how a free market operates, may predispose them to prefer it over government regulation, since the greater the role of free markets, the more valuable their knowledge is. But there is a counter-acting factor. Because we know more about markets than about government regulation, more of this training focuses on how and why actual markets differ from idealized markets, than on how actual regulations differ from ideal regulations, and that may swing some students towards liberalism.

The left-wing charge that academic economists have sold out to business is implausible, if only because you can sell only what someone else is willing to buy. Perhaps because they don't take us academic economists all that seriously, few, if any, business interests try to bribe us. And when a firm hires an economic consultant it is usually interested in how well she can forecast, not in who she voted for. To be sure, there are some foundations that sponsor conservative research, but there are also ones that sponsor liberal research. Given the predominance of liberals over conservatives in the better economics departments, an ambitious academic careerist who wants to move into a better department is, if anything, somewhat better off as a liberal than as a pro-business advocate.

Bias among economists can also result from trying to influence policy. Suppose you believe (rightly I think) that industrial policy, that is, the government attempts to pick certain industries as future winners that should be subsidized, is likely to be unsuccessful. To avoid "confusing" the public you are then tempted to deny that there have been any cases in which this policy has succeeded, even if you can think of one or two such cases where it was at least partially successful. The more one wants to improve the world, the harder it is to stay honest.

I have left to the last a probably much more serious bias. It arises because the aim of most applied economics is to enhance the economy's efficiency, and thus raise per capita income. This being what they are trained to do, economists overvalue the contribution that efficiency, in particular the allocation of productive resources to their highest-value ends, makes to the good society. To be sure, in talking about GDP in introductory courses, teachers spend some time explaining why it does not accurately measure true welfare, but in their day-to-day thinking they are likely to emphasize, if only by the topics they pick for their teaching and research, the importance of getting rid of inefficient policies and eliminating market failures that reduce income. If confronted with Oliver Goldsmith's classic lines: "Woe to the land, to hast'ning ills a prey/Where wealth accumulates and men decay," they may agree, in principle, or they may respond by saying that rising wealth causes men to improve rather than decay, but, in their day-to-day thinking, most of them are likely to be more than somewhat reluctant to make efficiency merely one of several goals.

This emphasis on economic efficiency and the resultant growth has been challenged in recent years from a new direction: "happiness studies." These are surveys, many of them undertaken by economists, which ask people how happy and satisfied with life they are. The response was surprising, seeming to show that beyond a quite modest level of income, a person's happiness and life satisfaction – although they depend on his income relative to others in his country – is independent of his absolute income. This means that raising GDP across the board does not increase happiness; what I gain if I become richer I lose from my neighbor becoming rich too. Hence, why should we bother to raise per capita GDP? However, a recent, very thorough, study came to a totally different conclusion: happiness and life satisfaction do increase with income.[5] In particular, it found no effect for relative income and a significant effect for absolute income on happiness when differences in income are measured in percentage terms. Hence, although a $200 increase in income makes a person whose regular annual income is $2000 much happier than it does a person whose regular income is $200,000, a, say, 10 percent income increase makes both equally happy. This implies that raising GDP matters after all, and so do charitable contributions, since transferring a given dollar amount from a rich person to a poor person raises the latter's income by a larger percentage than it lowers the former's.

3.5 Disagreement among Economists

The extent of disagreement among economists is the butt of many a joke; e.g., "if you laid all economists end to end they would not reach a conclusion," or, "if you ask three economists you get four opinions." But there isn't nearly as much of it as appears on the surface.[b] In general, economists agree much more among themselves than they agree with non-economists. Thus, Steven Landsburg reports that when talking with another economist about taxing Styrofoam peanuts, they reached different conclusions:

> as we have reached different conclusions on every other subject we have ever discussed. Yet we have much in common . . . [We] have never voted for the same candidate, but I am sure that in the most important senses, my views are closer to his than to those of 99 percent of the people who always vote as I do. We both approach the world as economists.[6]

Here are three other examples of how economists agree on economic issues regardless of their political orientation. Former Democratic Vice President Al Gore and Gregory Mankiew, a former chairman of President George W. Bush's Council of Economic Advisers, both advocate raising the federal gas tax. Most economists advocate free trade. Just about all economists agree that if a city imposes an income tax, the burden of this tax will fall on those who own land in the city at the time the tax is imposed.

The *PBS News Hour* and similar programs try to be fair by presenting both sides. Even when dealing with an issue on which almost all economists agree, they hunt up one of the few economists on the other side. The audience then observes half the economists saying one thing, and half the opposite. Moreover, there are enough economists around so that a lobby advocating a policy that nearly all economists oppose can find an economist to testify before a Congressional committee on its behalf.

All the same, there is much more disagreement among economists than among natural scientists. One reason is that in every active subject there is a research frontier seething with disagreement and a peaceful hinterland of settled issues. Not surprisingly, economics being less advanced than the natural sciences, has a relatively greater untamed frontier and a less settled hinterland. A second reason is the readiness of economists to offer answers to just about any economic question that arises. And when people take positions on which they have only frail evidence it is not surprising that some read this evidence one way, some the other. Now that environmental problems have impelled natural scientists to answer the public's questions on some issues

---

[b] Disagreement in economics is not quite as bad as an urban myth about the Nobel prize in economics has it. Yes, Friedrich von Hayek, a leading proponent of capitalism and Gunnar Myrdal, a socialist, shared a Nobel prize in economics. But they did so not for their work on capitalism and socialism, but on monetary theory, a topic on which they had followed similar lines.

on which they, too, lack solid information, such as the detailed effects of global warming, they also disagree.

Neither natural scientists nor economists should be blamed for their willingness to offer guesses, because not doing so is likely to result in the decision being made on the advice from those who know even less. Whether the certitude with which they usually express their guesses is appropriate, is another matter. One might try to justify it by the need to counter the even less informed who often claim absolute certainty, but even reciprocal dishonesty is seldom a good thing. However, being overly confident of one's opinions is a common failing, and not just that of economists.

A third reason why economists disagree so frequently is that the policy questions they are addressing are often not purely economic questions, but combine questions about how the economy works with questions about the ability of the government to carry out certain policies. For example, one economist might advocate a tax cut during a recession in the belief that it can be reversed when the recession is over. Another economist who agrees that a tax cut would have favorable effects right now during the recession might oppose it, because she believes that the government lacks the political strength to reverse it when it is no longer needed. Insofar as economists disagree about policies because they disagree about what is politically feasible, they are not disagreeing about economics.

Perhaps the most widely accepted – but not necessarily correct – explanation for why economists disagree is that they make different value judgments. Many people seem to believe that economists (or at least those economists who happen to disagree with them) allow their value judgments to overwhelm an objective evaluation of the evidence. This seems more plausible for issues closely related to policies with a strong ideological flavor than for the purely technical questions which take up more of economists' time, such as the relation between short-term and long-term interest rates. Fortunately, even on ideology-saturated issues there is a powerful force working – at least some of the time – against economists' ideological bias.[c] This is, that academic economists seek, above all, the applause of their colleagues. And those colleagues, most of whom vehemently insist that economics is a science, do not like the odor of ideology. So, even if an ideologically driven wish to reach a certain conclusion lurks in the background of their analysis, economists have an incentive to keep their explicit arguments confined to objective, technical issues.

---

[c] I do not want to get bogged down in the convoluted issue of the definition of ideology. For my purpose, the description of ideology (inadequate as it is for many purposes), as the acceptance or rejection of evidence, largely on the basis of the conclusions that it implies, will do.

I know of only two studies that have tried to quantify the role of ideology in the disagreements of economists. One found a fairly substantial bias, and the other (see appendix 3.1 in this chapter) found a much smaller one. (Is that itself the result of ideological bias?) Nowadays, when natural scientists comment so frequently on ecological problems, value judgments may play a role in their conclusions, too. I suspect that economists are more self-aware in this regard than are natural scientists, to whom this problem, or at least its importance, is relatively new.

Disagreement among economists is sometimes exacerbated by the tendency of some economists to divide into different "schools." These schools may form along ideological lines, but also along methodological ones, such as the extensive use of mathematically formulated theory versus more informal empirical analysis. And once you feel allegiance to one school because you agree with it on some issues that are important to you, you are likely to agree with members of that school also on other issues without carefully evaluating their evidence, if only because you lack the time to investigate it yourself and you trust their judgment. All very human. And so is the reluctance to relinquish, even in the face of fairly persuasive evidence, the conclusions you reached in previous papers, or for that matter the conclusions reached by your graduate-school teachers and former fellow students. Both loyalty to schools and stubborn defense of previous results make for disagreements. Such tendencies exist in the natural sciences, too, but there they are usually greatly attenuated by the greater conclusiveness of the evidence.

Finally, before getting caustic about the disagreement among economists, one should ask whether this disagreement might indicate that things are not quite as bad as they could be. Compare two cases. In one, policy is handled very badly, say, the Fed has set the federal funds rate much too high. Most economists then agree that it should be cut. In the other case, the Fed has set it at close to the correct level. With the difference between the actual and the correct rate now being small, it is hard to say whether the funds rate should be slightly higher or slightly lower; so economists disagree about that.

APPENDIX 3.1

Survey of American Academic Economists' Opinions

In 1999 I sent a questionnaire to a sample of American academic economists who were members of the American Economic Association. About half of all American academic economists are members, with nonmembers probably concentrated in smaller schools, so that my sample is not fully representative of all American academic economists. A response rate of almost 35 percent is not bad for a survey, but it does imply the danger that the respondents were not a sufficiently random sample of all those surveyed.

The questionnaire asked respondents their reaction to the statements shown in table 3.1 as well as to some others. In the first six questions they

Table 3.1 The opinions of American academic economists

		Mean	*No. of respondents*
1	Suppose technical change would raise the level of output permanently by 2 percent, but would cause a totally arbitrary 5 percent redistribution within each income decile, while leaving the distribution between quintiles unchanged. Would you favor this development?[a]	1.9	142
2	Whether GDP grows at a 1.5 percent or a 2 percent rate is not nearly as important as enhancing social justice.	3.3	152
3	The government has a moral right to redistribute income if a majority supports this.	2.9	156
4	Maintaining or, preferably, enhancing, freedom from government control should be the main goal of economic policy.	3.1	161
5	In general, the law of unanticipated consequences ensures that most programs to help the poor harm them more than help them.	3.2	95
6	Government spending as a percent of GDP should be reduced.	2.8	156
7	Government intervention that would substantially reduce the inequality of the income distribution would have major social and political effects. On the whole, these effects would be [strongly detrimental . . . strongly favorable].	3.0	150
8	Compared to the current situation, the federal government's role in the income distribution should be [larger . . . smaller].	3.0	160

Note: [a] Deciles are groups encompassing 10 percent of a population, when this population is ranked by some numerical criterion such as income. Quintiles are similar groups encompassing 20 percent of the population.

were given five choices ranging from "strongly agree" to "strongly disagree," and also a "cannot say" choice. The next two questions used the somewhat differently worded choices shown. I allocated a value of 1 to "strongly agree," a value of 5 to "strongly disagree," and corresponding values to the other choices, so that, for example, a mean of 2.0 denotes weak agreement, and a mean of 4.9 strong disagreement.[7]

NOTES

1   See Nancy Cartwright, *The Mottled World*, Cambridge, Cambridge University Press, 1999.
2   On this, see Daniel Hausman and Michael McPherson, *Economic Analysis and Moral Philosophy*, Cambridge, Cambridge University Press, 2006.
3   Nell Gross and Solon Simmons, "The Social and Political Views of American Professors," unpublished, Department of Sociology, Harvard University.
4   David Colander, *The Making of an Economist: Redux*, Princeton, Princeton University Press, 2007, p. 21.
5   Betsey Stevenson and Justin Wolfers, "Economic Growth and Subjective Well-Being: Reassessing the Easterlin Paradox," *Brookings Papers on Economic Activity*, 2008, forthcoming.
6   Steven Landsburg, *The Armchair Economist*, New York, Free Press, 1993, p. 145.
7   For more information on the survey and its implications for attributing disagreements among economists to ideology, see Thomas Mayer, "The Role of Ideology in the Disagreements of Economists," *Journal of Economic Methodology*, June 2001, pp. 253–73.

PART II
SOME INFRASTRUCTURE

4

Beguiling Words

This is a book on economics, not semantics. All the same, since emotionally laden, ill-defined, and generally misleading terms frequently play important roles in popular arguments about economics and politics you need to learn how to detect such impostors if you are to protect yourself from misleading arguments. Hence this chapter.

There are some words and concepts that seem almost destined to sow confusion. That is not to say that those who use them necessarily intend to confuse you. Most of them are passing on a verbal counterfeit in the belief that it is a genuine coin. Nor do I mean that such terms are always counterfeits; occasionally they are genuine coins. I am, therefore, not suggesting that you refuse to have anything to do with them – indeed some are almost indispensable, and I use them in this book. But when you come across these words, look them over carefully before slipping them into your mental purse. I will not attempt to nail all of these villains, but just to pillory a few to show how careful one must be. The list starts with a few terms that are widely used and then goes on to those that are used more frequently in the context of economics or politics.

But before turning to these specific examples let's consider briefly a general semantic error. This is to change the meaning of a term in the middle of an argument. For example, a book might correctly point out that the distribution of political power influences scientific theories: for instance, political power has some effect on what type of research and development (R&D) the government finances, and thus influences what scientists discover. So far, so good. But, a few pages further on, "influences" has morphed into "determines," which implies that the objective quality of the evidence does not matter, so that scientific theories have no truth value.

4.1   Some Widely Used Terms and Phrases

4.1.1   "May": the logic-defying leap from "conceivably might be" to "is"

Let's start with the simple, oh-so-innocent-looking word, "may." It has a perfectly legitimate use, but it can be a serious troublemaker because it can be used in two very different senses. One is when someone uses "may" to suggest merely that something *could* happen, that we cannot rule out the possibility that, say if A occurs, it will result in B. Since all sorts of things may happen, and A can have many direct and indirect effects, it is often hard to deny the *possibility statement* that, yes, indeed, B may follow from A. But how probable is it? We are not told. Yet a few pages later, implicitly,

---

Box 4.1: Many "Likelies" Make an "Unlikely"

Suppose that you plan to toss a coin that is fair so that the probability of getting a head is 1/2. Suppose also that you toss it a second time. What is the probability of getting heads both times? Well, there are four possible outcomes on the two tosses: H, T, H, T, and only one of them is two heads, so it's one in four. In other words it is 1/2 times 1/2, or $1/2^2$ (if you are unfamiliar with squaring, see box 10.1). Similarly, if you toss the coin ten times, the chance of getting all heads is $1/2^{10} = 1/1024$. Now suppose there is a 50 percent chance that A will lead to B, and a similar chance that B will lead to C and so on down to H (the eighth letter). If A does occur what is the chance that it will cause H? It is less than one quarter of one percent.

An aside: suppose you have tossed a fair coin five times and it has turned up heads every time. What is the probability that it will turn up tails on the next toss? Many people think that it must be extremely high because getting six heads in a row is highly unlikely. But that is wrong. It is true that *before* you toss the coin the first time, when you don't know the result of the first five tosses, it makes sense to say that getting six heads in a row is extremely unlikely. But after you have tossed the coin five times, you have additional information – that you got all heads on these five tosses. You should take that into account by asking not, "will there be six heads in a row," but by asking, "given that there have already been five heads in a row, will there be an additional, and hence a sixth head in row?" And the probability of that is one half – the coin being tossed does not know and respond to what happened on previous tosses.

the meaning of "may" has changed to imply a substantial probability, not just a possibility, so that we are told something like: "having shown that A leads to B . . ."

Moreover, sometimes several "mays" gang up on the reader. Suppose A may lead to B, B may lead to C, C to D, D to E, and E to F. To find the probability that A will lead to F you have to multiply the probabilities denoted by each of these mays. (See box 4.1.) Even if every one of them is, say, 80 percent (and they are independent of each other), then as you multiply 80 percent by itself five times you get only a 26 percent probability. Yet, I suspect that many unwary readers come away with the impression that, since every step in the argument has itself a high probability, the probability that A will lead to F must be high. This could be a major reason for the popularity of slippery-slope arguments, such as, that if you allow any abortions at all, the inevitable end result will be death camps. (See box 4.2.) Beware of long chains of mays.

"May" is not the only word that lends itself to the confusion of what is possible with what is probable. "Can," "could," and "might" are also capable of creating such a confusion, though to a lesser extent, since they at least hint at the distinction between possible and probable.

Unfortunately, our language often gives us no convenient way of indicating how likely is a process that we describe as possible by saying "may." Quantifying the probabilities as percentages or proportions often requires more precision than we can provide, and besides, in many contexts it sounds nerdy, while "perhaps" or "likely to" are vague terms, and also if used frequently makes you sound mealy-mouthed.

4.1.2   That "accounts" for it, but does it "cause" it?

Another chameleon word is "accounts." When decomposing some event into its constituent parts it makes sense to tell the reader how large each of these parts is: to say, for example, that the rise in investment accounts for – that is represents or equals – 40 percent of the rise in our GDP. Or, suppose you wonder why prices rose so much last year. Being told that, say, 80 percent of the rise is accounted for by the prices of services, and 20 percent by the prices of goods provides information that can be useful for some purposes.

Fine so far. But there is a problem. The term "accounted for" can be read not only as "represents," but also as "caused by," that is, to use the above examples, that 40 percent of the rise in GDP is *due to* a rise in investment and that 80 percent of the inflation is *due* to the rise in the prices of services. And that is a very different kettle of fish. To invest, firms have to buy capital

Box 4.2: Slipping Down a Slope

Slippery slope arguments proceed along the lines of the following example: if you decide to tolerate A, say voluntary euthanasia for the incurably ill, this will lead people to tolerate B, say voluntary euthanasia for those with only a slight chance of recovery, because B is not all that different from A, which, in turn, will result in tolerance for C, and so on, until you get to X, which is truly horrible (Nazi death camps). In principle, such reasoning is unexceptionable, *if* you can show that the consequences B, C, etc., will necessarily follow. And here is the rub. In most cases at best all you can show is that there is a high probability that each of the steps will follow. But, as shown in the previous Box, even high probabilities when multiplied by other high probabilities tend to become low probabilities. So when people throw a slippery-slope argument at you ask them to state the probabilities of each step and then do the multiplications.

Another problem with slippery-slope arguments is that one needs to distinguish between a logical slope and what one might call a psychological or political slope. Suppose you could show that tolerance of Nazi death camps is a *logical* implication of the toleration of voluntary euthanasia of the incurably ill. It would still not follow that, were the latter permitted, sooner or later there would be death camps. Political decisions are not always and everywhere made on the basis of logic. Voluntary euthanasia might perhaps not stir most people's emotions, death camps would. Admittedly, once people have become accustomed to voluntary euthanasia they might be less reluctant about the next step in the chain. As Alexander Pope wrote:[1]

> Vice is a monster of such frightful mien
> That to be hated needs but be seen
> Yet seen too oft, familiar with the face,
> We first endure, then pity, and then embrace

But whether or not that will actually happen is an empirical question, not a matter of logic. At some point people may dig in their heels and say: "thus far and no further." Even if live birth abortion could be shown to be logically indistinguishable from infanticide, most of those who support the former are unlikely to support the latter.

Thoughtful slippery-slope arguments are compelling, but not all slippery-slope arguments are thoughtful.

---

[1]   Cited in http://en.thinkexist.com/quotations/vice_is_a_monster.

goods, and as those employed in producing these goods spend part of their newly acquired incomes, the incomes of others rise too, so that the rise in investment might be responsible for – that is in a *causal* sense of "account for" – much more than 40 percent of the rise in GDP. A similar story can be told about the rise in prices. That the rise in the prices of services accounts for – in the sense of representing – 80 percent of the overall rise in prices, does not mean that the rise in service prices caused 80 percent of the overall price rise. The following mental experiment will readily show this. Assume that service prices had not risen at all, but that the Fed had caused the money supply to increase by 5 percent. With the prices of services not rising, people would then have had more money to spend on other items. As a result, the prices of these items would have risen more than they actually did. Holding down the prices of services would not have reduced the inflation rate by 80 percent. Here is another example: the Tyndall Center for Climate Change Research estimated that in 2004 net exports accounted for 23 percent of China's emission of greenhouse gases.[1] Suppose that China had reduced its exports, and to avoid a massive increase in unemployment, had stimulated domestic demand instead. Its net exports would no longer account for 23 percent of emissions, but would China's emissions' be any less?

4.1.3   "Root cause": privileging one cause

Another example of a confusing term, and one that, I suspect, has had a telling effect in many an argument, is "root cause." We all know that plants grow from roots, and that effects grow from causes, so why not combine the two words and cash in on a metaphor from nature? For a good reason. Since causation is an extremely complex and difficult concept, let's by-pass it and look at the "roots" part. Does it have any meaning, or is it, like the word "pitched" that journalists so often attach to "battle," merely a way of using two words where one will do? Not necessarily. It can have two uses, one that is legitimate and one that is not. Here is an example of the legitimate one. Suppose that we identify three important causes of a phenomenon. Someone might then point out that these three causes, in turn, all have a single cause. That cause would deserve the adjective "root."

But that is not how "root cause" is commonly used. Instead, the word "root" is used to sneak in the idea that this particular cause is somehow more important or noteworthy than any of the other causes. I say "sneak in," because usually no reason is adduced why this cause should be singled out. It is highly likely that when someone says "the root cause of crime is poverty," she calls it the root cause, not primarily because she believes that it is the cause that underlies all the other causes that she can think of, but because she thinks that reducing poverty is an important policy goal for other reasons, too. Suppose a conservative says: "the root cause of crime is the decline in family cohesion," and a liberal replies: "No. the root cause is poverty." They have two things in common; they are both pointing to *a* cause of crime, and claiming – without offering any justification – that this particular cause is much more important or noteworthy than are the other causes.

This does not mean that all causes are born equal, that when we talk about the causes of *x* we must list all the conditions required for *x* to occur. That would be impossible. We can treat all but one of them as background causes, and concentrate on the one we want to stress. But we should be able to give good reasons for why we have selected this one and not others, or give a reason for thinking that it provides a ready handle for controlling *x*. Just calling it a root cause does not suffice. Nor would replacing "root" with "basic," "fundamental," etc.; an explanation, not a synonym, is needed.

4.1.4　"Founded on" feet of clay

Phrases like "the foundation of," "founded on," and "rests on," are other examples of metaphors that crumble at the first touch. When we speak of a physical object resting on a foundation, we have a clear picture, but when we speak of an abstraction like democracy resting on another abstraction this clarity is lost. Take, for example, the statement that "political freedom is founded on a fundamentally religious belief in the sanctity of the individual" (or "on curbing religious zealotry"). Here "founded on" can mean at least three quite different things. One is that there is a logical relation between the two, that is, that a logically coherent defense of political freedom can be given only if one accepts the assumption of the sanctity of the individual, and that this assumption, in turn, can only be derived from religion. A second possible meaning is historical, that, at the time when political freedom became established, the balance of political forces was such that, had it not been for the prevailing religious belief in the sanctity of the individual, those who advocated political freedom would not have won out. A third, more sociological, meaning is that, never mind the political line-up at the time when political freedom was first established, generally (or at least now), the elimination of the religious belief in the sanctity of the individual would set in motion forces, such as the granting of greater power to the police, that would result in the elimination of political freedom. Any and all of these explanations may, or may not, be true; my point is only that the analogy with a physical foundation hides the absence of a coherent argument.

4.2 Some Terms and Phrases Relating to Economics and Politics

4.2.1 "Left" or "right" or just confusing?

The French revolution did some good things, and some bad things. Among the bad things was that in the National Assembly the more conservative members were seated on the right, and the more radical ones on the left. Presumably, this is the source of the simplistic idea that one can apply plane geometry to politics and classify everyone as either left or right. It is simplistic because it assumes either that all politics can be reduced to a single issue or else, that people who take a left position on one issue will normally do so on other issues too, and that a similar story holds for the right. Sometimes one or other of these conditions does hold, but sometimes neither does. Where, for example, does it leave fascism or contemporary American populism? Or for that matter when Democrats speak against free trade and Republicans for it, who is on the left and who is on the right?

If the terms "left" and "right" are almost incoherent in the contemporary political context, how about "liberal" and "conservative"? They too are rambling. In part, the problem is that the Democratic Party, having adopted some major positions that can meaningfully be called "liberal" and the Republican Party having adopted some that can legitimately be called "conservative," other positions that the Democrats adopt to enhance their appeal to certain voters are called "liberal," and a similar thing holds for the Republicans.

This leaves me with three choices: to try to develop a coherent set of alternative terms; to avoid concepts like liberal and conservative altogether; or to use these terms (or cognates) in their loose everyday sense. The first of these would require a book on political thought, and this is not it. The second, avoiding these terms, would require clumsy circumlocutions that would probably result in more confusion than elucidation. I will, therefore, with apologies to the reader, use the terms "liberal" and "conservative" in their standard, loose version.[2]

4.2.2 Bureaucracy

We usually associate bureaucracy with government, and conservatives use our inbred aversion to bureaucracy as a politically potent argument against government intervention. That, for example, is how they killed the Clinton health-insurance plan back in the mid-1990s. But identifying bureaucracy as uniquely a disease of government is wrong, since bureaucracy is an attribute of all large modern organizations. To avoid inconsistencies and to curb arbitrary decisions by low- and middle-level employees, and also to prevent them from making decisions contrary to the goals of the organization, large organizations have to sacrifice flexibility and operate by formal, written rules, and presto: bureaucracy. The owner-manager of a small store can bargain with a customer and if necessary reduce the price. If a large department store were to allow its clerks to freely bargain, some might cut prices too much, particularly to friends, since they have little incentive to maximize the store's profits. Similarly, if a casualty insurance company were to avoid formal rules and tell its adjusters to use their common sense, then there would be too many discrepancies in the treatment of similar claims.

Why then do we hear so much more about government bureaucracy than about business bureaucracies? One explanation that I will come to in a moment is that for good and sound reasons there is more bureaucracy in government. Another is the peculiar division of labor whereby conservatives slam government for being bureaucratic, while liberals slam business for being greedy. Actually, businesses, too, are bureaucratic, and governments, too, are greedy: most government agencies are eager to expand their budgets. Third, the blunders of government bureaucracies make juicy meat for the media, feeding as they do our sense of rebellion against those who impose rules on us and act like an elite. A story that the air force paid $7,000 for coffee pots finds eager readers, particularly if they are not told that commercial airlines also pay about that much for coffee pots for aircraft as large as the air force's troop carriers. And we don't hear many bureaucratic horror stories about business because journalists have less access to what goes on in business. In general, one should be wary of the media's horror stories. The very fact that some atrocious behavior receives much media attention tells us that it is highly unusual and not typical.

As just mentioned, quite part from the effect of their usually much greater size, government agencies are indeed more prone to the bureaucratic disease than are businesses. And this is as it should be. In firms, employees who deal with the public are more exposed to the supervision of managers who are motivated by the goal of the business, maximizing profits, than government employees are to the supervision of voters. Government employees, therefore, need to be bound by more rules. Moreover, for many government activities there is no clear yardstick by which to judge a manager's efficiency. There is, therefore, a greater risk in allowing them discretion. Many firms can give their managers considerable discretion in hiring and firing because they know that a manager has an incentive to hire and retain the most efficient workforce; his or her own rating depends on it. Instead, governments rely on a civil service system. Those who complain about government bureau-cracy would have even more to complain about if we went back to the old "spoils system," which allowed the party in power to fire employees who belonged to the other party and to hire their own adherents.

4.2.3 "Middle class"

Just what is "middle class"? Most Americans call themselves middle class, but the term is also used to mean people with an income not much larger than the median, and that differs from "most people." At other times it is used to denote people who are not poor, or people who hold certain values, or "respectable" people, or "us."

In one way, the unstable meaning of the term "middle class" has enhanced the role of government. When some interest group seeks public support for a government program that will benefit it, it can often call itself "middle class," conjuring up the picture of a hard-working blue-collar family, struggling against substantial odds to make ends meet, when, in fact, most of its members are fairly well-to-do. Or it can initially confine the proposed program to families that approximate to what most people consider middle class, and then, over the years, step by step, raise the income ceiling for eligibility, until the "middle class" which the program covers includes rich people. But in another way the broad use of the term "middle class" has reduced the role of the government, because, with even relatively poor people considering themselves middle class, there is less political support for programs to help the poor.

4.2.4 Necessary luxuries or luxurious necessities?

When thinking about our own purchases, "necessities" and "luxuries" are convenient terms because in this case we have a readily available standard – our own normal purchases – that allows us to say whether or not we should feel at least a tiny bit guilty about an intended expenditure. But such stand-ards are subjective, varying from person to person, and depending upon their incomes and tastes. For example, hot running water was once a luxury. The notion of luxuries is, therefore, of little use to economists and better left to moralists engaged in deploring the foibles of humankind.

If we discard the notion of luxuries we can also discard its converse, neces-sities. From time to time some people have tried to resuscitate the idea of necessities, arguing that we need a certain minimum amount of food, clothing, and shelter to stay alive. Moreover, to function adequately as social beings we need to meet a certain minimum level of consumption, particularly in clothing, that our society calls for. All other expenditures should then be called luxuries. But "social needs" cannot be demarcated unequivocally, so that what we call luxuries is more or less arbitrary. And it does not do any good to say that certain goods, like food, are necessities, so that, for example, food purchases should be excluded from state sales taxes. Not all food is a necessity. The expensive Belgian chocolate I buy is not. All in all, it is best to adopt George Stigler's definition that a luxury is something we think other people should do without, and leave it at that. That at least avoids making the value judgments that are intrinsic to terms like luxuries and necessities.

All the same, economists have given in to people's insistence that there be categories called "necessities" and "luxuries." Accordingly, they have allowed them back into the discussion by giving them a rigorous definition; necessities are those goods and services on which we spend a smaller percentage of our incomes as incomes rise, and luxuries are those on which we spend a larger percentage. But even so, these terms are hardly ever used by economists.

4.2.5   Is it really a waste?

Everyone is against waste, and there is a lot of it in government. It is, therefore, not surprising that politicians, particularly conservative ones, promise to eliminate it. It is also not surprising that they largely fail because one person's waste is another person's valuable program. You may consider the National Science Foundation's support for economic research to be waste, and federal flood insurance to be a valuable program, while I think just the opposite. Until we can get much more agreement than we have now on what is waste, waste will proliferate even if governmental officials try hard and intelligently to avoid it, and right-wing politicians flourish by denouncing it.

4.2.6   Trade: "free" or "fair"

Something that helps the advocates of free trade is that the word "free" has a positive connotation. Their opponents counter that advantage by advocating not "unfree" or "restricted" trade, but "fair" trade. By this they mean that it is unfair to allow importers to take advantage of lower wages in other countries to drive domestic producers out of business, and cause their workers to lose their jobs. But is it "fair" to deny far poorer workers in foreign countries the opportunity to compete with better-off workers in the United States? Granted that allowing such competition drives down the wages of some American workers, it also raises wages of foreign workers. And since these are earning less than their American counterparts, worldwide income inequality is reduced.

4.2.7   A tax on dying?

Taxing someone for the act of dying seems both bizarre and unfair, so by calling the federal estate tax a "death tax" the Bush II administration succeeded in getting Congress to phase it out, at least temporarily. But it is not a tax on dying. It is a tax on large estates that are passed on to heirs. You don't have to pay it to be allowed to die, and most people die without paying it. Very broadly, its effects are similar to taxing the recipients of bequests, and that seems neither bizarre nor unfair. The arguments here should turn on a discussion of whether the wealthy should be able to pass on all worldly riches to their heirs – when the heirs have already benefited from access to better education, schools, travel, friends, environment.

4.2.8   Should growth be sustainable?

We are told that we should aim at *sustainable* growth. And there is something to that. It focuses attention, if only indirectly, on the possibility that sometimes the unfavorable effects of growth outweigh the favorable ones. It also induces us to look at future, not just present effects, and that is important. But as a more specific injunction it is mistaken. Suppose a new durable good like the computer or TV appears on the market and becomes very popular. It will grow rapidly until its use has become widespread, and much more slowly after that. Would it be better if it were to grow at a sustainable rate by making some potential buyers wait longer for it? Or, looking at the economy as a whole, suppose one policy causes per capita income to grow by 5 percent next year and by 2 percent from then on, while another policy causes it to grow at a 2 percent rate in every year? Wouldn't the former be preferable? Yes, sustainable growth sounds warm, cuddly, and sensible, but is it always better than unsustainable growth? I suspect that all that the advocates of sustainable growth mean to say, is that we should pay attention to environmental effects. In this they are right, but why not say just that?

4.2.9   "Democratic" or "egalitarian"?

The way the word "democratic" is often used conflates two distinct meanings. One is as a system of government by elections with a widespread franchise, along with rules that give the opposition an adequate opportunity to make its case for replacing the government at the next election. The other meaning is egalitarian, as when someone remarks: "Sending your children to a private school is not democratic." Such a use of the term "democracy" to denote egalitarianism provides egalitarians with a powerful weapon. Practically all Americans have strong positive feelings about democracy in the first sense of the term. They, therefore, feel uncomfortable opposing policies and practices that are labeled "democratic," even if these are democratic only in the second, egalitarian sense. Yet many of them would not hesitate to oppose these policies if they were presented instead under the egalitarian label.

4.2.10   What's so bad about greed?

Surely, greed has a bad name. But just what is greed? When we see a well-fed man rapidly shoveling food down his gullet while casting covetous looks at the one remaining item on the serving platter, or when we see a child that has many toys grabbing toys away from other children, then we can say "yes, that is greed." But, in economics, things are usually not that simple. A few years ago the *New York Times* published an article on over-fishing in the Gulf of California under the title "In Mexico, Greed Kills Fish by the Seaful."[3] The article describes the activities of corporations, governments, and fishermen, many of the latter obviously poor people who depend on fishing to keep themselves alive. Should the *Times* have described them as greedy? Could it be that it used the word "greedy" because there are also corporations involved? If so, were these corporations "greedy" because they tried to make an immense profit, or were they just earning a normal profit? We are not told. And would the *Times* itself object to making an immense profit?

Here are three other troubling questions about what we mean by greed and about our attitude towards it: suppose an academic is eager to have his papers cited frequently, a standard measure of scholarly achievement. So he includes in his own papers many unnecessary citations to papers by colleagues in the hope that they will reciprocate. Is he being greedy, or does money have to be involved before one can speak of greed? If so, then perhaps some of the "greed talk" is nothing more than an attempt by sanctimonious academics, who are rewarded more by collegial prestige than by money, to claim that they are morally superior to businesspeople whose rewards come primarily in the form of money. Second, insofar as academics and journalists also strive for monetary rewards, are they innocent of the sin of greed because their monetary rewards come as salaries rather than as profits? Third, why are intellectuals and the media so much more troubled by the vice of greed than by other vices? Is it because they see themselves as less greedy than other elites, and are, therefore, less sympathetic to the sin of greed than to other sins? One hears little nowadays about the sin of pride. Has some of the old, traditional pride-talk morphed into greed-talk, the better to castigate the "other"?

Finally, aren't corporations supposed to maximize their profits? Isn't that their fiduciary duty to their shareholders, as well as being the force that impels them to seek increased efficiency and to generate (as will be explained in chapter 6) an efficient allocation of resources? Saying that they should strive only for "reasonable" profits and not for "obscene" profits is not an adequate answer. How do we define these terms? Moreover, if their profits fluctuate substantially it may take obscene profits in one year to offset heavy losses in other years. Similarly, for very risky ventures the prospect of obscene profits if the venture succeeds is needed as a lure to offset the much greater likelihood of losses.

This does not mean that *all* greed is virtuous. When Adam Smith praised self-interest, it was enlightened self-interest that he had in mind. And that often requires a moral sensitivity to the claims of others. In the dictator game discussed in chapter 2 a first player who tries to keep 99 percent of the total for himself will fare badly. (There is a saying on Wall Street: "You can make money being a bull, you can make money being a bear, but you cannot make money being a pig.") Moreover, the self-interest that drives greed is not, as already discussed in chapter 2, synonymous with selfishness.

4.2.11 Exploiting the affect of "exploitation"

Exploitation, like greed, is something that it is easier to denounce than to define. To talk seriously about workers being exploited one needs a criterion for determining the appropriate wage. And that's where trouble arises. It is emotionally – but not intellectually – satisfying to characterize the appropriate wage as at least a living wage. But that raises two problems. First, the term "living wage" is itself vague. If we apply the standards of industrialized countries, then most workers in most developing countries are being exploited. But what sense does it make to say that even workers receiving what is more than the median wage in their country are not being paid a living wage? Second, does it make sense to talk about a worker being exploited if her wage is equal to the value of what she produces, or more precisely her marginal productivity, that is, the change in the value of output due to her having been hired? And how can one tell how much that is, and why assume that it is at least equal to a living wage?[a] There is at least a presumption that,

---

[a] It seems offensive, perhaps even racist, to say that some workers have a marginal productivity of less than $1 a day. But it is not a worker's ability and productivity in the abstract that determines her wage, but her productivity in the specific setting she works in. And that can be one of poor education, bad roads, unreliable power supply, corrupt government officials, uncertain property right, and little capital.

given competitive labor and product markets, by and large, workers are being paid their marginal product, because if the marginal productivity of workers exceeds their wage, then firms have an incentive to employ more workers until the two are brought into equality. Admittedly, this presumption is not all that strong, because we often observe firms paying substantially different wages for the same type of work, but on a gross, overall, level, this presumption does seem reasonable. And where does that leave all the talk about systemic exploitation? None of this is meant to deny that in some countries there are cases of exploitation, in some countries even slavery, but only that exploitation is not an inherent and systemic characteristic of a market system.

4.2.12   Big business or just business?

There are many things that we are told about big business, that it is excessively concerned with profits, etc. Let's assume for the sake of the argument that all of these charges are correct. That still leaves the question why those who make them are so modest that they claim to tell us something only about big business instead of about business in general. Are large firms more concerned about profits and greedier than small firms? I doubt it. Although those who manage large firms usually do have a big personal stake in the profitability of their firms, it seems highly likely that, when measured as a percentage of their wealth or as a percentage of the net worth of the firm, their stake is less than that of managers of small firms, so that they have less incentive to snap up every penny of potential profits. This seems likely to offset, or more than offset, the fact that managers of large firms have less personal contacts with their customers and employees than managers of small firms. Admittedly, I have no data to back up this surmise, but then neither do those who focus their charges on big businesses. Is it perhaps that the critics focus on "big business" because most of us are more likely to know (and appreciate the humanness of) CEOs of small businesses, than of large businesses? Are they demonizing the other?

4.2.13   The law of supply and demand

Whether economics has "laws" in the same sense that the physical sciences do, is by no means obvious; the only example frequently cited is that ceteris paribus, the lower the price the more is bought. Nonetheless, some people assure us that: "you can't repeal the law of supply and demand." Perhaps you can't, but you can, or should be able to, define what you mean by it. While the statement is true if carefully circumscribed, it is not true if used, as it often is, as a club with which to attack proposals for government intervention. Suppose that the government finances an expansion of health insurance by lowering the fees that Medicare pays to physicians. If those who object by citing the law of supply and demand mean that this will result in some Medicare patients experiencing more difficulty in finding a physician they are right – but only to a limited extent since most physicians could not stay in business without some Medicare patients. If they mean that it will result in physicians using various devices, such as ordering more unnecessary tests, to cushion the decline in their incomes, and also that in the long run it will result in a lower quality of physicians, they are right too. But if they mean that the program, being contrary to the law of supply and demand, will break down entirely, they will be wrong.

4.2.14   Yes, of course, I support "social justice," but what is it?

The term "social justice" also provides a potent rhetorical weapon. Who, after all, can be opposed to justice? And if individual justice is commendable, how can the just treatment of members of different social or economic groups not be commendable? But just what is it that we mean by social justice once we get beyond some obvious cases? And unless we can specify what it is, how can we use it as a basis of policy? Here are some examples of the difficulties that arise when getting specific.

If Jane and Marlene expend the same amount of effort, but Jane, being cleverer, is more productive, is it fair that she should earn more? Or, if Jane and Marlene are equally clever, should Jim's income be less than either of theirs because, instead of inheriting superior genes, he inherited stocks and bonds? Should Bill and Joe, who work equally hard and like their jobs equally well, be paid the same, even though Bill is an accountant, a field in which talent is scarce relative to the demand for it, while Joe is a poet, a field where talent though equally scare, greatly exceeds the demand for it in the workplace?

Second, suppose that you think all types of inheritance are unfair, and so are income differences due to environmental factors, so that there is no moral justification for any income differences.[b] Since elimination of, or a significant reduction of, income differentials would reduce work effort and also cause a misallocation of resources (for example, too few accountants, too many poets),

---

[b]   Here we are getting too close for comfort to the issue of free will versus determinism.

as well as reducing saving and risk taking, how much productivity are you willing to give up to attain greater fairness?

Finally, suppose that you prefer a substantial reduction in productivity to living in an unjust society. Does that mean that you should favor a policy of taking from the rich to give to the poor? Not necessarily. There is still the question of whether the state has a moral right to redistribute income and wealth. Does all wealth belong to society, which can then allocate it to various individuals, as it does for instance in John Rawls' philosophy, or does it, as in Robert Nozick's more Lockian view, belong to the particular individuals who produce it, and who then decide to contribute some of it to the state to finance the public services that they want? Some people's moral compass will not give an unequivocal answer to this fundamental question. They might think that the income a person earns belongs to that person. But they also think that society contributes to the ability of individuals to earn their incomes, so that it has some legitimate claims on these incomes, and, further, that allowing people to suffer extreme poverty is morally wrong and that private charity is insufficient, so that the state is morally compelled to redistribute some income. Being, therefore, uncertain whether to go with Rawls or with Nozick, they do what is often reasonable in the face of uncertainty; they split the difference some way. But what trade-off should they settle for?

None of these vexing questions means that appeals to social justice are per se invalid. Although different persons will answer them differently, we should attempt to answer them; when considering any policy we do need to ask whether it is just. But what we should not do is use the term social justice as though its meaning were obvious to anyone of goodwill.

4.2.15   My rights or yours?

Another term that is effective in appealing to emotions is "rights." As Thomas Sowell has noted: "One of the most remarkable – and popular – ways of seeming to argue without actually producing any arguments is to say that some individual or group has a 'right' to something you want them to have."[4] Thus Lenard Liberal tells Cathy Conservative that "people have a *right* to decent housing," and Cathy Conservative responds that "people have a *right* to keep what they earn, and not have the government take some of it away to give to other people." Such assertions are more likely to result in raised voices than in reasoned discussion. One might ask both Len and Cathy to explain what they mean by "right," and whether they are not just saying respectively that even poor people *should* have decent housing, and that people *should* be allowed to keep their earnings. Putting it in terms of "should" opens up their assertions to serious discussions of the resultant costs and benefits, and by, so to speak, secularizing the rival claims, makes them amenable to negotiation and compromise. By contrast, "rights" has an almost religious aura, the adjectives, "inalienable" and "non-negotiable" come to mind, and with it the further connotation that this issue is beyond discussion and the give-and-take of negotiation. Rights-talk fosters an attitude of "I will not compromise, because every right-thinking person must agree with me, and if you are not that type of person, I am not interested in discussing anything with you."

Perhaps this fundamentalist connotation of rights comes from the frequent use of this term in a legal setting, combined with the rather questionable belief that legal rights are absolute. But what we have here are rights that are asserted not on the basis of some legal document, but on the basis of moral feelings, and these feelings may be in conflict. What do we do, for instance, if I assert the "right" of unhindered access to a beach, and you assert your "right" as a property owner to keep me out? All rights constrain what someone else can do, and hence limit that person's rights. Perhaps compromise is called for, and talking about "rights" makes that difficult.

A good illustration of how an appeal to "rights" can muddle a discussion is the following statement of Congressman Dennis Kucinich: "Every human being has the right to clean water . . . I strongly believe that public control and public administration of the public's water supply is the only way to guarantee the universal human right . . . to clean water."[5] Would anything be lost by replacing in this passage "has the right to" by "should have"? Yes, there would be. Speaking of clean water as a "right" invokes a warm glow that distracts attention from the subsequent more mundane and debatable assertion that public control and administration is the only way to get clean water. While I do not want to accuse Congressman Kucinich of consciously doing so – it is very easy to slip into this mode unconsciously – what is going on here is that the first part of the statement evokes fervent agreement, and this fervor is then used as a bridge over some slippery ground. Not only does it take attention away from the choice between outright public ownership and public control (which may involve only the setting of minimal standards), but it seems to suggest that everyone at all times must be provided with clean water, irrespective of the cost. For example, clean water must be provided on hiking trails where this would be very expensive and may require funds that could be spent better to provide more food stamps.

The enthusiastic expansion of alleged rights has a nasty by-product: as dubious "rights" proliferate, the status of genuine rights, such as free speech, is diminished. When I hear something that I am not certain is a genuine right called a right, the whole notion of rights loses some of the reverence I attribute to rights. Sooner or later we tend to think of rights, or almost all rights, as little more than claims by special-interest groups.

4.2.16   Social conscience

Let's consider the following story. The doorbell rings, John answers, and there stands his neighbor, Mary, with a petition to raise the minimum wage to $15 an hour and to instruct the Federal Reserve to aim at an unemployment rate of less than 3 percent. He refuses to sign it. This puzzles Mary because she knows that he is kind and decent. She concludes that, while he has a well-developed conscience in his personal dealings, he fails to understand that he should extend his decency and sympathy to people he does not know personally, in other words, that he lacks a social conscience. Mary is wrong, profoundly wrong. The reason Bill did not sign is not that he fails to sympathize with low-wage earners or with the unemployed, but because he believes that raising the minimum wage to $15 would cause many low-skilled workers to lose their jobs, and that an unemployment rate as low as 3 percent is an unattainable goal that would generate accelerating inflation.

The moral of this story is that favoring or opposing any policy requires two decisions: a value judgment about the desirability of the ultimate goal of the policy, and a positive judgment about whether the proposed policy would achieve this goal, and at what cost.[c] That distinction seems both just a matter

---

[c]   Many postmodernists argue that one cannot distinguish between normative and positive statements, that even so-called positive statements involve implicit value judgments. For instance, if you say it is sunny today, you cannot be *absolutely* certain, since, conceivably, your eyes are deceiving you. Hence, in deciding to say that it is sunny you are making the value judgment that it is alright to risk the small probability that you are wrong. And the decision that you should take this risk requires a value judgment. Thus, attached to every positive proposition there is a normative proposition playing hide-and-seek. Yes, that is so, but what follows from that? The problem is less serious than it appears at first glance. Someone saying that it is sunny does not claim God-like certitude, and her audience knows this. Making a value judgment that is shared by the entire audience is consistent with a moderate version of the positivist project. In this version a scientist should not see himself as Promethean figure who provides his readers with a God-certified truth; the validity of all evidence and proofs is contingent on a certain world-view, and someone with a different world-view can, with a good conscience, brush this evidence aside. But that should not bother the scientist; his job is to provide information to those who share his world-view and accept his presuppositions. Doing that is a worthy task. Think of the scientist or scholar in a mundane way: he provides a product, knowledge, to his customers, that is, to people who find it of interest because they share the same world-view. Most gas stations do not carry diesel fuel, but that does not prevent them from being useful to most motorists.

of common sense, and yet is something that many people find convenient to ignore, because this allows them to bask in a moral glow when they express certain opinions. And some of them, though of course not all, will then feel less of a need to act decently in their personal lives. We buy our bread where it costs least, why not do the same when buying the satisfaction of feeling moral?

4.2.17 Unions have bosses, firms have CEOs

Here the bias is too obvious to need discussion. Perhaps the distinction could be explained by saying that CEOs are selected by success in their prior work as determined by a search committee. Union heads are selected by the allegedly less reliable process of election by union members. But is this really true? Do politicking, luck, and personal connections play no role in the selection of CEOs, and ability to benefit union members play no role in the election of union leaders?

4.2.18 Conclusion

This listing of misleading words and concepts, though perhaps exhausting, is hardly exhaustive. But I hope it suffices to put the reader on his or her guard. This is not say that in economics we should avoid all vague terms and all terms that carry some emotive charge. That cannot be done; if something is important but cannot be precisely defined, then ignoring it carries its own danger. But we should be on our guard against being misled by such words and concepts.

NOTES

1 Judith Chavalier, "A Carbon Cap That Starts in Washington," *New York Times*, December 16, 2007, BU5, p. 5.
2 For an excellent reformulation of the usual left–right debate in terms of a constrained versus an unconstrained vision of human nature and human reason, see Thomas Sowell, *A Conflict of Visions*, New York, Basic Books, 2007.
3 Tim Weiner, "In Mexico Greed kills Fish by the Seaful," *New York Times*, April 16, 2002, pp. C3 and C6.
4 Thomas Sowell, *The Vision of the Anointed*, New York, Basic Books, 1995, p. 99.
5 Cited in Thomas Sowell, *Applied Economics*, New York, Basic Books, 2004, p. 27.

5

Important Economic Ideas: Often Misunderstood

Much scientific progress comes about through a more precise statement of ideas. For example, in a pre-Newtonian world, all objects are pulled downward. But to understand the force of gravity, Newton had to free himself of thinking that gravity makes objects fall "down." A large mass has a pull in all directions. Similarly, economics has been by built by taking some words in everyday use and giving them very precise meanings in an economics context. The ideas discussed in this chapter will not only will put you on the road to thinking like an economist, but they will help you spot a lot of nonsense.

5.1   Levels versus Rates of Change

One prevalent error is to confuse the level of a variable (e.g. the current value of the consumers' price index, or of GDP) with its rate of change, or to put it another way, to confuse "high" (a level) with "rising" (a rate of change), or "low" with "falling." In principle, the distinction between the level and the rate of change should be clear to everyone – a 30-year-old man is taller than his 3-year-old daughter, but she is growing at a faster rate than he is. Yet, in practice, high and rising, and low and falling are easy to confuse (even a Nobel laureate in economics got caught by this once), in part because we have separate words for some variables that merely denote the change in another variable: for example, inflation denotes the increase in the level of prices. Hence, if you want to explain why the inflation rate rose, you have to explain, not why prices rose, but, why they did so at an increasing rate. For example, with prices rising by 3.3 percent in 1996 and by 1.7 percent in 1997, the inflation rate was falling even though prices were higher in 1997 than in 1996.

Here are three examples of how people sometimes confuse the level of a variable with its rate of change. Many people think of a recession as a period when output is low and unemployment high. But actually, a recession is a period when output is *declining*, and it usually starts when output is above its trend. Hence, in the initial stage of the recession, output, though falling, is still above its trend. In a symmetric cycle the level of output, though falling, is above its trend during the first half of the recession, and below its trend during the first half of the expansion – see figure 5.1. Hence, to stabilize output you don't want monetary and fiscal policy to raise it during the entire recession phase and lower it during the entire expansion phase. You want these policies to increase output when it is low, even though the economy may already be in an expansion.

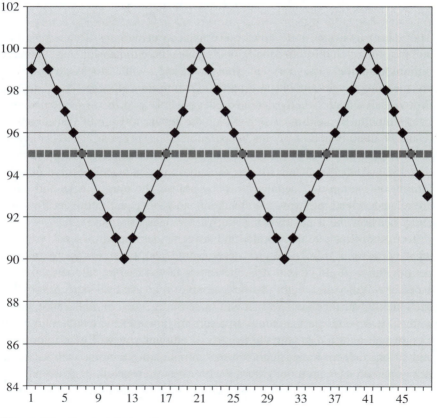

Figure 5.1 Symmetrical cycles

Here is another example: in 2007–8 when oil prices rose sharply some people told us that this was due to oil companies having a high degree of market power (that is, the power to set the price instead of having to meet the price that competitors set independently), and greedily taking advantage of it. But that can't be right, unless oil companies acquired *additional* market power and there is no reason to think that they did. At the time when a company acquires market power, or not long after that, it raises its prices, and then keeps them high so that market power by itself might explain why a price is high, but not why it is currently rising. For example, to explain the sharp rise in oil prices in 2007–8 it makes more sense to look at the rising demand for oil and the falling value of the dollar in terms of other currencies than at OPEC.

5.2   Stocks versus Flows

The ideas of "stock" and "flow" are crucial in economics. Related as they are, they are often misunderstood. Flows have a time dimension, e.g., so many billions of dollars per year, feet per second, etc., while stocks do not; they are measured as an amount at a particular time. For example, your income is obviously greater when calculated over a whole year than when calculated over a month. By contrast, when stating the square footage of your house, it would be literally non-sense to add "per month" or "per year." Another everyday example of a stock is the water in your bathtub that (ignoring evaporation and leakage) stays at a fixed level, unless you induce a positive flow by turning on the tap or a negative flow by pulling the plug. Stocks and flows are related in a simple way: the change in stocks is equal to the net flow and every net flow, be it positive or negative, changes the stock.

To further illustrate the distinction between stocks and flows, ask yourself what happens if from now on you consume just 1 percent more calories per day than you do now, that is, increase a flow variable, calorie intake, by 1 percent. Will your weight (a stock variable) increase by 1 percent too? No such luck! Over time your weight will increase by much more because, being a stock, it depends on the cumulative sum of flows: to the trivial amount of weight you gain today you add the trivial amount you will gain tomorrow, and so on. Indeed, if you ignore some complicating factors, such as that a heavy person uses up more calories with every step taken, or that you may die in the meantime, you will gain an unlimited amount of weight until something gives and you explode!

One reason why the distinction between stocks and flows is so important is that it is easy to get unnecessarily upset when you see a large change in a flow. Suppose that, after tariffs on some imported good were removed three years ago, imports have doubled each year. Does that mean they will continue to double every year and soon destroy the domestic industry? No, it does not, at least not necessarily. Suppose that, given the tariff, firms found it profitable to import 30 percent and to produce 70 percent in the United States. This 30 percent is a stock variable because it does not have a time dimension. (It makes no sense, for example, to say that it is 30 percent per year, and, therefore, 2.5 percent per month; it is the same 30 percent regardless of whether you look at the data for a year, a month or a minute.) Now suppose that when the tariff is removed firms find it profitable to import 50 percent of this good. Since they imported only 30 percent earlier, imports increase by two-thirds (20 percent divided by 30 percent). But once imports have risen to their new 50 percent level, they will cease to increase (assuming all else equal).

As another example of an unnecessary scare, involving both stocks versus flows and levels versus rates of change, suppose a new law now makes it easier to get a divorce. The number of divorces quadruples. Should we "view with alarm?" Not necessarily. It does not mean that from now on the divorce rate will be four times what it was before. Many of the split-ups were those of marriages that were bad, but not quite bad enough to lead to a divorce under the old law. These couples now divorce, and this shows up as a blip in the divorce rate. Once the stock of marriages has adjusted to the new law, the divorce rate (a flow variable) will fall again, and perhaps will be not much higher than before.

While focusing on a flow variable instead of on the corresponding stock variable can sometimes scare people unnecessarily, at other times it can lull them into a false sense of security. The United States has had a trade deficit for many years, which foreigners have financed by buying American stocks and bonds. (When foreigners buy American stocks and bonds they have to pay for them in dollars and thus provide dollars for American importers.) Can we assume that this flow of foreign money, that is, buying American securities, will continue forever? That depends, in part, on what is happening to the stock of wealth of foreigners. Suppose that their stock of American securities is rising at the same rate as their total stock of assets, so that the ratio of their American assets to their total assets remains constant. In that case they may well be willing to continue financing the American trade deficit indefinitely. But not if their stock of American assets is growing substantially faster than their total assets, so that over time a larger and larger proportion of their assets consists of American securities. Long before this proportion reaches 100 percent, they will cease to buy American stocks and bonds and, therefore, stop or at least reduce financing our trade deficit.

Here is an example from everyday life. You probably noticed that when a new item, such as cell phones, first appears it occupies a lot of shelf space in stores. It is a hot product because many families have less of it than they want; indeed most have none. But once they have acquired as much of it as they want, they stop buying it. Indeed, if this item is durable, i.e., does not wear out, or is made obsolete by a new variant or a new product, and if the population and its income and tastes are unchanged, then its sales will fall to zero, and stores will no longer carry it. One implication is that the temporary booms in the sales of new items that we notice do not necessarily mean that consumers are driven by fads.

An important implication of this relation between a flow variable and a stock variable is that a small percentage change in the demand for capital, that is, in the *stock* of capital, can result in a much larger percentage change in the level of the flow variable which we call investment. (Investment is simply the change in the capital stock.) Suppose, for example, that a firm currently has its appropriate stock of capital, but that 10 percent of this capital wears out each year and has to be replaced, so that its annual rate of gross investment (a flow variable) equals 10 percent of its capital. Now suppose that its sales increase by 5 percent, so that to produce this additional output it wants to increase its capital stock by 5 percent. Suppose, further, that it wants to attain this new capital stock within one year. This 5 percent of its capital that it now wants to add is equivalent to 50 percent of its previous annual rate of investment, so that a 5 percent increase in sales has led to a temporary 50 percent increase in investment. No wonder the capital goods industries are so volatile.

It is not only in economics that the distinction between stocks and flows is important. History departments currently give high priority to studying the history of previously oppressed and silenced groups, such as women and homosexuals, which means that they have fewer resources to devote to such traditional subjects as diplomatic and military history. Conservatives object that these traditional subjects are just as, or more, important, than the subjects that are now favored. Both may be right. Suppose, purely for the sake of the argument, that diplomatic history and women's history are equally important in the sense that we want an equally large stock of knowledge of both subjects. Since over the years we have accumulated a much larger stock of knowledge of diplomatic history than of women's history, it makes sense to direct a larger proportion of the current flow of new knowledge, i.e. research, to women's history than to diplomatic history, until the two stocks are equal. However, that does not necessarily mean that historians are right in deemphasizing diplomatic history to the extent that they have done. That depends on whether we really want equal stocks of diplomatic and women's histories, and on how rapidly we want to equalize these two stocks.

Finally, if you believe that economists are Philistines, or at least that this one is, here is an example that will cement your belief. The available stock of musical compositions grows over time. Assuming for the moment that neither incomes nor tastes change, we will eventually accumulate – and perhaps already have accumulated – the optimal stock of musical compositions, so that there is little left for composers to do. To be sure, some contemporary composers may be so talented that we want their compositions to replace inferior ones in our accumulated stock. But as we do this, the quality of the stock rises, so that the bar for new composers is set ever higher and higher. At some point, there might not be room for even the most talented composer of a generation. In actuality, of course, incomes are rising, and we can, therefore, afford to satisfy the desire for greater variety as well as minority tastes by adding new compositions to our stockpile. Moreover, changes in taste create a market for new compositions. All the same, one would expect the increase in our ever-rising stock of old compositions to reduce the demand for new ones. We would also expect modern composers to cater more to niche tastes and to try to expand their markets by changing our musical tastes. The same principle applies to literature, though here one would expect tastes to change more rapidly as conditions of life change. And in the visual arts perhaps much of the installation "art" that we see can be explained by artists wanting to sidestep the competition from previous paintings, a competition that has been aided by the greatly improved quality of reproductions.[a]

---

[a] This paragraph has dealt with only one aspect of the economics of art and therefore ignored the "Baumol disease" (named after its discoverer, William Baumol). This is, that while technological progress has rapidly raised labor productivity in most sectors of the economy, it still takes four musicians to play a string quartet. And with technological progress having raised wages in the rest of the economy, musicians have to be paid more too. As a result, the relative price of concert tickets has risen, and that has reduced the employment of musicians. However, Tyler Cowen (*In Praise of Commercial Culture*, Cambridge, Harvard University Press, 1998) presents a much more optimistic picture than either Baumol or I do, by stressing how greatly technological advances have increased the accessibility of art. Now, a vastly greater proportion of the world's population has access to Mozart's music than was true in his lifetime.

5.3   Real versus Nominal

Suppose that instead of denominating wages and prices in dollars, we would denominate them in pennies. Nothing would essentially change. Or suppose that we would double everyone's income, wealth, and debts, and also double prices. Again, nothing of substance would change. What determines your standard of living is not your income in dollar terms, what economists call your *nominal* income, but your *real* income, that is, your income as measured by its command over goods and services. Sounds pretty obvious, but it seems that many people don't quite grasp this point, or at least don't appreciate its importance. On October 4, 2006, the *New York Times* reported that the Dow–Jones index had finally passed its previous peak set in January 2000. Not until the eighteenth paragraph did it mention that this was so only in nominal terms, that in real terms it was still well below its previous peak.[b] Or consider the following mental experiment. Suppose that last year prices rose at a 3 percent rate but you got only a 1.5 percent raise. Next year, there is a steep recession, prices *fall* at a 2 percent rate and your employer cuts your nominal salary by 1 percent. You might feel more resentful about this 1 percent cut in your nominal wage, even though it represents a 1 percent rise in your real wage than you did last year when your nominal wage rose but your real wage fell.

It is astonishing to see how many businesses and people compare financial outcomes today versus yesterday with the notion that today's outcome it so much better. And they are rarely right about their great gains. The person who boasts "I bought my house for $300,000 and sold it for $450,000" is usually ignoring that all the years in between purchase and sale, there was an annual inflation devaluing the dollar each year. (We won't even get into the issue of where her new house is and how much it costs.) Every Monday morning Hollywood studio weekend grosses for movies are given, and comparisons are often made to the previous year or previous top movies. Nearly always, the inflation of earnings is ignored in today's statement of success. So *Spiderman 3* earned more than 1939's *Gone with the Wind*. But the admission charges for *Gone with the Wind* ran from $.10 to $.25, versus *Spiderman*'s $7 to $10. You might also check the inflation rate since 1939, to see that the winner financially was this old movie.

---

[b]   Throughout this book I criticize the *New York Times*, not because it is worse than other newspapers, but because it is the paper I read and therefore know. Besides, being our premier newspaper makes it the appropriate target. Editorials in the *Wall Street Journal* would also have yielded some choice targets.

The confusion between nominal and real income is probably even worse with respect to interest income. Everybody knows that "the dollar isn't what it used to be," but how many people know that if you earned, say 3 percent on a one-year CD in 2007 you bought in the first quarter of 2007, and were in the 33 percent marginal tax bracket (counting both federal and state taxes), you lost on the deal. After paying the tax you earned 2 percent, but with prices rising at a 2.3 percent rate, the purchasing power of the after-tax $1.02 you got back from the bank for every dollar you had put into the CD was only $0.997 = (1.02 − 0.023). To find the *real rate of interest* − that is the interest rate adjusted for inflation − you have to subtract the inflation rate from the *nominal* interest rate. If you ignore the distinction between the nominal and the real rate, then, whenever prices are rising, you will overestimate what you earn on your savings. And you will also overestimate the actual interest cost when you borrow.

The confusion between nominal and real values also infests the way the federal budget is stated. Suppose government revenues are $100, and government expenditures on goods and services are $98. Suppose also that the value of the national debt is $50, and the interest rate is 6 percent, so that the government has to pay $3 as interest. The budget then shows a deficit of $1 = ($100 − $98 − $3). If there is no inflation, that is correct. But suppose that the inflation rate is 4 percent. Then the *real* interest rate the government pays is only 2 percent, so that the interest cost you should include in the budget is $1 (2 percent times $50) and not $3. Thus, when you look at real magnitudes the government is running a surplus of $1 = ($100 − $98 − $1), and not as the budget states, a deficit. The *New York Times* ignored the distinction between nominal and real interest rates when it reported that in fiscal year 2006 interest payments on the national debt amounted to "$220 billion, more than what is being spent on Medicare."[1] It should have compared *real* interest payments to the cost of Medicare. And lest you think that only the government would misstate its budget that way, corporate income accounts and balance sheets, too, are generally not adjusted for inflation, because adjusting them would require making many more or less arbitrary assumptions.

5.4   Future versus Current Dollars

You *can* add apples to oranges, and what you get is fruit salad; but if you add up one dollar today and one dollar next year what you get is a meaningless mess. The reason is not only that, unless prices are constant, the purchasing power of these two dollars differs, but also that, if you receive a dollar this year you can invest it and earn interest for a year, so that you are better off than if you receive it only next year. Or suppose you want to spend it this year. Then, if you receive it this year that's fine, but if you receive it only next year, you will have to borrow and pay interest on that dollar for a year.

This raises a question. There are many situations in which you are offered the prospect of a stream of payments spread over several years: for example, when you buy a bond. If you cannot just add these future dollars, how can you find out how much to pay for this bond, or how to value a commitment you undertake to make a stream of payments, such as rent, in the future? You can do that by finding what is called the *"present value"* of each one of these future payments, and then add these present values, and not the dollars themselves.

Here is how to find this present value. To keep things simple, suppose you can earn 5 percent on a completely safe investment and can also borrow at 5 percent. Then, receiving $1 a year from now is worth only $0.95 to you right now, because you are missing out on the $0.05 of interest you could have earned had you received the $1 right away. In symbols, if PV is the present value of a dollar you will receive next year, and i the annual interest rate, also called the "discount rate," then: $PV = \$1/(1 + i)$, so that in the current example the present value is $\$1/(1 + 0.05) = 0.95$. Similarly, suppose you have to pay $1 next year. The present value of this obligation is only $0.95, because in the meantime you can earn $0.05 interest on the $1 that you will not have to hand over until next year.[c]

That takes care of the one-year case, but what is the present value of $1 two years or ten years from now? That means dealing with compound interest. Let's take it in easy steps by first looking at the value of $1 you will receive two years from now. To do that, initially consider what the value will be *next* year of the $1 you will receive in the *following* year. As before, a one-year wait is required, so that *one year from now* the value of the $1 you will receive two years from now is again $\$1/(1 + i)$. To find the value *this* year of something that has a value of $\$1/(1 + i)$ *next* year, you have to multiply it again by $1/(1 + i)$, and that gives $\$1/(1 + i)(1 + i)$, which is usually written as: $\$1/(1 + i)^2$. Similarly, the present value of $1 ten years from now is $\$1/(1 + i)^{10}$.

---

[c]   A warning: I have simplified the examples in this paragraph by taking the case where interest is paid and compounded at the end of the year. Most bonds pay interest twice a year, and some investments pay compound interest daily or continuously.

Table 5.1 Present value of $1 (examples)

	Present value of $1 to be received in:			
	1 year	*5 years*	*10 years*	*20 years*
Interest rate:				
1%	0.99	0.95	0.91	0.82
5%	0.95	0.78	0.61	0.38
10%	0.91	0.62	0.39	0.15

One final step: how about the present value of a permanent income stream, for example, the promise to pay $1 in perpetuity or the value of an environmental improvement that pays off by saving $1 of clean-up costs each year for the infinite future? Since it keeps on giving forever, it might seem that its present value is infinite. But that's not so. A mathematical theorem (which you will have encountered if you studied calculus) tells us that if each successive receipt is less than 100 percent of the preceding one, then the sum of these infinite receipts approaches an upper limit regardless of how far out you go. To find its present value, you divide the payments you will receive each year by the interest rate expressed as a percentage of the principal, e.g. a 5 percent interest rate becomes 0.05. For example, at a 5 percent interest rate the present value of receiving $1 for an infinite number of years is $20. To see why this is so, consider that if you invest $20 at a 5 percent interest rate you get $1 each year.

Table 5.1 shows some examples of the present value of $1 to be received at different times and at various interest rates.

As you can see, both the length of time and the interest rate matter. At a 1 percent interest rate the dollar you will receive twenty years from now is worth 82 cents, but at a 10 percent interest rate it is worth only 15 cents. Not surprisingly for short periods of time the effect of different interest rates is less. A dollar one year from now is worth 99 cents if the interest rate is 1 percent, and 91 cents if the interest rate is 10 percent.

If all this sounds too complicated and you are willing to settle for an approximate, but surprisingly close answer, there is a simple way you can calculate how long it will take for a sum of money to double. Just divide the number 72 by the interest rate, and that's the number of years. Similarly, you can find the interest rate required for a sum of money to double in, say, 7 years by dividing 72 by 7.

Box 5.1: Getting Rich from Compound Interest?

Steve Status is dying. A cure for his disease it is still ten years away. So Steve decides to have himself frozen upon death. But that is expensive and will leave Steve with only $100,000 to invest for his future needs. In his fast-moving field his skills will be outdated when he is revived, so it will be hard for him to find a well-paying job. And Steve does not like the idea of being poor. But he has an idea. He will leave instructions not be woken up for three hundred years, and at a *real* interest rate of 3 percent his $100,000 will have grown to over $700 million (expressed in 2008 dollars). He will finally have achieved his goal of being super rich.

Great idea? Not quite. When Steve wakes up he will indeed be worth over $700 million, but if labor productivity has also grown at a 3 percent rate, his $700 million will amount only to about twice the yearly income of the median family. Compound interest is not the great threat to equality that at first glance it appears to be.

To dramatize the effect of compounding, suppose that in 1507 one of your ancestors had been fortunate enough to buy a drawing by the young, as yet unknown, Raphael for the equivalent of $10, by borrowing at a 3 percent interest rate to be compounded annually until the loan is repaid. In 2008 you, the lucky heir, sold the drawing for $25 million, but when you went to repay the $10 loan plus the accumulated interest you found yourself more than a million dollars in the hole.

Such is the power of compound interest. Sounds awesome, and makes one want to save, save and save. Fortunately, as box 5.1 shows, the compounding of interest does not mean that virtually all wealth will land up in a few hands. But for unsophisticated or weak-willed borrowers, compound interest does create a problem.

So far it's all been a matter of mechanical calculation. But things become less certain when you ask how you figure the appropriate rate of interest at which to discount income from an investment? If your alternative to making the investment is lending the money, then you should use the interest rate you could earn on an equally risky loan. Or, if you have to borrow to make the investment you should use an interest rate equal to the interest rate that you have to pay for the money you need to make the investment. So don't buy a 5 percent government bond by borrowing on your credit card.

This brings up some rather nasty questions. First, why do so many people lend to a bank at, say 5 percent by buying its CD, when at the same time they

---

Box 5.2: Why Lend at a Low Interest Rate While Borrowing at a High Rate?

That people borrow on their credit cards while simultaneously earning a much lower rate on their bank deposits or securities is hard to explain plausibly, if you assume that they are entirely rational and dispassionate utility maximizers, who have no problem in disciplining themselves. Let's, therefore, turn to behavioral economics.

Its explanation is that people are afraid that if they take money out of their bank deposits they will lack the self-control needed to replace it. And even if they do succeed, it may require an unpleasant internal struggle. Paying a credit-card bill requires less self-control. Hence, while on one level borrowing high and lending low may be irrational, on another level, a level that acknowledges the existence of human weakness, it may be rational. The next best thing to being fully rational is being aware of your irrationalities and counteracting them.

---

are borrowing on their credit card at, say 15 percent? Box 5.2 tries to explain that. Second, it is easy enough to say that if you are a borrower you should use the interest rate that approximates the interest rate you have to pay. But what interest rate is this? If you borrow only to make this particular investment and will not borrow again, that question is easy to answer. But suppose you will be borrowing in the future as well. Then you have to take into account that by becoming more indebted now you lower your credit rating, and hence raise the rate you will have to pay when you borrow in the future. And as box 5.3 shows, the choice of the correct interest rate also raises a troublesome question for environmental policy.

Obvious though it may seem, the principle that you have to discount future dollars before adding them to current dollars is sometimes forgotten. Suppose opposition from environmentalists delays the construction of a bridge, which results in a substantial cost increase. This alleged "increase," for which environmentalists will then be blamed, might be considerably less of an increase or no increase at all, when the cost is stated correctly in present-value terms. Another example of the failure to discount future costs and benefits is the claim that many people ignore the environmental damage they do because they lack foresight; that to avoid having to spend $1 right now, they inflict damage that it will cost $2 to clean up later. I certainly agree that a lot of serious damage is done to the environment, and some of it could be due to thoughtlessly ignoring future costs, but another factor may perhaps play a

Box 5.3: Global Warming and the Discount Rate

The discount rate plays a major role in deciding what to do about global warming, because the costs of current actions to ameliorate it have to be compared to benefits, most of which will occur only in the distant future. The appropriate discount rate is not easily determined. At one extreme some have argued that we should use a zero, or close to zero, discount rate since to do to otherwise would amount to treating a dollar of consumption of future generations as less valuable than a dollar of our own consumption, and such selfishness is immoral. If, by spending one dollar now, we can save some future generation more than one dollar, then we should do so.

But there are weighty counter-arguments. First, future generations will presumably (though not necessarily) be much richer than we are, so that the marginal utility of a dollar of consumption is greater for us than it is for them. Second, in their everyday lives people act without apparent qualms as though the value of a dollar to their heirs is less than it is to them; otherwise, given the magic of compound interest, they would save much, much more. Moreover, it seems highly unlikely that many people think of their fourteenth-century ancestors as immoral because they did not save more for the benefit of our generation. Should such widespread moral intuitions be ignored?

But if we, therefore, decide to use an interest rate substantially greater than zero, what should it be? The interest rate currently prevailing in the market is not *necessarily* the right rate since it depends on the savings rate of the current generation, a decision about which future generations have no say. However, if you take a natural-rights view of ownership you might respond that the current income belongs to the current generation, and that future generations have no right to say how much of it we should save, they did not earn it. But, one might respond, we earned it with the capital that previous generations had accumulated. By now the debate has now veered off into philosophical issues outside the scope of this book.

However, this uncertainty about the discount rate does not mean that we should do nothing about global warming. Even at a high discount rate some action is warranted, particularly if one takes into account the great uncertainty about how bad the effects of global warming will be. Since people dislike uncertainty it may be reasonable to spend a dollar now even if the most likely discounted benefit from that expenditure is less than a dollar. Perhaps a stronger case for action against global warming can be made, not by arguing that it will have this or that bad effect, but by arguing that we do not know what its effects will be, and want to protect against quite unlikely but *potentially* immense losses.

bigger role. If the interest rate is 4 percent, and the $2 clean-up cost will not be incurred for eighteen years or more, then it is rational to spend the $2 then rather than the $1 now. A stitch in time may save nine, but if the nine stitches will not have to be made for seventy-five years, and the interest rate is 3 percent or more, it costs more to do the one stitch now.

5.5   The Price Level versus Relative Prices

Suppose one morning you find that your supermarket now charges more for a pound of your favorite coffee. That could be due to a change in the *price level* – also called "absolute prices" – that is, in the exchange rate of money against goods and services in general, or a change in a *relative price*, that is, in the exchange rate of coffee relative to other goods. This difference is important because the price level depends on macroeconomic factors, such as changes in the quantity of money, while relative prices depend on microeconomic factors specific to particular industries or firms, such as shifts in consumer demand, technological improvements in a certain industry, or changes in the market power of a particular firm.

Let's put this distinction to work. Suppose that there is a 50 percent increase in the price of an imported good, which directly (and indirectly as raw material for other goods) accounts for 10 percent of total sales. A simple-minded analysis that demonstrates greater virtuosity at arithmetic than at economics would say that the price level will rise by 5 percent (10 percent × 50 percent). But this assumes that other prices will be unchanged, and that is a dubious assumption. To take an extreme case, assume that the Federal Reserve does not allow the money supply to rise at all. Then, if the price level were to rise by 5 percent, the real value of the nominal money that you and everyone else holds would fall by 5 percent. But since nothing else has changed, if you previously found it convenient to hold a certain amount of real money you will now still want to hold the same real amount of real money, and that means holding 5 percent more nominal money. (Of course, unless you are a monomaniac economist you will not think of it that way, but will say to yourself something like: "I better keep some more cash around.") To do that, you will spend less money buying goods and services, stocks and bonds, etc. And as you and other people do so, demand falls, and unemployment and the excess capacity of firms increase. This results in downward pressure on wages and on profit margins. Ultimately, this brings the price level back to where it was before. At that point all the adjustment that has occurred has been in relative prices. The imported good and goods that require it in their production are now more expensive, but other prices have fallen enough to offset these price increases. This is just a hypothetical example to illustrate the point; in actuality the Federal Reserve is likely to intervene and generate *some* increase in the nominal money supply, so that prices of other goods do not fall, but just rise less than they otherwise would have.

One final point on relative prices. They change all the time as supply and demand change because of factors such as shifting consumer demand or technological changes. Some rise in real terms, that is, they rise in nominal terms by more than the overall inflation rate – and others fall in real terms. There is no reason to wax indignant about some price rising at a faster rate than inflation. All that means is that some others are rising at a rate less than the average inflation rate.

5.6   Stable Prices versus Low Prices

This is a distinction that some special interests have an incentive to hide. Suppose you are the head of a farm cooperative that wants to raise the prices of its products by restricting supply at times when they are falling. (It's legal, since farm cooperatives are exempt from anti-trust laws.) If you announce that you want to raise your prices, consumers are likely to object. You, therefore, announce instead that all you aim to do is to "stabilize" prices by restricting output only when prices are falling. That sounds fine, and few people object to keeping prices stable. And it sweeps under the rug the fact that if you eliminate instances when prices are falling without also eliminating instances when they are rising you raise the average. Beware of producers when they offer you "stability."

5.7   Gross versus Net and Single versus Double Counting

Let's listen to Jerry Booster, Hometown's convention manager report to the City Council. "Wouldn't it be great if our city could secure the 2012 convention of the National Association of Left-handed Hairbraiders? Granted, it would require giving a $2 million subsidy to this association. But when you add up the $3 million that the left-handed hairbraiders will spend on hotels, the $2 million they will spend on food, and the $1 million on entertainment, and add to that the $4 million that these industries will pay out as additional wages, plus the $1 million in increased tax receipts that the city stands to gain from all this additional spending, you can see that we stand to make a substantial profit: $11 million in receipts for just a $2 million subsidy. Isn't that a great deal?"

No, it isn't: because the $13 million figure is a meaningless jumble that counts some items twice, and also confuses net and gross receipts. Thus Jerry added to the $6 million that the hairbraiders will spend on hotels, restaurants, and entertainment, the $4 million that these industries will pay out as wages. But these $4 million of wages have already been counted once as part of the $6 million received by the hotel, restaurant, and entertainment industries. Or, put another way, to calculate the *net* gain to the hotels, etc., we have to *subtract* from the $6 million receipts the $4 million they have to pay out as wages. Only then can we count the $4 million of wages received by workers in these industries as part of the benefits from the convention. And, similarly, the $1 million of taxes that Jerry added in are part of the $6 million he has already counted once as receipts.

Moreover, even if Jerry had not confounded gross and net numbers and stated correctly that Hometown, its businesses, and employees will receive $6 million from the convention, he would still not have made a case that it should offer the $2 million subsidy, because the $6 million revenue is not directly comparable to the $2 million subsidy. The subsidy is a net loss to the city that will eventually have to be made up by raising taxes or cutting city services. By contrast, the $6 million received from the convention is not a *net* gain to the residents of Hometown. The hairbraiders receive goods and services in exchange for their $6 million. Hometown workers will have to work more, hotel furnishings will depreciate faster, and Hometown will be paying for food and liquor imported from elsewhere.

5.8   Opportunity Costs versus Monetary Costs

Opportunity costs is one of the most basic concepts in economics that shows up whenever you consider taking one action rather than another. It differs from the conventional, everyday notion of cost, by looking at costs as fore-gone opportunities. This does not necessarily conflict with the conventional notion of costs. But if you think in terms of opportunity costs it is less likely that you will overlook some not so obvious costs, because opportunity costs put front and center that, since your resources are limited, the more resources you use to attain one objective, the less you have available to pursue your other objectives. Suppose a firm owns a machine it could use to produce either toasters or electric irons. Assume that operating the machine does not involve any significant costs, such as electricity and wear and tear, so that the cost – as conventionally measured – of using it to produce toasters is zero. Does that mean that in deciding whether to produce toasters the firm should treat the cost of using this machine as zero? No: it should not. The relevant cost of using it to produce toasters is what the firm could have earned by using it to produce electric irons.

Here is an example from everyday life. Suppose you generally buy reduced-calorie jam, but on your last shopping trip bought regular jam by mistake. You decide to eat it rather than waste money by throwing it out. Should you consume only one tablespoon per day instead of your usual two? No: whether you eat two tablespoons or only one of the high-calorie jam determines how soon you will finish the high-calorie jam and eat low-calorie jam again, not the total amount of high-calorie jam that you will eat. The opportunity cost of eating two tablespoons per day is, therefore, the cost (in terms of calories and money) of eating more low-calorie jam, and you previously decided that you can allow yourself two tablespoons of that.

Or take the question whether many of the products we buy should be sturdier and longer lasting. The obvious answer is, "of course they should," until you ask what making them sturdier would do to their costs and hence prices. The optimal degree of sturdiness depends among other things on the extent to which they become obsolete due to technical improvements and on the rate of interest at which we discount their future services. Box 5.4 gives another example.

Policies, too, have their opportunity costs. For many economic policies their monetary costs are more or less adequate approximations to their opportunity costs. But not for all. Here is an example. Some people advocate reinstituting the draft because they think that it would act as a curb on military adventures, or that military service is a duty of citizenship, or else, that it would provide young men (and women?) with much needed discipline. They may, or may not, be right in making these claims. But they are clearly wrong if they go on to talk economics, and claim that a draft would be less costly to the country because a draftee would not have to be paid as much as a volunteer. Although the government would pay a lower wage to a draftee, it would still be using up more resources – the true measure of costs – than it would if it relied on volunteers. Here is why. Suppose the army wants to add one soldier and, therefore, offers to pay $40,000 a year to either Jack or Bill. To keep the example simple, assume that, apart from any gains or losses of income, both are indifferent to whether they are soldiers or civilians. Jack says no because he earns $70,000. Bill who earns $39,000 says yes. By contrast, if there were a draft, so that the army would not have to compete with civilian employers,

---

Box 5.4: Another Example of Opportunity Costs

In February when tickets went on sale Cindy Careless bought a ticket to a concert on July 17 for $40, and then forgot all about it. A week before the concert she spent $80 for a theater ticket on the same night. At 5 p.m. on July 17 she realized her mistake. Too late to sell either ticket now. Which performance should she go to? Her first impulse was to say, well it is better to waste $40 than $80, so I'll go to the play. But then she dimly remembered what she had learned about opportunity costs in Econ.101; that what she had paid for the tickets was sunk costs, spilled milk, and should not influence her decision. The opportunity cost of going to the concert was missing the play, and vice versa, regardless of what she had paid for the tickets. The only relevant consideration is which performance she would enjoy more, and that was the concert.

The next day when she told her mother about it, her mother told her sternly: "Buying the theater ticket was silly, you should not have been that careless, and you should have remembered that you had a concert ticket for that night." "Oh no," Cindy replied, "being more careful would have required time and mental effort, and since I am a highly paid professional, the opportunity cost of ensuring that I don't occasionally miss a concert for which I have a ticket is too great." So you see, economics is useful after all.

---

it might pay its draftees only, say $30,000, and use a lottery to select either Jack or Bill. If it is Bill who is selected he is $9,000 worse off than if there had been no draft and he had continued to earn $39,000. But suppose the computer had picked Jack. He is $40,000 ($70,000 minus $30,000) worse off. But the army's gain is only the $9,000 less than what it would have had to pay to get Bill to volunteer. Since we don't know which one the computer will pick, it is reasonable to set the average loss from the draft at $24,500 (0.5 times $9,000 to Bill plus 0.5 times $40,000 to Jack). With the government's gain from the draft being only $9,000, the draft does not make economic sense. It appears to be cheaper only when one looks just at the money the army pays out, and not at the opportunity cost.

Having reached what seems like a definitive conclusion on the cost of a draft versus a volunteer army, I must admit a qualification. The money that the government pays its soldiers does not somehow descend from heaven in a gentle rain, but comes from taxing the public. And taxes impose a dead-weight cost on the economy. For example, if income is taxed at a 33 percent marginal rate, someone who can produce $30 worth of goods and services by working an extra hour, but who values her leisure at $25 per hour, will not work that extra hour, because that would yield her an after-tax income of only $20 ($30 × 0.67), $5 less than the benefit she gets from enjoying leisure. This generates inefficiency, since the economy as a whole, loses $30 of output, while she gains only $25 worth of leisure. It is conceivable that with the higher pay of a volunteer army requiring higher taxes, this excess burden of taxation exceeds the previously discussed benefit of relying on volunteers. But as a practical matter that seems most unlikely.

Here is another example. You buy a $10,000 bond paying 5 percent interest. Right afterwards interest rates rise to 6 percent and the value of your bond is now less than the $10,000 you paid for it. (For why interest rates affect bond prices, see box 5.5.) Your obnoxious brother-in-law commiserates with you and tells you about his own successful investments. So you tell him curtly that he is wrong, your bond is still paying you the same $500 a year as before, and will be redeemed for the same $10,000 as before, so where is the loss? Fortunately for your peace of mind, your brother-in-law does not know about opportunity costs, so he mumbles something and slinks off. Not so, your sister-in-law. She points out that if you had waited with buying a bond you would now be receiving $600 a year instead of $500. Now it is you who mumbles something and slinks off, because in terms of opportunity costs you *do* have a loss.

For additional examples lets turn to the oh-so-earnest people who tell us things like: "we must ensure that the workplace is as safe as we know how to make it" or "we must do whatever is technically feasible to prevent air crashes, regardless of the cost and its impact on profits."

5.9   Cost–Benefit Analysis

And this brings us to cost–benefit analysis which, as the name implies, compares the benefits and opportunity costs of a particular policy. That seems the obvious way to evaluate a policy. But it is far from uncontroversial because usually, though not always, costs and benefits come in different units. When they do come in the same units things are simple; for example, if you have $10 million to spend on safety, and you know that spending them on an improved ambulance service will on average save ten lives per year, while spending them on improved guard rails will save twenty lives, you know what to do. But suppose you can also spend them on providing courts with more public defenders which you estimate will result in one hundred fewer wrongful

Box 5.5: Interest Rates and Bond Prices

What happens to bond prices when interest rates rise? "They rise, since bonds now offer a greater return," is the quick and obvious – and wrong – answer. It is wrong because the interest rate on previously issued bonds does not go up when the interest rate on newly issued bonds does. A firm that issues a $1,000 bond carrying a 6 percent interest rate will pay you $60 per year regardless of whether new $1,000 bonds pay $10 or a $100 per year. But if you want to sell the 6 percent bond before its maturity date and the interest rate on new bonds with the same degree of risk and the same liquidity is 10 percent, then nobody will pay you a $1,000 for the right to receive the $60 per year that your bond provides. You will, therefore, have to sell your bond at a loss. Conversely, if the interest rate on new bonds falls to 3 percent you can sell your 6 percent bond at a profit.

How big a profit (or loss) depends on two factors, the difference between the interest rate on new bonds and on your bond, and on the maturity of your bond. The longer the buyer of your bond can enjoy a 6 percent interest rate when newly issued bonds pay only 3 percent, the more she will pay for your bond.

In one special case, you can quickly calculate exactly how much your 6 percent bond is worth. This is the hypothetical case of a perpetual bond that will never mature, but keep on paying 6 percent evermore. In that case if your bond pays 6 percent and new bonds pay 3 percent your $1,000 bond will sell for $2,000, because $2,000 invested in a bond that pays 6 percent brings the buyer the same $60 as $2,000 invested in 3 percent bond.

There is one wrinkle you have to watch out for: corporate bonds usually have a provision allowing the borrower to repay the bond ahead of its maturity. So if interest rates fall to 3 percent you may be unfortunate enough to get a check from the corporation that issued the bond, repaying it. Buyers of bonds know this, and if they think the corporation will repay the bond ahead of its maturity they will not be willing to pay much more than $1,000 for your 6 percent bond when interest rates fall below 6 percent.

convictions. Now to decide which is the best policy you somehow have to price, i.e., express in dollars, the value of saving a life and of preventing a miscarriage of justice. How do you do that? For the value of saving a life you can try to estimate the monetary value that people put on their own lives by comparing the wages required to attract workers into jobs that require similar levels of skill and effort, but one of which is more dangerous than the others. This is far from ideal both because workers may have an unrealistic appreciation of the danger of losing their lives in the riskier job, and also because those who take risky jobs may value their lives less than the average person, but it gives you *some* idea. Estimating the loss from being falsely convicted of a crime is even dicier. But, if you are a policy-maker who has to decide how to allocate the $10 million, dicey or not, you have to make some sort of guess, just as a donor has to decide how much to give to famine relief and how much to the local symphony.

Some people find such reasoning morally repellant. They consider putting a finite dollar value on human life as similar to the mentality that brought us Gulags and Nazi death camps. To them the economist with her cost–benefit analysis has only one answer: "Do you in your personal life put an infinite value on human life? If so, do you drive, and if you do, do you at least have the brakes on your car checked every day and never drive at more than the safest speed?" And it is no use replying that you are allowed to put a value on your own life, but not other people's because when you drive you do put other people's lives at risk.

5.10   Wage Rates versus Labor Costs

From 1976 to 2006 real per capita GDP rose by 81 percent. Yet average real earnings per hour were 4 percent *lower* in 2007 than in 2006. What is going on here? Well one thing is that, as will be discussed in chapter 10, appendix 10.2, the consumer price index used to convert nominal into real earnings over-states the inflation rate, so that real earnings did better than the data show. Another, and probably more important one is that we are looking at the wrong concept, and hence the wrong numbers. Employees receive extensive fringe benefits, such as medical benefits and retirement benefits, which are not included in "average real earnings." When we look at another measure, real total employee compensation per hour, which includes these fringe benefits, that went up in this period, so that employees were better off in 2007 than in 1976.

Moreover, the data on average hourly earnings include along with full-time workers part-time workers, who on average are paid less per hour than full-time workers. And the proportion of part-time workers has been rising. The moral of this story: make sure that the data you look at are the ones relevant for the question you are asking.

This is not to deny that blue-collar employees fared poorly relative to college graduates in this period, nor is it to deny that one should be seriously concerned about this. But it does mean that those who cite what has happened to real hourly earnings to show how badly workers have fared have gotten hold of the wrong concept and data.

5.11   Capital Goods versus Human Capital

If asked to name the biggest component of our capital stock some would reply factories, others residential buildings, and perhaps some would say land. But, to economists, it is none of these. Their reply would be human capital and other forms of intangible capital. Human capital is the present value of the income that employees will earn as they apply their skills. Roughly 0.67 of our income consists of the earnings of labor. And very little of this labor is raw, untutored brawn; it is instead the application of knowledge and skills that have been acquired by education and training. This acquisition has been costly since it includes not only the tuition costs but also the earnings that students had to forego to acquire this education and training. Investment in human capital in 2004 has been estimated as $46 trillion, while only $12 trillion were invested in plant and equipment.

Compare two brothers, John and Bill, who each inherit $300,000. John uses it to buy several trucks and establish a hauling firm. Bill uses it to go to medical school. Though many people tend to think of John as someone who owns capital and as Bill as someone who does not, this distinction is not reasonable. Both had foregone alternative uses of their money, such as spending it on corporate bonds or on wine, women, and song, and both expect to earn a certain return on their investment. Both take risks. John's risk is that his firm might be unprofitable, and Bill's that he might flunk out of medical school, or that he might die before he has amortized the investment he made in his education. It is true that Bill's decision to invest in a medical career may well have sprung primarily from motives other than making money, but that may also be true for John's decision, since he may have been eager to be his own boss. And even if non-financial motives did play a larger role in Bill's decision than in John's, the same may be true for someone who establishes an art gallery rather than a trucking firm, and yet we consider the cost of setting up the art gallery to be investment.

Broadening the idea of capital to include human capital is not a new idea. It goes back to at least John Locke (1632–1704) who treated a worker's ability to earn an income as a form of property. It has several consequences. One is that it highlights the importance of education. It also helps to explain why areas that were destroyed by wars or natural disasters recover so quickly.

The destruction of human capital is usually less than the destruction of buildings and other physical capital that we see. It even explains something that may puzzle readers of Victorian novels, the great emphasis on inherited wealth. At that time human capital was much less important than it is now, and if a woman married a man with little nonhuman capital she was unlikely to enjoy a decent standard of living. Similarly, a man with no nonhuman capital had a much stronger incentive to seek an heiress than he does now. The increased importance of human capital also explains the declining role of the traditional dowry. A bride's high school, college, and professional degrees now take its place.

Intangible capital, though it resides within human beings and is, therefore, human capital, consists of more than the technical skills that people bring to their jobs. It includes attitudes and habits like the "puritan ethic," and also our laws, habits, attitudes, and other informal institutions, such as protection of property rights and the belief that people should be honest

5.12   Marginal versus Average Utility

Although the study of economics can be traced back to the ancient Greeks, the iconic figure among the fathers of economics is Adam Smith, whose *An Inquiry into the Nature and Causes of the Wealth of Nations* appeared in 1776. One of the major questions that concerned Smith and his immediate followers (called classical economists) was to explain the relative values and prices of goods. While it seems obvious that their relative values should depend on how useful they are to potential buyers, classical economists were stymied when they tried to develop this line of thought systematically. There seems to be little relation between what is useful to man and what is expensive. The classic example was the contrast between a lump of coal (remember that was in the late eighteenth and early nineteenth century) and a diamond. Why does a diamond sell for more than does a so-much-more useful lump of coal? Surely, we would suffer more if we were deprived of coal than of diamonds.

The breakthrough came only in the second half of the nineteenth century, when economists distinguished between average utility and marginal utility. Suppose you were confronted with the choice of either buying your entire gasoline supply for next year at $10 per gallon, or not getting any gas at all. You would probably agree to pay the $10. But if it were just a matter of doing without the last – that is the marginal – gallon, or buying it for $10, you would probably decide that you can do without it, and eliminate the least useful trip you had planned. It is not that the marginal gallon is, in and of itself, different from any other gallon – your car gets the same mileage on the last gallon as on the first. In economics "marginal" does not have the connotation of "barely adequate," it just means that you put it to a use you value less than the one to which you put any of the other gallons you buy. Hence, the more you consume of something, the less is the utility you derive from having one more unit of it. Economists call this "declining marginal utility."

Once one focuses on the *marginal* purchase decision it is no longer puzzling that consumers are willing to pay as much for an additional unit of a good they could easily do entirely without (diamonds), as for an additional unit of a good that, *in toto*, they could not do without, such as food. The value of a good does depend, as common sense tells us, on its utility, but it is its marginal, not its average utility. The fact that we cannot live without *some* food does not enable farmers to hold us to ransom. If food prices rise, we just cut back on marginal purchases. And we consume as much food, diamonds, coal, etc., until the last dollar spent on any of these goods provides us with equal utility. If it did not, we could increase our utility by switching expenditures from a good with a low marginal utility to one with higher marginal utility.

5.13   Marginal versus Average Costs

The marginal–average distinction applies not only to utility, but also to costs. The cost of producing an additional unit of output, that is, its marginal cost, *could* equal the average cost for all previous units, but there is no reason why it should. Not only are there the familiar economies of scale, there are also offsetting diseconomies of scale, that is, factors that raise the average cost as you produce more units.

One of factors that – in the short run – raises costs as a firm produces more is that it has a fixed stock of capital. As it adds more workers, each worker has less capital to work with, and output per additional worker, therefore, declines. One can tell stories here, such as additional workers being used primarily to bring material to the previously hired workers who are tending the machines. But in the long run the firm can increase its capital stock, so that in the long run this reason for increasing marginal costs disappears. But there is a reason why costs should increase even in the long run as a firm increases its output. This is that the larger size, and hence greater complexity of the firm, inexorably increases bureaucratization with its resultant loss of flexibility. Moreover, as will be discussed in chapter 7, the larger the firm, the less efficiently are its manager's incentives aligned with those of the firm.

On the other side, are some factors that increase efficiency and hence lower average costs as a firm increases its output. One is that it can now spread its overhead costs over more units. Another factor that operates in the short run is that if a firm had previously cut its output, perhaps because of a recession, and is now increasing it, it can often do so without having to add very many additional employees because previously when it cut output it did not cut employment proportionately since it knew that in the subsequent expansion it would be hard to replace some specialized employees who have the particular skills and knowledge that the firm needs. So it had them work less intensely or work on less urgent tasks. But this factor is no longer operative once the firm reaches its old level of output.

However, in the long run, another factor that lowers costs as output increases enters the story. This is that a larger output allows a firm to take more advantage of the division of labor, and to use more specialized equipment. Whether these advantages of operating on a large scale are sufficient to offset the above mentioned disadvantages of greater bureaucracy varies from firm to firm.

5.14   Big Business versus Market Power

The identification of big business with market power is firmly established in the public mind. And there is something to it; size does have some connection to market power, if the market is large, it does take a large firm to dominate it. But the connection between firm size and market power is loose. A firm may be large in absolute terms, but if the market is very large, it may account for only a small proportion of the industry's output and have little market power: some steel mills are large, but not relative to the size of the American market for steel. Conversely, a small firm in a tiny market, for example, the only grocery store in a village, does have some market power. And even if the firm is small and the industry is large, if a significant proportion of consumers consider the firm's product so superior to that of its rivals that they are willing to pay a higher price for it, then this firm does have some market power. On the other hand, a firm may be both large in absolute terms and account for a large proportion of its industry's output, and yet its market power may be quite limited because it may be afraid that if it raises its prices new firms, perhaps from other industries or other countries, may invade its turf.

What then drives the tendency to overestimate the connection between size and market power? Probably the major reason is that people distrust bigness per se, because they feel a certain helplessness when dealing with a giant organization, be it in business or in government. It is more comforting to complain to the owner right in the store, or the next time you meet her on the street, and quite another to having to pick your way among the branches of an immense telephone tree to reach a "customer service" that cannot help you.

Whatever its cause, the popular tendency to identify size and market power adds support to the debatable notion that the government should protect small competitors rather than competition itself. For example, if the entry of Wal-Mart threatens small retail stores many people may demand that the city council prohibit it. Perhaps, though I doubt it, one can successfully make a case for this by arguing that, regardless of the economic consequences, it is socially desirable to have a lot of small shopkeepers. But economists tend to reply that the purpose of competition is to provide low prices for consumers, so that a policy of protecting competitors by preventing a large firm from underselling them misses the point.[d]

5.15   Pro-market versus Pro-business

Those who support the interests of business, either in general or of a specific business, often wrap themselves in the cloak of Adam Smith and describe themselves as "pro-market." This is by no means always wrong, because many measures that reduce business profits also interfere with free markets. But neither is it always right. Businesses and their sympathizers also advocate some measures that would curb competition and thus obstruct free markets.

For example, ship owners and maritime unions have lobbied Congress into requiring that much of American food aid must be sent in American ships. In some cities, building codes limit competition from cheaper materials, and states use licensing requirements to limit competition in services such as cutting hair. Those of us who urge reliance on the market are not necessarily advocates of business interests.

5.16   "Should" and "Can" versus "Will"

At first glance, it may seem strange that someone would mix up what should be or can be done with what will be done. Even infants know that the world

---

[d]   An exception is a situation in which a large firm lowers its prices to drive out small competitors, and subsequently raises its prices. But whether a firm is likely to do that is open to debate.

is not perfect. But apparently some of those who comment on economic policy do not, or at least do not always apply this distinction. Thus, those who advocate imposing some costs on firms, such as requiring that they pay a "living wage," sometimes tell us or imply that firms can absorb these costs. But that firms *can* absorb them does not mean that *will* do so. Instead, they are likely to pass at least some of them on to consumers through higher prices, and perhaps also to higher-paid employees through raising wages less than they otherwise would. Similarly, some who advocate lowering the corporate income tax argue that this will allow firms to invest more, and thus create more jobs. Yes, but it will also allow them to raise dividends instead. And those conservatives who advocate setting voluntary instead of mandatory pollution standards for firms also seem to confuse can with will.

5.17   Comparative versus Absolute Advantage

Now let's look at a distinction that is basic to understanding why we all don't grow our own food or sew our own clothes. We specialize and trade our services and goods. This principle applies to individuals, to exchange between regions of a country, and to trade between two different countries. Suppose country A can produce every good more efficiently, that is, with a smaller input of labor, capital, land, and entrepreneurship than can country B. It might seem that since it can make everything more cheaply itself, it has no incentive to import from country B, and that B cannot possibly compete in A's market.

Wrong! While A has what we call an absolute advantage in producing every good, for some goods its advantage is greater than it is for others, and it can benefit by exporting those goods in which its advantage is greatest, and importing those for which its advantage is least. That is why economists distinguish between "absolute" and "comparative" advantages, where "comparative" refers to a comparison – not between the same good in different countries – but between different goods within any one country. Suppose that in India it takes 2 units of labor and capital to produce a pair of shoes and 1,000 units to produce a tractor, while in the United States it takes only 1 unit of labor and capital to produce a pair of shoes and 300 units to produce a tractor, so that the United States has an absolute in both goods and a comparative advantage in tractors.

There is then a gain to be had from trading. How big a gain? Let's first assume that the prices of tractors and shoes stay put at their Indian levels, and look at how much India can then gain from trading. Without trade India would have to give up 500 (= 1,000/2) pairs of shoes to release the labor and capital it needs to produce one tractor, while if it trades it can obtain a tractor by exporting only 300 pairs of shoes. How about the United States? Assume now that the prices of shoes and tractors stay put at their American level. By exporting a tractor it can obtain 1,000 pairs of shoes instead of the 300 pairs it would obtain by switching its own labor and capital from producing one tractor to producing shoes.

In this example, I assumed, when talking about India, that trade takes place at the prices of shoes and tractors prevailing in India and, when talking about the United States, that it takes place at the prices prevailing in the United States. That does not make sense since the prices in India and in the United States differ. We have to allow for the fact that as India imports tractors the price of tractors in India falls, and that as the United States imports shoes the price of shoes in the United States falls.[e] But all that means is that, while both countries gain from the trade, neither gains all that it would if it were able to sell its exports and obtain its imports at the initial prices prevailing in the other country. But there is still a gain for both countries, and that's what counts.

One more wrinkle needs to be discussed. Assume that India has lower labor costs than the United States for both shoes and tractors. What prevents India from exporting both goods to the United States, while importing nothing? Let's see what would happen if India tried that. Indian firms would now receive a lot of dollars for their exports which they would have to exchange for Indian rupees on the foreign exchange market, since the costs they incur are primarily in rupees. At the same time, American firms would be scrambling to exchange their dollars for the rupees they need to pay for all their imports. As a result, let's simplify, by ignoring foreign investment and some other activities that create a demand for either rupees or dollars, and assume that the only thing going on is the trading of shoes and tractors. Then, since the foreign exchange market reaches balance only when the supply and demand for rupees are equal, the rupee will have to rise in terms of the dollar until Indian tractors are so expensive in the United States when measured in dollars, and American tractors so cheap in India when measured in rupees, that India stops selling tractors to the United States and instead imports them, while still exporting shoes to the United States.

That, except in very special circumstances, both countries gain from trade is an idea that seems obvious to economists, but alien to the general public, which being ever suspicious of the subtle machinations of ill-intentioned foreigners looks upon foreign trade as transactions in which one side's gain

---

[e] To keep the discussion simple, I am assuming that both India and the United States produce shoes and tractors at constant costs.

is another side's loss, a zero-sum game, or even worse a situation in which special interests gain at the expense of ordinary people in both countries. Many people would be surprised to learn that most economists think that we gain when we cut our tariffs even if other countries don't cut theirs. It is hard to say why the public thinks so, because it usually recognizes that within the country trade is beneficial to both sides of the deal. Perhaps it is a visceral fear of foreigners, that when we undertake foreign trade we are entering a dark jungle where the wicked "other" is all set to pounce on us. Perhaps it is the notion that there is a fixed number of jobs (sometimes this is called "the lump of labor theory") and that if foreigners or immigrants perform work previously done by Americans there will be fewer jobs for Americans. This ignores the fact that, by importing more, we are providing foreigners with the wherewithal to buy more American goods.

But negative-sum and zero-sum thinking, along with the fear of being exploited are not confined to foreign trade. Such thinking also flourishes among both left-wing and right-wing zealots. If a law is good for business it must be bad for the average man. If some countries are rich and others poor, it must be due to the rich former colonial countries having exploited their former colonies, and never mind that this requires some mental acrobatics to explain why Switzerland, which never had colonies, is rich, while Thailand, which, though forced to sign unequal treaties, was never colonized by the West, and Ethiopia, which was colonized only from 1935 to 1941, are poor.

PART III
ECONOMIC THEORY AND POLICY

6

The Crown Jewel of Economics: The Price Mechanism

How is it that firms, by and large, produce the goods and services that we want? This coordination between hundreds of millions of consumers and producers is an amazing feat – just think of how difficult it often is to arrange a lunch with just three friends. No wonder that when the last premier of the Soviet Union, Mikhail Gorbachev, visited Britain he asked the British prime minister, Margaret Thatcher, how she ensured that the British population got its food.[1] Adam Smith could have told him that already in 1776: it is the invisible hand of the free market's price mechanism, one of the great discoveries of humankind, because it permits the extensive division of labor that we find in all but the most primitive economies. We'll first look at how it works in an idealized world, and then at the warts it, like everything else, displays in the real world.

6.1   An Overview of the Price Mechanism

Suppose that a new study shows that apples are healthier than people previously realized. Consumers now want more of them, so more should be produced. But just how many more? While everyone knows how many apples he or she now wants, nobody knows how many apples other people want, nor do they know to what extent this increased demand for apples is at the expense of pears or iPods, etc. This information is stored only in the minds of many millions of people, and the economy needs some mechanism that combines and registers it, so that apple producers can respond accordingly. Or, suppose an innovation lowers the cost of producing aluminum. Obviously, the economy as a whole should now produce more aluminum and fewer of rival goods, such as steel and plastics. But, again, how much more, and how much fewer of what? And even if we somehow knew this for the economy taken as a whole, an individual firm that can use either steel or aluminum would not know in some magical way whether it or some other firm is the one that should switch to aluminum. It is an exaggeration, but not all that much of one, to say that all the numerous problems of economics essentially boil down to one grand problem: coordinating the information that exists in the minds of individual producers and consumers.

To see how the price system does this, let's start with a simple economy in which no such coordination is needed. This is an economy consisting of a single person, say, myself. I work until the utility of the additional goods I obtain by working another hour is just equal to the disutility I experience from having to work this extra hour. Then I stop. And I allocate my working time among the various goods that I can produce until at the margin the utilities of all the goods I can generate by an hour's work are equal, because if they are not, then I can increase my welfare by producing more of the good with the higher marginal utility and less of the good with the lower marginal utility.

But in an economy consisting of many persons, things are more complicated. Instead of producing in accordance with my inherent knowledge of what it is that I want, I now have to produce in accordance with what others want, even though I have no direct knowledge of what is going on in their minds. Since there are too many of them to ask, and since if I were to ask they might not tell me the truth, I undertake an experiment. I offer to sell my product, say apples, at a certain price. If at that price they demand more apples than I want to produce at that price, I raise my price. As I do this two things obviously happen. One is that they now demand fewer apples. The other is that at that higher price it is worth my effort to produce more apples. So I keep on raising my price until the number of apples I want to produce at that particular price is just equal to number of apples consumers want to buy at that price.

Consumers decide whether to buy my apples or some other goods in a way similar to the one I used to decide what to produce in the previous single-person story: that is, they look at the utility they obtain from the last dollar they spend on each good. Obviously, if the marginal utility they get from a dollar they spend on good A exceeds the marginal utility they get from a dollar spent on good B, they can make themselves better off, by shifting expenditures from the lower-valued good B to the higher-valued good A. Similarly, as a producer of apples I buy various inputs such as labor and fertilizer until the marginal dollar spent on each input brings me the same increase in output.

Now, consider producers and consumers jointly. Suppose a good costs $1. At the *margin* its value to consumers cannot be more than $1, otherwise they would buy more of it, thus bringing its marginal utility to them down to $1. Nor can it be less than $1 because then they would not buy it. So it must be $1. Similarly, the marginal cost to producers cannot be more than $1 otherwise they would not produce it. And if its marginal cost were less than $1 they would produce more of it, thus bringing its price down. Hence, the marginal cost of producing the good must also be $1.

What this means is that, at least in this simple story: *despite each consumer and producer knowing only his or her own preferences or marginal costs, and being driven entirely by self-interest, decisions about what to produce and how much to produce are made as efficiently as they would be in the single-person economy in which all knowledge about utility and production costs is stored in a single mind, and where (since the "public" consists of only one person) self-interest is identical with the public's interest.* With each consumer buying every product up to the point where the last dollar spent on it brings the same utility, and all producers minimizing costs by using productive resources up to the point where the last dollar spent on each unit of resources increases output to the same extent, there is no reallocation of consumer expenditures or productive resources that could make everyone better off. Another way of looking at this is to say that nobody has to spend his money on something when for the same money he can get something else that he values more highly.

This is not so when we turn to the government instead of the market. Through its power to collect taxes, the government might make you buy something that you value less than its cost (the tax) or even value negatively. Hence, relying on the price mechanism ensures that we live in the best of all possible worlds. Alright, I know that isn't so once we leave the simple world discussed so far and introduce nasty "details" like monopoly power, income inequality, pollution, etc. Then we will see that an actual market system is far from ideal, and that there is an important role for government in correcting the faults of the price mechanism. But let's leave that for later, and look now at the interrelation of prices.

The price mechanism is a web that connects all prices in the economy. On the demand side if the price of a particular good, say, apples, changes, then consumers respond by changing how many apples they buy, and (if their incomes and savings are constant) can do so only by changing the amount they buy of other goods, thus affecting output and prices in these other industries.

On the supply side, if demand for apples increases, apple producers respond by raising their output. Unless they happen to have enough excess capacity, they can do this only by bidding away labor and capital from other firms or by paying their workers overtime, so that their costs increase. When the process is completed, what with increased output reducing the price of apples, and the cost of producing apples being higher, apple production is no longer more profitable than it was before the demand for apples increased. How do we know this? Because as long as there are excess profits to be made in producing apples, more apples will be produced. The increased profits of apple producers were only temporary, though "temporary" may mean several years.

However, the price of land that is especially suitable for the growing of apples has risen permanently relative to the price of other land. The reason for this difference is that new producers can enter the apple industry and existing firms can expand, while the supply of land especially suitable to apples is fixed, unless some innovation in producing apples occurs, or the cost of importing apples falls.

As another example of how prices are connected, suppose oil prices double. Prices of substitutes like natural gas and coal will also rise, though not by as much. So will the prices of goods, such as plastics, that are made of oil or of substitutes for oil. Prices of machinery that economize on oil or its substitutes will also rise, but prices of gas guzzlers and of machinery that uses a lot of energy will decline. Real wages in some industries that produce substitutes for oil-intensive goods might rise as demand shifts to these goods. But, overall, real wages will fall since the productivity of workers is less when a greater share of the value of their product has to be paid to those who provide the fuel used in its production. As oil prices and the prices of goods whose production requires much oil rise, the Federal Reserve could, in principle, adopt a monetary policy that is restrictive enough to force down other prices enough, so that the price level as a whole is stable. But, if the increase in oil prices is substantial, it is most unlikely to do that, because forcing down other prices sufficiently could result in a recession.

6.2 Equilibrium

A standard procedure that economists use when analyzing the web that connects one price to another is to look for the set of prices that leaves markets in equilibrium. Economists copied this procedure from Newtonian physics, where equilibrium is characterized as a situation in which an object remains at rest because the forces pushing it in one directing are just balanced by equally strong forces pushing it in the opposite direction. In economics, what equilibrium analysis tells us is where – other things being equal – a price will settle after a particular disturbance to it, such as a 10 percent increase in demand. To be sure, other things are usually *not* equal; at any one time a multitude of disturbances impinge on prices, but we can analyze their effects one at a time. The appendix (6.1) to this chapter uses supply-and-demand diagrams to illustrate how equilibrium is reached.

How long does it take for a price to reach its new equilibrium? This depends on how far the price has to move to reach its new equilibrium, and on the type of market. In markets with a homogeneous product, and with many buyers and sellers who are well informed about the current price, and do not feel a sense of personal involvement in the price, markets clear almost instantaneously because to hesitate means to miss a profitable opportunity to buy or sell. Some examples are the stock market, the foreign exchange market, and organized markets for standardized commodities, such as Florida orange juice. Suppose that a hail damages a crop. Commodity dealers, who make sure that they hear such news right way, now raise the price to the point where they think that the resulting decline in demand for it will balance the reduction in supply. The time required is measured in minutes or seconds. For goods that are not homogeneous, such as houses, markets usually take much longer to adjust because potential buyers need to consider the specific features of the house, and normally do not just buy it sight unseen. And when the equilibrium price of houses drops would-be sellers tend to be slow to accept that their cherished homes are now worth less, particularly if the new equilibrium price is less than what they paid for it. Moreover, in an industry with only a few firms, each of them might be slow to cut its price out of fear of starting a price war.

One important market that is slow to clear is the labor market. Here conditions are very different from those in organized commodity markets. Neither employees nor jobs are homogeneous; employees have no way of finding out about all available jobs, nor employers about all available workers. Taking or offering a job is usually an informal commitment that lasts some time. Recently hired employees might feel reluctant to quit the job after a month or two, and some who have been with their employer a long time, might also feel that they should show loyalty to their employer. In addition, both employees and employers lack information about what wages other firms are currently offering. Moreover, to a considerable extent, employees view their wages as an indication of their personal worth, and may, therefore, prefer temporary unemployment to taking a wage cut.

Also, consider the situation of a firm when the equilibrium wage for some job falls. If it tries to cut the wage rate for this job it would upset the accustomed differentials between wages for different jobs, and make the firm look callous. Morale, and with it productivity, would drop, perhaps precipitously. Doesn't seem worth trying. Conversely, when the equilibrium wage rises, the firm will probably be reluctant to match this increase, because it would lower morale by upsetting wage differentials. Better to increase recruiting efforts, relax hiring standards, or just do without for some time, though eventually it will have to raise the wage.

In addition, is there a moral issue involved if an unemployed worker takes a position at a much lower wage until a better paying job opens up 2 or 3 months later. Most employers would have a fit if someone (after a long job search by the firm) up and quits after 2 months.

6.3   Shortages

The foregoing raises the following question: since the price mechanism balances supply and demand, does it ever make sense to talk about shortages? Yes, it does during a transition period in which wages and prices have not yet risen to their equilibrium levels. But over the longer run, shortages – the way economists define this term – can occur only if the government or a cartel of producers imposes effective price or wage controls. Otherwise, if you want to claim that there is a shortage you must, unlike economists, define "shortage" in normative terms, that is, as a situation in which buyers have to pay more than you think they should, or some people have to do without something you think they should have. That type of "shortage" depends on one's value judgments and, while certainly worth thinking about, is not amenable to the type of objective analysis that economists prefer.

A similar point applies to the term "affordable." If you define "affordable housing" as housing that takes no more than one-quarter of a person's income, then there certainly is a shortage of affordable housing. But why one quarter, why not more?

How then are we to interpret complaints, such as that there is a chronic shortage of nurses or math teachers? As a normative use of "shortage," we (society) have decided that we would like a certain ratio of nurses to patients, but are unwilling to pay nurses enough to induce the requisite number of people to become nurses. If nurses were paid, say, 90 percent of what physicians earn, there would be a surplus of nurses.

The essential point is that as a buyer you cannot – at the same time – control both the price and the quantity that you are offered. If you set a price that is not high enough to elicit the desired quantity, you just have to settle for a lesser, perhaps even zero quantity. Similarly, if a seller sets the price, she will be able to sell only as much, but no more, than is demanded at that price. All this may seem simple and obvious, but governments sometimes ignore it, set a price, and then seem surprised when they cannot buy (or sell) all they want to at that price.

Having rather arrogantly laid down the law to governments, there is something I should confess. Suppose you were to ask me about the scarcity of tickets to certain concerts or sporting events, or the unavailability of last-minute reservations for certain restaurants. I would be embarrassed. Why don't concert managers and restaurants maximize their profits by raising prices to the point where demand is no greater than supply? There are two more – or less – plausible explanations, which may both be partially right, but I find neither of them all that convincing. One is that their very scarcity makes tickets to performances, sporting events, and restaurant reservations seem more valuable. You may not be all that good a judge yourself, but you think the pianist or the chef must great, otherwise it would not be so difficult to get a ticket or a reservation. So, perhaps their scarcity is effective enough as advertising to make it worthwhile for the concert manager or the restaurant to leave some money on the table by not raising the price to the point where demand equals supply. The second explanation does not require that people judge value by scarcity, but assumes instead that people enjoy obtaining what is hard to get, and are, therefore, willing to pay more for it. You get satisfaction from mentioning, oh so casually, that you have just seen a world series game or a certain sold-out play. And even if you don't actually get to mention it, that may make you feel special and, therefore, happy.

6.4   A Digression: The Equilibrium of the Firm

To find the equilibrium price that a firm charges, we simply have to find the price that maximizes its profits. Let's look first at a firm that is so small compared to its competitors that its own decision about how much to produce has no discernible effect on the market price; a farmer (who to economists is a firm) is an example. Such a competitive firm takes the price as a given and maximizes its profits by setting its output at the point where its marginal cost, which we will assume increases as it raises its output, is equal to that price. If it produces any less, it is leaving money on the table, because it could earn something by producing one more unit, and if it produces any more it is making a loss on that unit.

Most industrial firms are not in that position. They account for a large enough share of their market for their decisions about how much to produce to affect prices. If they produce more they have to cut their price to get consumers to buy all of this larger output. When such a firm decides how much to produce it is also ipso facto deciding what its price will be. It, therefore, sets its output and price jointly. And it sets them at the point where its marginal cost is just equal to the increase in sales proceeds, taking account of the fact that it has to lower its price if it is to sell more. Economists call the sales proceeds that take account of having to sell all units at a lower price "marginal revenue," and state the optimal pricing rule as setting the price so that marginal revenue equals marginal costs.

The extent to which firms actually follow the rule of setting marginal revenue equal to marginal costs is not clear. A major problem for firms is that they lack accurate information on how demand would respond to a change in price. With demand changing all the time as consumer incomes and tastes change, that is not easy to determine. Moreover, they are unsure about how their competitors will react if they change their price. If a firm raises its price and its competitors do not, it will lose market share; if it lowers its price and competitors do the same, its price cut will not enhance its market share. Hence, instead of trying to get the price just right, firms may just calculate what their average cost is at a normal operating volume, add a mark-up, that while not fixed changes only moderately, and that's their price. The prevalence of this way of setting prices is a disputed issue.

6.5   What Happens in the Absence of a Price Mechanism?

It is not easy to appreciate the benefits of something one is so used to that one hardly acknowledges that it is there. So let's look at three examples of what happens when the price mechanism is short-circuited: government price controls, the economy of Soviet Russia, and an environmentalist's dilemma.

6.5.1   Price Controls

Suppose that the inflation rate rises sharply, or else suppose that while the overall inflation rate is low and stable, the price of gas doubles. In both cases voters want the government to "do something." And the most direct and obvious "something" is to set a price ceiling, typically by prohibiting any further price increases unless specially authorized, and then authorizing only those that are justified by cost increases. Both Presidents Nixon and Carter tried such controls, the former across the board, and the latter on gasoline.

Before that comprehensive price controls were also in effect during World War II and the Korean War. In the former episode many goods were rationed, that is, consumers were issued books of ration tickets that they had to surrender when making purchases. That was to prevent disruptions due to goods being sold out on a first-come-first-served basis, and to inhibit surreptitious price increases. Price controls are hardly a thing of the past. Some countries with lots of poverty have price ceilings on food and other basic "essentials" like gasoline, while other countries buy up food at market prices and then sell it to their citizens at below market prices.

Imposing such price ceilings interferes with the price mechanism. One way is by reducing the supply of the price-controlled goods because they discourage firms already in the industry from providing additional units that are expensive to produce, and, therefore, not profitable at the controlled price. Another way is by discouraging other potential suppliers from entering the industry. For example, rent control, a popular instance of price control, and one that in attenuated form is currently in effect in a few American cities, reduces the supply of apartments, both by discouraging new construction and by reducing the incentive that home owners have to rent out spare rooms.[a] I remember from my childhood in interwar Vienna, apartments of my parents' friends in which they kept some rooms permanently locked. They could no longer afford the servants needed to keep them up, but had insufficient incentive to sublease them, or to move to a smaller apartment.

Another problem is that price controls lead to an inefficient allocation of the available supply. If prices are left free to fluctuate, they ration the available goods by allocating them to the highest bidders. But if there is price control, then, unless there is effective rationing, priority goes to those assiduous or lucky enough to locate the goods, or to those having some connection to a seller (perhaps as a result of a bribe), or else to those willing to stand in line. Allocating goods by forcing people to waste time looking for goods or by standing in line is obviously inefficient, and relying on establishing perhaps illegal connections to dealers hardly ensures that scarce goods go to the right customers. If the ceiling price is $10, then a good may go to Mary, who values it only at, say $12, rather than to Jane who values it at $20. In the 1970s when the price of gas was controlled, and gas was consequently scarce, some people filled up their gas tanks whenever they found a gas station that had some left – an instance of the old principle of "let's

---

[a]   To substantially reduce the negative effect on construction, newly built apartments can be exempted. But potential landlords have no assurance that this exemption will be maintained.

get it before the hoarders do." That hoarding made the gas shortage much more severe than it otherwise would have been.

A third disadvantage of price controls is that they lead to evasion. Viewed from a distance, price controls may seem simple and straightforward, but not from close up. For example, when prices are held below equilibrium and producers can sell all they want, they can lower their costs by cutting quality, thus, in effect, surreptitiously raising their price. That is hard to control. Moreover, price controls also lead to black markets and to corruption, as firms and their lobbyists maneuver to get favorable provisions written into the government regulations.

And then there is the problem of what to do next. The inefficiencies of price controls are so great that eventually they have to be removed. Unless they were imposed to deal with a strictly temporary shortage, once they are removed prices shoot up from their controlled to their equilibrium levels. Thus, when the Nixon price controls were removed, prices rose approximately to where they would have been if controls had never been imposed. The government's good intention was to use monetary and fiscal policies to reduce aggregate demand enough, so that with there no longer being overall excess demand, price controls could now be removed without prices rising sharply. But, of course, once price controls were in effect, the pressure to impose restrictive monetary and fiscal policies evaporated and the good intention remained just that.

Beyond these strictly economic detriments of price controls, there is the loss of economic freedom and the extension of government controls and bureaucracy. There is also the moral decay that occurs when people are given yet another incentive to evade the law.

On the other side of the debate those who favor price controls can point out that they shift the distribution of income in favor of the poor, because if they are not accompanied by rationing, then the ability to obtain goods depends in part on pure luck in locating them. And, though the poor have less income than the rich, they have just as much pure luck. And if there is rationing a poor person gets just as many ration coupons as a rich person. However, since, for the reasons just discussed, price controls and rationing reduce the efficiency of the economy, and hence overall income, it is far from clear that in absolute terms the poor benefit from them. In any case, if one wants to redistribute income in favor of the poor, there are much more efficient ways of doing so.

All the same, it does not necessarily follow that price controls are *never* appropriate. In great emergencies, prices of some goods, such as food, might rise so high that they generate a redistribution of income that most people consider grossly unfair and a worse evil than the inefficiencies induced by price controls and rationing. But "never" is not inconsistent with "nearly always."

A modest form of price control is a law against "price gouging" – which in a bill that Congress considered in 2007 when gas prices rose sharply, was defined as setting a price that is "unconscionably" high or "takes unfair advantage of unusual market conditions." Such a law would suffer from many of the just discussed flaws of general price controls. In particular, it would create shortages and reduce the supply of gas in areas that need it most. Besides, the meaning of "gouging" is far from clear, and the just cited definitions do little to help, and there would be much costly litigation. Laws that can put people in jail should be clear. And besides, the moral argument for such a law is far from solid. In some industries prices fluctuate a great deal. If, when demand greatly exceeds supply, price "gouging" is to be prohibited, what should be done when supply greatly exceeds demand and prices fall sharply? Should consumers be prohibited from paying the low price?

6.5.2   Central planning

The communist regime in the Soviet Union allowed only a limited role for the market mechanism. To be sure, consumers were charged prices for their purchases. However, production levels for most industries and firms were set by central planners, though, in practice, central planning was ameliorated by the use of subterfuge, evasion, and corruption, Farmers were allowed to sell a substantial part of their output on free markets. While this industrial system proved effective in some major tasks, such as the amazing feat during World War II of evacuating much of Russian industry from western Russia to beyond the Urals and producing more munitions than Nazi Germany did, older readers from the 1950s through the mid-1980s may remember news reports about its inefficiency in meeting the everyday needs of consumers, and about the system's difficulty in generating innovations outside the defense sector. Central planning could not match the efficiency of a free-market system in discovering appropriate prices of goods. In the free-market system if too much of something is produced its price drops, and if too little is produced, so that there is a shortage, its price rises. By contrast, in Soviet Russia unsaleable goods piled up in stores, while consumers stood in long lines for goods in excess demand. The feedback mechanism that leads from the piling up of unsaleable goods to a reduction in their production, and from excess demand to more production did not work efficiently. Not many people who experienced that system want it back.

But although few people now advocate comprehensive central planning, "planning" still has a favorable connotation. Wouldn't you rather have your city plan for growth rather suffer the effects of "unplanned growth"? Isn't planning what reasonable people do? Ah, but here is the rub. As Thomas Sowell eloquently points out, the alternative to government planning is not mindless action or chaos, but private planning; nobody puts up a building without planning and thinking where it should be located. What economists typically call "planning" means that the government makes the decisions, rather than entrepreneurs. Sometimes the government's decisions will be better, but as Sowell's examples show, in many cases they will not be.[2]

6.5.3   The dilemma of the environmentally concerned consumer

Environmentalism presents a more contemporary example of the difficulty of operating without an extensive price mechanism. Suppose you are a conscientious person who does not want to leave a large carbon footprint on the environment. You just got a bonus and are thinking of taking a fancy vacation trip or else buying some new furniture. You plan to do whichever is less burdensome to the environment. But how can you tell which one that is, since neither the trip nor the furniture carries an environmental price tag? You know that airplane trips contribute to global warming. But you don't quite know how much, and you know even less about the environmental costs of producing furniture. Or suppose you love your SUV. Can you drive it without feeling guilty if you make up for it by setting your thermostat at 65° to save natural gas, and by increasing the materials you recycle, or by contributing $500 to the Environmental Defense Fund? Hard to know. But suppose prices, perhaps in the form of pollution taxes, were charged for environmental degradation. If they were set correctly that would allow you to compare the environmental costs of your various activities. Moreover, if you believe that these taxes are high enough to offset the environmental damage caused by your SUV you need not feel guilty driving it, because the amount you pay would offset this damage.

6.6   The Dark Side of the Price Mechanism

We live in an imperfect world. So you may have wondered how I could describe the price mechanism as such a magnificent device. The answer is that what I described so far is not our actual price mechanism, but an idealized model that we find in just a few, if any, markets. Let's look at several ways in which our actual price mechanism differs from this ideal. (Chapter 7 will then deal with two additional ways: the distortions caused by the principal–agent problem, and limitations on property rights.)

6.6.1 Income distribution

The price mechanism ensures that, subject to the caveats discussed below, the economy produces the types and quantities of goods that consumers are willing to pay for at prices that correspond to their costs of production. But is that necessarily good? Which goods consumers are willing to pay for is not inscribed in heaven, but depends in part on the distribution of income. A society with an egalitarian income distribution demands less caviar and more hamburgers than one with an extremely skewed income distribution. Put another way, the price mechanism is sometimes praised for being democratic because what it produces depends on how consumers "vote" with their dollars. There is something to this, but it is a "democracy" in which the number of votes that a person casts depends on his or her income. This is not *necessarily* bad. Insofar as income differences are due to differences in effort, ability, or in willingness to assume risk, one can make a reasonable – but I don't think conclusive – case that they are entirely appropriate. But unless the distribution of income is right, the allocation of resources will not be right either. More generally, the price mechanism provides us with an efficient way of reaching certain ends – but these ends while not immoral are amoral. (See box 6.1.)

A seemingly easy out for an economist, qua economist, but not qua citizen, is to say that such ethical and philosophical questions are for others to decide. And that once these decisions have somehow been made, and the income distribution conforms to them, the economist's favorite tool, the price mechanism, should be allowed to determine what to produce. In principle, that is a persuasive argument, but in practice it is not an *entirely* satisfactory one. Suppose you do prefer a more egalitarian income distribution, but you are outvoted on this issue. Should you then support a proposal to subsidize a good consumed disproportionately by the poor, such as low-rent housing, that has a better chance of political success, despite its interference with the price mechanism? This is, in large part, a philosophical question, so let's pass on it.

6.6.2 Unemployment

The story told so far was implicitly one of a fully employed economy, that is, an economy in which all who want to work at a wage corresponding to

Box 6.1: The Amoral Price Mechanism

The price mechanism steers by no moral compass. It allocates goods impartially to whoever will pay the most; to the starving man who will die without them, to the billionaire in his surfeit, and to the drunk reaching for another bottle. Its efficiency in heeding the clamor of whoever's dollars shout the loudest provides it with purpose, but it is an amoral purpose. There are, however, two saving graces. First, you can insert moral purpose into it. If, like some, you believe that people should be rewarded in accordance with their productivity (and with the productivity and generosity of those from whom they have inherited), then you will find moral purpose in the price mechanism's heeding the call of those who offer the most. And if, like others, you believe that the poor should be provided with more resources, then the price mechanism will also heed your wishes – after you have redistributed income from the rich to the poor. Those who oppose income redistribution should not do so by proclaiming the virtues of the price mechanism, and those who want to redistribute income should not disparage the price mechanism.

Second, the price mechanism plays a much smaller role in even the most capitalistic of countries than economics textbooks seem to imply. It coexists with a moral code based on religion and moral intuition that more or less constrains self-interested behavior. For example, people leave tips even in restaurants they will never visit again. Indeed, a substantial proportion (about a quarter?) of our economic activity is carried out, or at least supposed to be carried out, in a communistic manner. (Can you guess what it is?) It is economic activity within the family (that is housework and the allocation of goods and income between family members), where "from each according to his ability, to each according to his needs," and not "to each according to his marginal productivity" is the recommended principle.

what they produce (their marginal productivity) can readily find employment. In the real world there is "frictional" unemployment, that is, unemployment due to the difficulty that job seekers and potential employers have in finding each other, or being in different locations, or job seekers not having the particular skills that employers want. Some level of frictional unemployment is consistent with the price mechanism working optimally, because well before frictional unemployment is reduced to zero, the costs of providing more information on job opportunities, of facilitating labor mobility, and of retraining workers, will exceed the benefits from doing so. Remember that the world of economics is dynamic. Firms go out of business and jobs are lost. New firms grow and jobs are created. In an increasingly globalized economy, US firms with plants in the bigger cities of Michigan or the smaller towns of Pennsylvania close down some of these facilities as other firms open similar plants overseas with much cheaper labor. Not everyone in these towns, who see their main employers leave, is willing or able to just pack up and go. Thus those who stay behind face longer periods of unemployment and jobs that often pay less. Older workers are less mobile than those who are recent college graduates.

In addition to frictional unemployment, there is also the unemployment that appears during recessions. Some of this seeming "unemployment" could be due to recessions being periods in which productivity and hence real wages are falling, so that fewer people want to work at a real wage corresponding to their now lower marginal productivity. Some economists believe this to be an important explanation of cyclical changes in unemployment, but many others (including myself) very much doubt it, and attribute this cyclical unemployment to a deficiency in total demand, or "aggregate demand" as economists call it.

On average, unemployment, therefore, exceeds the optimal level of frictional unemployment. And that is not necessarily bad because we have to worry about inflation as well as unemployment, and the two are connected. As unemployment falls, firms find it harder to hire additional workers and to retain the ones they have. At first they are likely to respond primarily by increasing their recruiting efforts, but sooner or later they find that they have to offer higher wages. And they then pass these higher wages on in higher prices. Moreover, as employment and incomes rise, firms find that they can raise their profit margins, which further raises prices.

Could we just say: never mind, unemployment is a greater evil than inflation, so let's reduce unemployment to, say 3 percent? Most economists believe that this would not work. Suppose at a time when inflation is running at a 2 percent rate firms try to hire more workers, and unemployment falls. With labor now in short supply they also raise their nominal wages and prices by, say 4 percent. But with real wages, and hence the labor supply not having risen, they are still short of labor, so they raise money wages by, say 6 percent, knowing that this does not represent a rise in real wages, because prices will also rise over the long run by 6 percent. Thus the inflation rate accelerates until the Fed realizes that its goal of a 3 percent unemployment rate is too low, and, therefore, raises interest rates. What its policy of low interest rates has done is to reduce unemployment temporarily at the cost of an ever-rising (and hence intolerable) inflation rate until the Fed abandons this policy.

There is a certain unemployment rate called the "natural rate of unemployment" or the NAIRU (short for "non-accelerating inflation rate of unemployment") that is just high enough to prevent inflation from accelerating, and this is the unemployment rate we usually aim at, at least over the longer run. Unfortunately, we are unlikely to hit this rate exactly. One reason is that we know only vaguely what this unemployment rate is, since it fluctuates. Thus, although we can be sure that at present it is greater than 3.5 percent and less than 6.5 percent, whether it is 4.5 or 5 percent is something we cannot be sure about.

In addition, our tools for managing aggregate demand, that is, monetary and fiscal policies, are imprecise and slow acting. Because fiscal policy overtly redistributes income, it is a highly charged political issue, and hence clumsy to implement. When we want to increase aggregate demand by cutting taxes, there is likely to be considerable time-consuming debate about just whose taxes to cut, and when we want to increase expenditures many claimants demand to be heard. (The speedy adoption of the 2008 tax rebate was an exception.) Moreover, monetary policy takes about a year or so (we are not sure how long) to have a substantial part of its effect, and just how large its effect will then be is uncertain. Because of these lags, we have to rely on forecasts of where the economy will be when our monetary and fiscal policies finally take effect, and these forecasts are far from perfect. All in all, although we have the knowledge and tools needed to counter really major recessions or inflations, our ability to offset minor fluctuations in employment and inflation is like driving at night a car with a foggy windshield that responds to twists of the steering wheel only with some delay, and then responds sometimes substantially more than at other times. Thus while – arguably because of better policies – the economy has at least so far fluctuated less since the mid-1980s than before, the problem of excessive unemployment is not likely to disappear in the foreseeable future.

6.6.3   Consumer misinformation

Letting output be guided by consumer demand will give us the right products only if consumers choose those goods that provide them with the most satisfaction. Obviously, they don't *always* do this, we all know that from our personal experience. But probably most of us are disposed to say that despite (or because of?) extensive advertising, on the whole, people know what makes them better off, or at least know this better than any government agency would. If we are disposed to criticize the choices of consumers, most of us, though not the critics of materialism, usually focus our attention on what we think of as special cases, such as highly manipulative advertising, or the surprisingly widespread undervaluation of the future that makes someone borrow at 18 percent on a credit card, or the inability of patients to evaluate a physician's recommendation for treatment, which is one reason why the private market for medical services (fee for service) does not work well.

However, this idea that, by and large, consumers both know what they want and want what is good for them, is far from universally accepted. Many critics of the price mechanism view the consumer as a pawn in the hands of advertisers. (For one aspect of advertising see box 6.2.) More fundamentally, as discussed in chapter 3, some value systems put a low value on meeting what consumers *perceive* to be their preferences. They derogate much

---

Box 6.2: Why Do Sellers, But Not Buyers, Advertise?

When you are buying something you are bartering money for some item. Often, the seller of that item will try to persuade you to buy it by advertising how wonderful it is. But you, the buyer, do not normally bother to advertise how wonderful the money you are willing to pay for it is. Why is it that it is the seller and not the buyer who advertises?

One reason is that the purpose of advertising is either to inform others that you have some particular item to sell, or to inform (or misinform) them about its high quality or low price. But there is no need for consumers to inform sellers that they have money to barter in exchange for goods. Nor do they have to inform them about the quality of the money they are offering: one person's dollar is exactly as good as another's. Another reason is that it saves time if only one party to the transaction gathers extensive information, and informs the other. Since the seller undertakers many more transactions in this particular item than does each individual buyer, she is the one to do it. And, having this information, she is also the one to make the sales effort of communicating it – often along with much misinformation – to buyers.

But this does not mean that the buyer never undertakes sales effort in the broad sense of that term. In bargaining, say for a car, the buyer might argue that he cannot afford the price the dealer asks, that is, that his money is more valuable to him relative to the car than the dealer thinks. Another example emerges under price control and rationing. Here, both the buyer and the seller may have to exert much effort to find each other.

consumer choice as a consumerism that satisfies superficial and artificially induced, rather than deeper and more worthy, choices.

Let's look at a specific case. As I am writing this, there is a debate about requiring airlines to adhere to a "passenger bill of rights." At first glance, this looks like unnecessary government interference. If an airline treats its passenger badly by, for example, keeping planes sitting for hours on the tarmac with toilets that do not work, then unless it offsets this with lower fares, it will lose business. Why not let passengers decide whether to fly cheaply and get treated badly at times or to pay more for better treatment? But this assumes that passengers know what to expect from each airline. To be sure, some magazine, or else the government, could make this information available, but it would take passengers time and effort to obtain and digest this information. Should they have to make this effort? On the other hand, punishing airlines for occasionally mistreating passengers by overbooking would require airlines to keep spare planes on hand, which would raise fares.

6.6.4   Monopoly and other types of market power

In most of the story told so far, all firms are competitors who lack market power. They are so small that they believe that their individual output has no effect on the price of the good they produce, which is a homogeneous commodity. If any firm were to raise its price when other firms do not, it would lose most of its customers. And firms do not effectively collude to raise prices, not only because it is illegal, but also because it is relatively easy for a firm to cheat on its agreement with other firms and cut prices. They are, therefore, price takers, not price makers. (Economists refer to such a situation as "perfect competition.") But that is not the real world, where a few firms are monopolies, and many more have some significant market power. As we shall see in a moment, that is not entirely unfortunate. But first let's look at the harm that monopoly does. Its higher prices inevitably redistribute income from poor and middle-income families towards its richer stockholders. It is this "hurt-the-poor-and-help-the-rich" effect of monopoly which critics of monopoly who are not economists usually focus on.

Economists, while more or less accepting their argument, add another charge: monopoly causes productive resources to be misallocated. Suppose that the marginal cost of producing a pair of shoes, and hence the price in a competitive market, is $100, but that shoe manufacturers now form a cartel by colluding to price them at $120. If the shoes are worth only $105 to you, you will then not buy them, so that $5 of potential value goes down the drain.

Moreover, monopolistic firms have an incentive to suppress, or to induce the government, to suppress, innovations that threaten their control. Also, innovation often comes from a firm's R&D department, but the monopolist need not spend much on R&D without competition on the horizon. And even if they don't consciously try to suppress innovations, the "group-think" that comes naturally to a close-knit group like a monopolistic firm does not make for an innovative industry. In general, although a monopolistic firm, like a competitive firm, tries to maximize profits, it does not feel as much pressure towards greater efficiency as does a competitive firm. This difference is hard to formulate in a theoretical framework or to measure empirically, but it *may* make a substantial difference.

But there is another side to monopoly. While monopoly can result from firms colluding, or from a firm having established a widely respected brand name, monopoly, particularly a temporary one, can also be the result of innovation. Suppose you develop a voice recognition system for word processing that is so efficient that it sweeps away all competition. You now have a monopoly and will earn monopoly profits. But you have made the world better off. In an innovative economy, some temporary monopoly is both almost inevitable – because someone is going to be first – and also desirable, because without the spur of monopoly profits there would not be sufficient incentive to innovate. But that type of innovative monopoly differs sharply from the stagnant type of monopoly that results when producers get together and agree to raise prices or even worse, to stifle innovation, or when there is a single firm just chugging along because its market power or the government's edict prevents other firms from entering the industry.

Monopoly can also arise from economies of scale that are so large relative to the size of the market that there is room for only one or a few producers. Even in a major industry, the production of large, long-distance passenger planes, there seems to be room for only two companies in the world, Boeing and Airbus, with a Russian company serving primarily that country's captive market. And, towards the other end of the spectrum, economies of scale may also prevent a small town from having more than one shoe store. A monopoly need not be a big business, and a big business need not be a monopoly.

One can also point to economies of scale in countering the argument that monopolies and firms with extensive market power inhibit innovation. Large firms often have considerable market power – and also large the R&D programs that smaller firms with less market power cannot afford. When AT&T had a monopoly over telephone service it could afford to maintain Bell Laboratories, the source of some great innovations. The problem is that small and competitive firms have a strong incentive to innovate, but often lack the means, while large firms which usually have some market power, have the means, but less of an incentive. Whether the existence of large firms is better for innovations, is a still unsettled issue.

So far I have talked only about monopoly firms. While such firms certainly exist – indeed, our patent and copyright systems are designed to grant temporary monopolies – perfectly competitive firms and monopolistic firms are only the two ends of a continuum. In most industries firms are not just price takers, but have some limited leeway in setting prices. There are firms whose products are similar enough that, while some customers treat them as homogeneous, and decide between them purely on the basis of price, to other, more discerning (or fussy?) customers, they are distinct products in which each firm has a monopoly, while to still other customers there is a difference, but it is worth only a small premium.

There are also in many important industries, called "oligopolies," in which there are only a few firms, each of which takes account of the responses of other firms to the price that it sets. In a perfectly competitive industry, producers, so to speak, do not know each others' names and addresses, or at least act as though they don't. But in an industry with, say, five firms, each firm knows that if it lowers its price the others may well respond by lowering their prices too, perhaps for the very purpose of disciplining the price cutter. Such interaction in the price setting of firms can be highly complex, because what firm A does depends on what it thinks that firms B and C will do, and what firm B does depends on what it thinks firms A and C will do, and so on. Economists usually employ game theory to analyze such interactions, though not always with great success. Many sophisticated models have been built embodying different specific assumptions about how firms react to each other's behavior, but it is hard to go from these specific models to a general theory of how most oligopolists actually behave. Idiosyncratic factors, such as the personalities of their CEOs may determine whether oligopolistic firms coexist peacefully and avoid cutting prices to gain market share, or whether they try to drive out their rivals.

A good example of an oligopoly is the market for textbooks at the university/college level. There are three firms that control around 70 percent of the market, but if we look at only freshmen-level courses, that market share is a bit greater (and not by accident). Meanwhile, the market share of the remaining 30 percent is divided amongst many firms. Of the big three, one has as its top manager someone who worked many years at one of the other big three (so two of the three top managers worked together for a decade). How much price competition is there amongst these top three?

But even monopolists and cooperating oligopolists face some constraints and cannot charge, as some people complain, "Whatever they want." One constraint is the familiar one that if the price of a good rises, consumers will buy less of it. In some sense monopolists, too, have competitors – all other sellers who clamor for the consumer's dollar. Second, even with only a single producer or only a few producers in the United States, there may well be foreign producers eager to enter the American market when high monopoly prices make that profitable. Third, if the few currently existing firms in an industry raise their prices, other domestic firms, either newly formed ones, or, more likely, established firms in another industry, might invade their market. Unless the old firms can block new entry, the mere threat of such entry limits, at least to some extent, their power to charge excessive prices.

Firms, therefore, have an incentive to set up barriers to entry, such as establishing a strong brand name, controlling important patents, or obtaining government regulations that require firms to meet costly standards that they hope new entrants will not be able to meet. For example, the large established airlines have tried to limit low-cost upstarts through their control of gates at airports. To management and stockholders alike, a dollar of profits won by keeping out competition is just as valuable as a dollar won through greater operating efficiency. And even if strong market power will eventually be eroded away by new entrants and innovators, in the meantime it can be very profitable.

Large or even "obscene" profits are not necessarily a sign of market power. They could be due to some temporary factor, such as a sudden shift of consumer demand, as for example when some item becomes a fad, to a reduction in supply perhaps caused by a natural disaster, or they could be due to greater efficiency, perhaps embodied in successful innovations. Unusual profits do not mean that this firm is greedier than others; other firms would also like to make that much profit. Conversely, a firm's market power need not show up as abnormally high profits. Instead, it might provide average profits or even below-average profits to a firm that is inefficient, or is in a declining industry.

6.6.5   Externalities

Until now, I have assumed that buyers and sellers are the only ones affected by a transaction, so that if it leaves both of them better off, the whole society of which they are a part is also better off. But surely that is not always so. Many transactions affect others too; they have what are called "externalities." Such externalities can be large, in some cases even larger than the "internalities" that the buyers and sellers themselves experience, and thus invalidate the case for relying on the price mechanism.[b] These externalities can be either positive or negative.

Negative externalities

Suppose you sell your house in a fine residential neighborhood to Chevron, so that it can build an all-night gas station on this lot. You are better off, and so presumably is Chevron, but the gains from this trade are outweighed by the losses to your neighbors – unless you are a particularly obnoxious neighbor. Such externalities can be large, very large. Suppose a developer builds a major suburban mall. The retailers who leave the city to locate there are better off, and so are their customers, who otherwise would not shop there. But the central city decays. Perhaps this decay makes those who now shop in the mall worse off than if they had continued to shop in the central city because they do not want the central city to decay. But because they are acting on their own, they cannot stop the decay by deciding that they, themselves, will shop in the central city. In this case the market, by not giving "voice" to the customers' desire for a vibrant central city, has failed to reach the right decision.

A major source of negative externalities is pollution. For example, the process of manufacturing autos may require burning coal. If unchecked by regulations and scrubbers, this dumps soot on local neighbors and generates acid rain that destroys forests hundreds of miles down wind. Moreover, those who drive these cars are burning up lots of gasoline that shortens the lives of those who breathe the local air. Woe to those who reside at busy inter-sections with lots of idling cars awaiting their turn to move ahead. In some of the major eastern industrial cities of China, trucks are only allowed to enter town at night – and yet people who leave white sheets out overnight to dry will find blackened sheets the next morning.

When transactions inflict damage on third parties, taxes on these transactions that just equal this damage would improve the way we allocate resources, since they would render activities that do more harm than good unprofitable by, in effect, turning an externality into an internality that a firm takes into account, just the same way as it takes its cost of raw materials and labor into account. But usually we do not impose taxes, or at least sufficient taxes, on activities that have negative externalities.

---

[b]   For a well presented case along these lines, see Tom Slee, *No One Makes You Shop at Wal-Mart*, Toronto, Between the Lines, 2006.

Sometimes we handle negative externalities by regulations, such as zoning. But laws and regulations are clumsy tools (see box 6.3). For example, zoning regulations may be used not only to combat externalities, but also to limit new housing and thus raise the property values of already established homeowners. Another solution, discussed in chapter 9, that is occasionally feasible, is for those who are potentially harmed by the externality of a transaction to pay one of the partners to the transaction to refrain from it. Still another solution is for such a third party to exercise social pressure or to appeal to the conscience of the other parties.

Box 6.3: To Regulate or Not to Regulate?

Given all the serious shortcomings of the market system, isn't there a good case for government regulation? Yes, and no; in some situations there is, but there is not a good case for presuming that whenever something is not regulated it should be. In 2007, when the sub-prime mortgage crisis broke, some people were outraged that certain types of mortgage lenders were totally unregulated. This outrage seemed based on the belief that regulation can only bring good, because if some business practice harms the public interest the regulators will prohibit it, and if it does not then they will allow it.

This is not the way the world works. Regulation, while sometimes desirable or even necessary, has its drawbacks. One is that it tends to stifle competition and innovation. In an unregulated market a new idea has to pass the acceptability test of a single entrepreneur, in a regulated market it has to pass the additional test of also being acceptable to the regulators. And these regulators may be influenced (perhaps through political pressures arising from campaign contributions) by the desire of existing firms to keep out new entrants, particularly innovative ones. Moreover, even without outside pressures, regulators have an incentive to oppose innovations that biases their decisions. Suppose regulators are asked to pass on a new type of mortgage. If they approve it and it turns out to be safe and sound, they neither gain nor lose. There are unlikely to be editorials or ed-op pieces praising them for approving it. But if turns out to be unsound and leads to many foreclosures, they will be blamed for permitting it. Better play it safe: when in doubt say no, and be often in doubt.

In addition, to protect high-cost firms from becoming unprofitable, some regulators may prohibit low-cost firms from cutting prices or fares. They see this as keeping the industry "healthy," and indeed regulatory agencies are sometimes explicitly charged with that task. Until abolished under the Carter administration, the regulators set minimum fares for the airlines and trucking industries, and severely limited entry by new firms.

Pressure from the industry is not the only factor that may warp the regulator's judgment. It could also be pressure from other special interests, such as particular types of consumers, e.g., natural gas pipelines that want the well-head price of natural gas held down, or from those who have an ideological axe to grind.

Does that mean we should eliminate all, or most, regulations? Of course not. While it may well be true that the Food and Drug Administration holds many useful drugs off the market for too long, without the FDA the proliferation of dangerous, even deadly, drugs would create a much worse problem. Neither Chinese nor American drug companies should be be trusted to have the consumer's welfare at heart: their job is to maximize long-run profits. And on the local level, while residential-zoning power is much abused, few people would like to see zoning regulations abolished entirely.

Liberals are right to complain about free-market fundamentalists who, on principle, oppose reasonable regulations; and conservatives are right to complain about anti-market fundamentalists who on principle advocate regulation. Better look at the specifics of each case. For example, I believe that our financial system needs much more regulation, but oppose the regulations Congress is currently (2008) considering. The financial system has undergone immense change and has become much more complex since our present regulations evolved. What we need now is a high-level presidential commission to spend perhaps two or three years to see what regulatory changes are needed.

Self-aggrandizement, envy, and prestige goods

There is a particular externality arising from envy. If you buy a luxury car, or for that matter write a successful book, your peers are apt to feel envious and, therefore, worse off. One might respond that, since envy is an unworthy feeling, we should disregard it in totaling up a society's welfare, and should not treat the gnashing of the teeth of others as a negative externality to the winners' success. But since the impulse to feel superior to others is so common, I am not at all sure that, however much moralists disdain it, economists are in the business of making the moral judgment required to dismiss envy. All the same, mainstream economics does pay little attention (I suspect too little) to it, or for that matter, to the distinction between what are primarily prestige goods used for "conspicuous consumption," and other goods.

Taking envy seriously has a disconcerting implication. Consider the extreme and highly implausible case where all additional output is used for conspicuous consumption, and then make the further admittedly strong assumption that – contrary to the latest findings in happiness studies – the pleasure that the purchaser of a status good obtains from thus getting ahead of her peers is just equal to the displeasure that these peers jointly experience when she does so. In that case the economic progress that the GDP data show is just an illusion.

A less extreme implication of the role played by prestige goods is that we should discourage consumption of those goods for which conspicuous consumption plays a disproportionate role. If it were not for the administrative mess, misallocation of resources, and the inequities that they generate, taxes on luxuries should play a prominent role in our tax system. Similarly, since it is harder to flaunt before your acquaintances the savings that you have accumulated than the jewelry you own, perhaps there is a case to be made for subsidizing saving, possibly by taxing consumption instead of income. And if, as discussed in the next chapter, the tax system discourages work and induces people to consume more leisure, *perhaps* that is not all bad. There are, however, counter-arguments. First, if you work harder, you are offering more of your services in exchange for the goods and services of others, and that makes them better off. Second, you benefit others by paying more income taxes. Third, if you work less and take more leisure, you might use it to acquire status "goods" like aesthetic expertise which in the competition for status would devalue the expertise of others.

If we treat these counter-arguments as unimportant, one might draw a more general implication from the prevalence of prestige goods and envy. This is, that we should aim for a more equal distribution of income, despite the negative effects on incentives, since the rich spend a larger proportion of their incomes on prestige goods than the poor do. Even the natural-rights case against redistribution, that is, that people are entitled to what they produce, is at least somewhat tarnished, though not really refuted, if inequality leads primarily to pride. However, as is so often the case, there is an "on the other hand." The importance of envy and pride can also be used to defend a highly unequal distribution of income. On a crude level one can claim that the objection to income inequality is based largely on envy, and, as already discussed, that such an ignoble objection should not be given much weight. On a more subtle level one can argue that if the urge to feel superior is such a powerful force, then it is better to channel it into outdoing others in the acquisition of material goods than in the acquisition of political power. No, this is not paleo-conservative ranting. Keynes, the most influential liberal economist of at least the last two hundred years, made this point.[3] As Dr. Johnson observed:

"There are few ways in which a man can be more innocently employed than in getting money."[4]

Favorable externalities

By no means all externalities are unfavorable. A beautiful garden that you plant and that is enjoyed by your neighbors as well as by the local deer has a favorable externality, and so does the construction of a large store that raises the value of a nearby parking lot. A special type of favorable externality is the network effect; for example, the more people are on the internet, the more valuable it is to those already on it. Since anything that raises values elsewhere in the economy without fully charging for it has a favorable externality, favorable externalities *could* be just as, or even more important than unfavorable externalities. (Perhaps we hear less about them only because the inclination to complain is stronger than the inclination to give thanks.) And just as the market tends to produce too much of goods with unfavorable externalities, it tends to produces too little of those with favorable externalities. That suggests that they should be subsidized. But there is a problem: the government is not an efficient allocator of subsidies – particularly not after lobbyists do their work.

However, there are many forms that regulation of externalities can take. In many new housing developments in the US, especially in California, neighborhood associations require all residents to maintain both minimal and maximal efforts in lawn care. Both positive and negative externalities due to attractive gardening or weed-covered property are prohibited in favor of a uniform look.

An extreme case of positive externalities: public goods

Public goods are those things that, if made available to one person, benefit others too, without the first person being made worse off, or without any additional cost being imposed on the producer. For example, your tuning in on a TV program does not prevent others from watching it or cost the station anything. Charging you for watching it is, therefore, inefficient. Suppose that cable TV costs $40 a month, and you do not subscribe because it is only worth $30 to you. This means that the economy foregoes $30 worth of a useful service that would have cost it nothing to provide. But firms cannot charge a zero price and stay in business. Hence, there is a case for having the government providing public goods, or subsidizing their production by private producers. But that means raising taxes, which creates inefficiencies of its own, and also may be unfair to those taxpayers who themselves derive no enjoyment from these public goods.

There are also what are called "*pure* public goods." Here, not only can the good or service be made available to others at no cost, but, also, there is no technically feasible way to exclude those who do not pay, so that any firm that would want to supply them could not make a go of it. If supplied at all, pure public goods have usually to be supplied or subsidized by the government which can use its police power to make everyone, including non-users, pay through taxes. National defense expenditures are an obvious example.

Occasionally, we rely on the user's sense of fairness to make a suggested payment, but there are always free riders who do not pay. Recently the downloading of copyrighted music has brought this problem to the fore. Those who want to download songs argue that, since they were not going to buy the CD in any case, nobody loses from their downloading. Unfortunately, there is no way the copyright owner can distinguish between these people and those who, if they cannot get it free, are willing to pay.

With the information industry becoming a larger and larger share of the total economy, the public-goods problem *may* eventually become so important that it can no longer be treated as a minor qualification to the proposition that the price mechanism provides a near-optimal allocation of resources. Perhaps we will have to develop new economic theories and new economic institutions. But such long-run prediction is difficult, so let's change the subject.

6.6.6 Decreasing costs

Take the case in which the larger a firm's output the lower is its marginal cost: that is, there are economies of scale. If the firm were to sell its output at this low cost of producing the last unit, then it would make a loss on all its other units and go bankrupt. But if it sets a higher price, then some consumers who are willing to pay the marginal cost but not the price that the firm charges will forego buying this product, so that the economy foregoes something that costs, say $3 to produce but has a value of $4, an obvious inefficiency. In such an industry of otherwise similar firms in which marginal costs fall with rising output, the largest firm can drive the others out of business and enjoy a monopoly.

6.6.7 Some factors limiting trade

Another reason why actual markets do not correspond to the rosy picture of a market economy described at the start of this chapter is that some hypothetical markets that would be highly beneficial do not exist, so that some trades are not feasible. For example, you are generally unable to sell a claim to your next year's salary, and thus insure against the risk of your salary falling greatly. One reason is called the problem of asymmetric information. You are likely to have better information about your future salary than does a potential buyer. Suppose you, who are currently earning $200,000 a year, offer to sell me your next year's salary for $100,000. Before jumping at this bargain I would ask myself why you are offering me such a seeming bargain, and would wonder whether you know something I don't, such as that you are about to be fired. Hence, even people who are sure that they will earn $200,000 next year will not be able to sell a contract for this $200,000 salary, except at a discount great enough to compensate for the probability that they will earn much less next year. But if they can sell claims to their next year's salary for only, say $50,000, they will be unlikely to do so if they expect their salaries to be much above that next year. And since you know that, you won't offer even $50,000. This does not mean that in cases where one party knows more than the other, trade cannot take place at all; there is a market in used cars. However, the risk to the buyer lowers the price, and hence the amount supplied, and thus reduces the volume of trading.

Fortunately, the trade-inhibiting effect of asymmetric information can often be reduced by signaling. If a student wants to convince a prospective employer that she is highly intelligent, saying so won't do it, but getting A's in advanced math, physics, and philosophy courses will, even if nothing in the particular job requires knowing these subjects. Similarly, offering a money-back guarantee or an explicit or implicit warranty may clinch a sale. So may something that allows dissatisfied customers to retaliate. A hotel that is part of a chain signals its quality, and thereby attracts customers, because if it does not come up to scratch (or even worse, if the next day you find yourself scratching) you can retaliate by avoiding that chain in the future, and the chain knows that. But where effective signaling is either not feasible or is expensive, many otherwise profitable trades do not take place. And even when signaling is feasible, it may be costly or inconvenient.

A further factor that restricts trade is what economists call "moral hazard," the fact that the contract itself gives you an incentive to change your behavior in a way unfavorable to the other party. If I insure my car against theft, I am less likely to lock it; if I buy life insurance, I have less incentive to stop smoking. In 2008 when the Fed stepped in to keep Bear Stearns from going bankrupt it created a serious moral hazard because it gave those who buy bonds issued by such large investment banks or otherwise lend to them, good reason to think that the Fed will again rescue them if a large investment banks fails in the future. They, therefore, have little incentive to gauge the risk carefully, or to charge an interest rate that makes due allowance for risk.

To some extent, elaborate contract provisions can, though perhaps at considerable cost, guard against moral hazard. But it is usually difficult or impossible to write contracts that provide for all sorts of contingencies, so that certain types of insurance, for example, insurance against gaining weight, are simply not feasible.

Some people find it impossible to borrow at all, and all of us find it impossible to borrow sums that are very large relative to our income or wealth, because we cannot provide sufficient assurance to potential lenders that we will be able to repay, even though we ourselves know that we will be able to (asymmetric information), or else, because we cannot convince lenders that we will make sufficient effort (moral hazard). And if we try to offer an extremely high interest rate to offset such risks, that won't work – since the very size of the interest payment makes it less likely that we will be able or willing to meet the payments on the loan.

Still another factor limiting the extent of, or the very existence, of markets is the cost of setting them up and managing them. When eBay greatly reduced the cost of buying and selling second-hand goods, such trades increased substantially. But not everything can be sold efficiently on eBay: if you intend to retire in ten years and move to Florida you cannot sell your house in New York for delivery ten years from now. In addition, as discussed in the next chapter, markets require a legal system that will establish and impartially enforce claims, such as property rights.

6.6.8   Market irrationality

Since market participants have an incentive to behave rationally, and since a Darwinian process favors those who are most rational, one would expect participants in financial markets to behave rationally. Usually they do, but there are exceptions. Sometimes they are subject to what psychologists call "group think." Mob psychology can take charge, even if the "mob" wears expensive tailored suits – think of the dot.com boom or the investment bankers who bought all those bonds secured by sub-prime mortgages. Wishes and hopes then masquerade as unbiased forecasts and "irrational exuberance" takes over. At other times irrational fear masquerades as commendable caution, and bargains go begging.

6.7   The Upshot

Nothing works as well as it should, and the price mechanism is no exception. Yet there is, and rightly so, a widespread consensus among economists that, on the whole, it works better than any other way of organizing economic activity.[c] That, in actuality, it does not work as well as it would in an ideal world, is irrelevant. Nor is it relevant that its success could well be due more to its dynamic efficiency, discussed in the next chapter, than to the static efficiency of matching prices to marginal costs, which this chapter is about. This dynamic efficiency, often referred to as "creative destruction," is a process whereby the development of new products and new ways of doing things ensure that the firms and products that will lead fifty years from now are not the ones that lead today. This is painful to those who see the value of their old assets or skills destroyed by the new, but it does raise living standards.

None of this means that we should always bow our heads before the dictates of the market. The voices of justice and of simple decency need to be heard. Moreover, even if the price mechanism were to ensure an absolutely efficient satisfaction of people's wants, not everyone thinks that this is a necessary and sufficient condition for a good society. If your value judgments tell you that rampant consumerism is reprehensible then you should perhaps reject the market system that fosters it. In addition, there are the just discussed problems of unemployment, market power, externalities, decreasing cost industries, and restricted or missing markets, and depending upon your philosophical predilections perhaps income inequality.

But, beware of jumping from the obviously correct proposition that the invisible hand of the price mechanism sometimes lacks dexterity, to the, by no means obvious, proposition that the visible hand of government is dexterous. No government is run by a philosopher-king. Few are run by even those pathetic substitutes for one, technocrats and intellectuals. The best, the democratic ones, are run in part by politicians responsible to a public that is not only badly informed, but has little incentive, when voting, to rely on reason rather than emotion.[5] As a result, not only are silly policies adopted,

---

[c]   Indeed some socialists advocate that while the government should own most industries, it should run them in accordance with the price mechanism, by telling managers to set their prices equal to marginal costs, and thus simulate the operation of a capitalist market system, but one in which all property income belongs to the state or to employees. Would this system provide the right incentives for innovative management, and protect the process of creative destruction from the pressures of those whose interests it threatens? I doubt it.

but they can persist. (For example, federal law prohibits gas stations from charging extra for using a credit card, but they are allowed to offer a discount for cash.) Moreover, governments are subject to the sway of lobbyists for various interest groups. For example, many occupations require unnecessary (or unnecessarily arduous) licenses that, by limiting the supply, benefit the interests of providers at the expense of consumers. And even when governments are not run by interests, or are subject to the views of an electorate often governed by emotional thinking, they are run by bureaucrats, with their tendency to group-think.

And government bureaucrats, too, are not immune from self-interested behavior. They are likely to support policies that increase the budgets and prestige of their own agencies and their chances for promotion. For example, a problem in using World Bank loans to reward those countries that follow sound policies and not others, has been that the World Bank's staff is organized by country departments, and each of these departments has an incentive to seek more loans for its country, and thus enhance its own budget.[6] As someone once pointed out, in policy-making the truth is just another special interest.

This certainly does not mean that government intervention can never compensate for the weaknesses of the market, but it does mean that, before invoking the supposedly benign guiding hand of the government, one should ask not how this hand *should* function, but how it is likely to function in this particular case. Chapter 8 gives several examples of how well-intentioned policies for improving upon the market's decisions have made things worse rather than better. Deciding whether a particular intervention would be beneficial or harmful does not call for sweeping ideological declarations but for careful analysis of the particular case (see box 6.4).

If one decides that in a particular case government intervention can improve upon the unaided workings of the market, one should still try to make use of the market mechanism in designing the intervention. Chapter 9 describes an example of this: taxing pollution instead of setting mandatory pollution limits for each firm.

One final point: admiration for the price mechanism does not necessarily imply agreement with everything advocated by those who declare themselves pro-market or conservative. Thus, although they wax lyrical about the virtues of the competitive market, they are often less enamored of tough anti-trust policies that help to keep it competitive. Yet it was Adam Smith, not Karl Marx, who wrote: "People of the same trade seldom meet together, even for merriment and diversion, but the conversation ends in a conspiracy against the publick, or in some contrivance to raise prices."[7] One message of this book is not: "Always vote Republican," but is, instead, "try to design

Box 6.4: Privatization

Those who are enthusiastic about limiting the size of government often advocate that the government should privatize some services it now performs. For example, while a municipality has to ensure that garbage is collected, it can have firms bid for this work, and get it done cheaper, since they are less shackled by bureaucracy and political pressures than is the municipality and because they are subject to the spur of competition. Currently, the major battleground on this issue is school vouchers.

There are many tasks that can be efficiently privatized, but one should not get overly enthusiastic. Unless their work is adequately monitored, firms that contract to perform public services can and will maximize their profits by skimping on the quality of the service they provide. Whether a certain government activity can be successfully privatized, therefore, depends on how well the government can evaluate the quality of the service provided. For garbage collection, a municipality can readily do this, because if the garbage is not picked up, it will hear about it. By contrast, the criminal justice system should not be privatized, because without costly duplication of the work of private courts, the government would not know whether a private court has dealt fairly with a case. The civil justice system, however, could, and indeed has been, partially privatized since litigants can agree to binding arbitration by a private-sector referee.

Each case for privatization should, therefore, be evaluated on its own and not settled on fact-blind ideological grounds. Nor should it be settled by surrendering either to the pressures of government employees who want to maintain their cushy jobs, or to the lobbying of private-sector firms that want to make a buck. One must also watch out for the government's bias, which may go either way. Some officials and politicians may want to foster their prestige and influence by being in charge of a large workforce, while some governments may want the money that they could obtain in the process of privatization from selling some public assets, such as refuse trucks. The bizarre rules of government accounting allow them to treat proceeds from such sales as though they were current revenue, so that they can increase spending or cut taxes.

whatever policy you support so that it goes with, and not against, the grain of the price mechanism." To be pro-market, the government may need to work against the immediate interests of a particular business through anti-trust action or pollution regulation of some sort.

APPENDIX 6.1

More on Supply and Demand

Much of this chapter has discussed supply and demand. But it is often easier for many readers to look at diagrams for understanding of these ideas and thus you will find them in this portion of the chapter.

DEMAND

Demand for a good is determined by many factors: its price, the prices of competing goods, as well as of any goods that are used in conjunction with it (e.g. gas with automobiles), the incomes of consumers, and also their tastes. (Economists use "tastes" as a dumping ground for all factors other than prices and income that affect demand.) While we can estimate econometrically the role that all of these factors play in determining demand, economists often single out for special attention the relation between the price for a good and the demand for it. By contrast, they usually take tastes as a given and as stable, leaving that topic mainly to psychologists and sociologists. Relating the demand for a good to only one of its determinants, its price, has the advantage that we can then show this relationship as a line, called a "demand curve," in a two-dimensional diagram. In figure 6.1 the demand curve DD (drawn arbitrarily as a straight line) shows how much is bought at each price. It takes all the other determinants of demand as constant. If any of these change, you get a new demand curve such as D^1D^1, which could be, but certainly need not be, parallel to DD. There is, therefore, a sharp distinction between moving between points *along* the demand curve – as happens when the price of the good changes and movements *of* the demand curve itself, such as a shift from DD to D^1D^1.

We can invoke rigorous economic theory to establish that, except in a particular case that can be precisely specified, demand curves slope downward, so that more is bought at a lower price. Fortunately, one can also establish this almost as well by ordinary common sense. Suppose that the price of clothing rises substantially. What will you do? You will probably decide to buy less clothing, to make that old jacket last another year. That much is obvious, but let's get a bit more specific. If the jacket now costs more, then to buy it you have to give up more of other goods you could have bought instead, and that is one reason, called the "substitution effect," why you decide to do without it. But there is also another reason, called the "income effect."

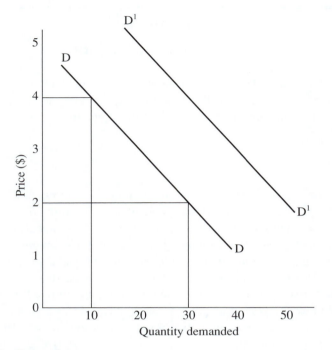

Figure 6.1   Demand curves

The rise in clothing prices has made you poorer – with your nominal income staying put and clothing prices rising, your real income has fallen. And with your real income being lower, your demand for most goods and services, including clothing, will also be lower.[d]

The slope of the demand curve measures how responsive the quantity demanded is to price. For example, in figure 6.1 a $2 decrease in price increases the quantity demanded by 20 units. This way of measuring the responsiveness of demand is not helpful because it depends on the particular units used. For instance, if changes in demand are measured in ounces, the responsiveness of demand is 16 times as large as it is when measured in pounds. Similarly, if the amount purchased is stated as the amount bought per year, the responsiveness of demand is 12 times as great as it is when expressed as the amount bought per month. Economists, therefore, measure the response in terms not

---

[d]   How about a prestige good? Couldn't a rise in its price increase demand for it by making it an even better vehicle for conspicuous consumption? Yes it could, but that would be a change in taste, and hence a *shift* of the demand curve, and not a movement along it.

of physical units, but in terms of percentages, that is, as the percentage change in the quantity demanded divided by the percentage change in price. This is called the "elasticity of demand." If this elasticity is greater than unity we say that the demand for this good is elastic, and if it is less than unity we call it inelastic. Elasticity has a useful implication; if a seller raises the price of a good with an inelastic demand her total receipts (price times quantity sold) rise, while if she raises the price of a good with elastic demand her total receipts fall. And if the elasticity of demand happens to be exactly unity her total receipts are unchanged.

People generally underestimate the elasticity of demand. For example, they think that if the price of gas were to rise they, as well as others, would have few opportunities to reduce their use of it. They believe this because they do not have an incentive to think seriously about all the things they could do to cut their use. But if the price of gas does rise and stays high, people will find many previously unsuspected ways of cutting back, and discover more feasible ways of using familiar methods, such as car-pooling, or public transportation. Necessity is the mother of invention. When gas prices are low and airport security systems are a general hassle (as well as charged back to the airline consumer), more people will drive. When gas prices rise, more people will fly long distance. However, all this takes time. Similarly, when a price falls, it takes people quite a long time to adjust fully, so that the long-run elasticity of demand is greater than the short-run elasticity. But eventually even the demand for addictive goods like alcohol, tobacco and drugs responds to their prices. Humans are wired so that the switch to the brain is located in the pocketbook.

Analogous to the demand curve, there is a supply curve, such as SS in figure 6.2, that tells us how much will be supplied at each price, holding constant other determinants of supply, such as the available technology and the firms' market power. Again, when these factors change, we draw a new supply curve. We measure the supply curve's elasticity as the percentage change in the quantity supplied divided by the percentage change in price. As in the case of demand, the long-run elasticity exceeds the short-run elasticity. At any one instance there is a fixed supply, but, sooner or later, producers increase their output while imports may rise as additional foreign suppliers enter the market.

THE INTERACTION OF SUPPLY AND DEMAND

Figure 6.3 combines the demand and supply curves of the previous figures to show the equilibrium price. If the price is P_a then, as the horizontal axis shows,

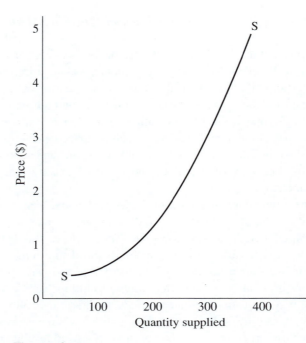

Figure 6.2 The supply curve

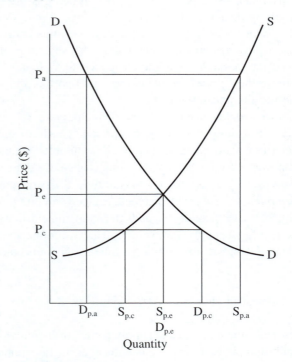

Figure 6.3 Combining supply and demand

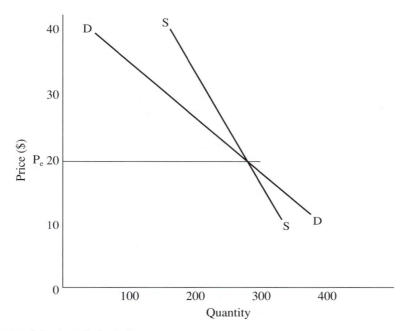

Figure 6.4   A pathological case

supply exceeds demand. At least some suppliers cannot sell all they want to, so they cut their prices. Conversely, at P_c demanders want more than suppliers have to offer, and suppliers take advantage of this by increasing their prices. Only at the price P_e, where the supply and demand curves intersect, does supply equal demand. This is a stable equilibrium. If the price should somehow happen to rise above P_e supply exceeds demand, so that it falls again, and at any price below P_e, such as P_c, demand exceeds supply, so that it rises again.

At least, in principle, there are also other possibilities. Figure 6.4 shows a case where due to strong economies of scale the supply curve slopes downward at a steep enough angle to intersect the demand curve from above. If the price falls even slightly below P_e supply exceeds demand and drives the price further down, and conversely, if the price happens to rise above P_e there is no stopping place. If either the supply curve or the demand curve is not a straight line, and there is no reason why they should be, it is even possible that the two curves intersect more than once. At which of these equilibrium positions the price will settle then depends on factors that are beyond this simple supply and demand model. But these are almost pathological cases of more interest to the economic theorist than to the student of economic behavior.

AN APPLICATION

Suppose the federal government imposes a tax on dry-cleaning because dry-cleaners use hazardous materials. Who ends up paying this tax? In a superficial sense of "paying," owners of dry-cleaning establishments do, because they are the ones who have to send checks to the government. But this does not necessarily mean that they are the ones who bear most of the burden. It is a fundamental principle of economics, one that chapters 8 and 9 will illustrate again and again, that people are not catatonic when prices change. When costs or opportunities change, firms react by changing the prices they charge, the amount they work, etc. So let's see whether dry-cleaners can do something to pass the burden of the tax on to others.

To do that, let's try to imagine what they might try to do, and see if that would be an equilibrium. One possibility is that they raise their prices by the full amount of the tax. That would not work. At the previous price, supply of and demand for dry-cleaning were equal. If the price now rises, figure 6.3 tells us that supply exceeds demand, and the price would have to fall. But it would not fall all the way back to its previous level. With the tax raising the costs of dry-cleaners, they would supply fewer dry-cleaning services at each price; in other words, the supply curve in figure 6.3 shifts upwards from SS_1 to SS_2, so that the new equilibrium price is somewhere in between the old price and the old price plus the tax, and dry-cleaners have succeeded in shifting some of the tax onto consumers. Just how much depends on the relative slopes of the supply and demand curves.

If they cannot pass the entire tax forward to consumers, will they pass some of it backward to their employees in the form of lower wages, or as lower prices to the suppliers of the materials they use? Let's assume that they will not, and see if that is a possible equilibrium. With dry-cleaners having to absorb the entire tax, their profits will be lower: indeed some might make a loss, and several will leave the industry. Some of their employees will now be unemployed, and some of their suppliers will find themselves with excess capacity. If these employees have skills that are specific to the dry-cleaning industry, so that for many of them the wages they can earn in other industries are less than in dry-cleaning, they will be willing to accept lower wages to remain in the dry-cleaning industry, and thus absorb some of the burden of the tax. (This does not necessarily require a cut in their current money wage, it could just be that their wages rise less than they otherwise would.) How much of the tax they will absorb depends on the slope of the supply curve of labor in the dry-cleaning industry. If this supply curve is horizontal because they can get jobs in other industries at the same wage as in dry-cleaning, then they will absorb none of the tax. A similar story applies to the suppliers of materials to dry-cleaners.

As you can see, determining the burden of even a simple tax on dry-cleaning is complicated. Hence, not surprisingly, there is much dispute about who ultimately pays the corporate income tax. But one thing is clear. While students who figure that they have nothing to lose if property taxes in their college town are raised because they are renters, are right if they graduate before rents have adjusted, but subsequent students will not be so fortunate.

As a second example, suppose that Congress raises the fuel efficiency standards for cars and trucks enough to reduce the demand for oil to be turned into gasoline by 10 percent, and that American drivers account for, say, 20 percent of the world's demand for oil. Does that mean that the world's consumption of oil will drop by 2 percent? No it does not: because such a simple calculation ignores the workings of the price mechanism as oil producers adjust to the decreased demand, and other consumers of oil adjust to the lower oil prices due to lower demand by American drivers by consuming more oil. To simplify the discussion assume at first that all oil is supplied by a monopolist whose marginal cost of producing this oil is $1 per barrel regardless of how much he produces. He sells it, of course, for much more than that, choosing a price at which marginal revenue equals marginal cost. Marginal revenue depends on the elasticity of demand. Suppose, for example, that up to some point beyond which demand disappears, the demand for his oil is completely inelastic so that the demand curve up to that point is a vertical line. The monopolist can then maximize his profits by setting his price at that point. Conversely, suppose that demand is completely elastic at a price of $3.00, that is, nobody will buy oil at $3.01, but that there is an infinite demand at $3.00, in other words, that the demand curve for his oil is a horizontal line. Assume further that although the increased fuel-efficiency standards shift the demand curve downward they do not change the elasticity of demand.

Now look at figure 6.5 where DD is the demand curve before and D^1D^1 the demand curve after the increase in the fuel efficiency standard, and P and P_1 the respective prices. What the increased standard has done is to lower the price of gasoline, but to leave the supply and consumption of oil unchanged as long as the price stays above $1 per barrel.

Now let's see what happens when we get rid of some of the assumptions. The assumption (made only for simplicity) of a monopoly producer is harmless. As discussed above, competitive firms also maximize profits by setting marginal revenue equal to marginal cost, and although each individual firm

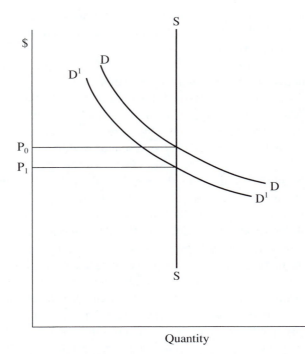

Figure 6.5   Effect of increases: FACE standards if oil supply is completely inelastic

faces a completely elastic demand curve, for the industry as a whole, the demand curve is the same as for a monopolist. The assumption that firms set prices so that marginal revenue equals marginal cost rather than charging average cost plus a mark-up does not create a serious problem, because, in the long run, firms are likely to charge the profit-maximizing price shown by marginal revenue equaling marginal costs. The assumption that higher mileage standards, while lowering the demand curve for oil, do not change its elasticity, is a reasonable first approximation. However, the assumption that the supply of oil is completely inelastic is not. It may be close to that for some OPEC countries that are low-cost producers, but there are other producers who will cut back their supply because their marginal costs now exceed the lower price.

What is the upshot of all this? It is that higher fuel efficiency standards – and other measures to reduce the demand for oil – will reduce oil consumption by less, probably substantially less, than appears at first glance. Just by how much less, depends on the elasticities of supply and demand. They will, however, have the side effect of lowering the price of oil. If the purpose of higher fuel efficiency standards is to reduce the emission of greenhouse gases then one has to look also at the effects on substitutes for oil. For example, the lower price of gas will reduce the demand for coal, another severe pollutant.

NOTES

1   Cited in Thomas Sowell, *Applied Economics*, New York, Basic Books, 2004, p. 23.
2   Thomas Sowell, *Economic Facts and Fallacies*, New York, Basic Books, 2008, ch. 2.
3   John Maynard Keynes, *The General Theory of Employment, Interest and Money*, New York, Harcourt Brace, 1936, p. 374.
4   Clive Crook, "Capitalism: The Movie," *Harpers*, March 2006, p. 46.
5   See Bryan Caplan, *The Myth of the Rational Vote*, Princeton, Princeton University Press, 2007.
6   See Paul Collier, *The Bottom Billion*, Oxford, Oxford University Press, 2007.
7   Cited in James Buchan, *The Authentic Adam Smith*, New York, W.W. Norton, 2006, p. 103.

7

Risk Taking and Incentives

The previous chapter discussed how efficiently the price mechanism allocates resources between the production of various goods. But such static efficiency is only one aspect of how well an economy functions. It leaves out of account the dynamic efficiency that determines how fast the economy is growing. That per capita income is now so much greater than it was in 1800 is not due mainly to a better alignment of marginal utility and marginal costs, but primarily to our greater stocks of knowledge and human capital, and, secondarily, to our greater stock of physical capital. Economists have, therefore, devoted much effort to developing a theory of economic growth in which the stock of knowledge is endogenous, with people investing in acquiring knowledge and not just in installing physical capital. But much work on this still remains to be done. Accordingly, this chapter discusses just two aspects of dynamic efficiency, aspects that are also relevant for economic growth: risk taking and getting the incentives right.

7.1   Risk Bearing and Entrepreneurship

By "risk" economists mean not just the possibility of a loss, what is sometimes called "downside risk," but include also the possibility that events may turn out better than expected, that is "upside risk." Downside risk and upside risk tend to occur together. In a market in which prices fluctuate violently, there are both large profits and large losses to be made.

Most economic activity, not just what is usually called "speculation," requires risk bearing, and some requires an immense amount. A firm that starts something completely new bears tremendous risks because it is operating in a fog of ignorance. But even in an established industry, say, shipping, a company ordering a freighter runs the risk that by the time it is built and delivered, other firms may have expanded and freight rates may have declined. And let us not forget the graduate student in a humanities Ph.D. program who runs the great risk that she will not be able to find a job in her field upon graduation. Nor should we forget her professor who initiates an innovative research program whose failure may deprive her of tenure, or the lawyer who works for a contingency fee. On a vastly lesser scale, someone trying out an unfamiliar brand of milk also takes a small risk.

One indication of the importance of risk bearing is the role it plays in generating high profits. A firm that produces a good that has been on the market for some time, and produces it in a familiar way, is not bearing great risk, but it will also not earn sustained high profits. For that, it has to do something different from what others do. But doing things differently involves risk, and usually the only reward for departing from the beaten path is scratches. Some unknown, but perhaps substantial, part of the income inequality that we observe around us is due to some people's greater willingness to take risk and the outcome of that crapshoot.

There are some people who like to take risks, even when they are not paid for doing so; indeed they are willing to pay to do it. They are called gamblers. But most of us like to avoid risk – that's why we buy insurance. Since there is more risk in the economy than can be absorbed entirely by those who like risk or are indifferent to it, the marginal risk bearer is someone who has to be paid to do it, and hence risk bearing carries a positive price. That the enhanced productivity that results from inducing people to shoulder risk is substantial is suggested by the high rate of return that American corporations have paid to those willing to assume the risk involved in holding their stock rather than holding bank deposits or very safe short-term securities. Over the 1926–2004 period, stocks paid a nominal rate of return as dividends and capital gains of 12.4 percent, while Treasury bills paid only 3.8 percent.[a]

The price of risk bearing, like the price of labor and capital, is determined by supply and demand. On the supply side, social attitudes matter. The willingness to take on risk is part of an entrepreneurial culture, the culture of the "go-getter" and the self-made man. Psychology matters, too; it is optimists, not pessimists, who become entrepreneurs.

---

[a] For readers who happen to know what a standard deviation is (it will be explained in chapter 12), the standard deviation of returns was 20.3 percent for stocks and 4.3 percent for Treasury bills.

Within the firm the predominant risk taker is the stockholder, who gets paid (earns a profit) only to the extent that the value of the firm's sales exceed what it has to pay its employees, suppliers, and creditors. With the value of sales fluctuating unpredictably and profits being a small residual, the rate of profit is highly variable. If a firm earns a 10 percent profit, and its gross receipts fall by 10 percent while its costs remain constant its profit is wiped out, but if its receipts rise by 10 percent its profit doubles. This is why profit sharing has not caught on. Most employees prefer to be paid a stable amount instead of receiving a share of fluctuating profits. Stockholders, who can spread their risks by holding shares in various firms, can assume the risk better than can employees, who cannot similarly diversify by working for various firms.

Moreover, financial intermediaries, that is, firms that obtain funds from savers and provide funds for investors and other spenders, generally – but not always – reduce the total amount of risk in the economy. For example, when a bank pools the deposits of savers and lends them to businesses, the law of large numbers allows it to reduce the risk of lending below what it would have been had savers made these loans directly – it is harder to predict whether any particular borrower will fail, than to predict what proportion of a thousand borrowers will. (Besides, small deposits are insured, and since banks ultimately pay the cost of this insurance, the risk is spread over many banks.) Another example is a financial institution that buys mortgages from their original issuers (whose mortgages are geographically concentrated, and hence share a common risk), and then sells bonds secured by shares in a large number of these mortgages. A further step is to "slice and dice" these mortgages by issuing several types of bonds secured by these mortgages, some of which pay a higher interest rate, but are first in line to take the loss when some mortgages turn sour, and others that will have to bear losses only if the former are insufficient to cover all the losses. But some of this "financial engineering" undertaken in the first decade of this century in mortgage markets turned out disastrous: it was predicated on rising house prices and few defaults in monthly payments. When these conditions failed to hold in 2007 and 2008 some financial intermediaries had devastating losses.

Yet, despite sophisticated financial engineering, and sometimes because of it, there is still a lot of risk that has to be borne in an innovative economy. Even so, despite its usefulness, some people treat being paid for risk bearing – particularly when it is labeled "speculation" (which all risk taking essentially is) – as less justifiable and honorable than being paid for working. This is an aspect of the culture that dates back to the Middle Ages and before, that paying interest on borrowing money is usury. There are still some prejudices against those people who bear financial risk.

7.2   Incentives

Steven Landsburg opens his excellent *The Armchair Economist* with: "Most of Economics can be summarized in four words: 'People respond to incentives.' The rest is commentary."[2] There is much to this; hence, incentives deserve a close look. Let's start by distinguishing between two types of incentives, intrinsic and extrinsic ones, and then ask whose incentives are the relevant ones. After that we'll look at four examples of incentives in action.

7.2.1   Intrinsic and extrinsic incentives

The usual procedure in neo-classical economics is to consider only extrinsic rewards, such as a high salary or higher profits. But as psychologists have rightly pointed out, there is also pleasure to be got from the very fact of doing a job, and doing it well, and never mind the pay. An amateur computer programmer might feel happy about having written a sophisticated program even if she does not expect to earn anything from it.

After all, many people greatly enjoy doing crossword puzzles. Similarly, some – let us hope many – people derive satisfaction from knowing they have done a good or honorable deed. This does not mean that neo-classical economists with their almost exclusive emphasis on extrinsic incentives are wrong, because, for most of the problems economists deal with, you get the same answer regardless of whether or not work provides a certain amount of intrinsic satisfaction along with its extrinsic rewards. You work until the marginal utility of the goods you can buy with what you are paid plus the self-esteem you obtain from doing the extra work and any other intrinsic benefits, balances the disutility of doing this work.

But this does not mean that the intrinsic satisfaction obtained from work can *always* be brushed aside. Economists have long recognized that when you compare jobs requiring the same level of skill, pleasant jobs pay less than unpleasant ones. A tobacco company may have to pay more than a public-interest law firm for a lawyer with the same abilities. Beyond this rather obvious point, empirical studies of employee behavior show that workers who are loosely supervised tend to work harder than closely supervised ones, because being trusted to work hard, they feel greater pangs of conscience when they don't. Similarly, paying previously unpaid volunteers might *reduce* the number of volunteers, because if they are paid, people no longer receive the satisfactory feeling that they are doing a good deed. Likewise, if people are fined when they violate a rule, they may conclude that paying the fine frees them from any moral obligation to obey the rule.

There is much to be said for an economy relying not just on the extrinsic incentive of money, but also on the intrinsic incentives that altruism provides. Great moral and religious teachers have praised altruism, and even among us lesser folk it is more widely admired than "a what's-in-it-for-me?" attitude. But reliance on altruism also has some disadvantages. One is that it is a clumsy way of directing the flow of resources. Suppose you decide to do some volunteer work. How can you tell whether you would do more good as a volunteer in a hospital or in a school? By contrast, to the extent that wages correctly reflect marginal social productivities, the extrinsic motive of pay directs you to the appropriate work. Second, there is an inherent unfairness in relying on altruism: good people make a sacrifice, while other people enjoy themselves.

Then, there is the question of what a greater reliance on altruism in one activity, say donating blood, does to the availability of altruism for other activities. Suppose that there is a fixed amount of altruisms, then the more we rely on it in one activity, the less altruistically people will behave in other activities. It may, therefore, be bad policy to induce people to act altruistically in a situation where we could easily rely on cold cash. Virtue is a scarce good and needs to be economized. But is the assumption that the amount of altruism is fixed correct? That seems unlikely. It seems more likely that seeing some people act altruistically induces others to behave altruistically too, if only by raising the bar they have to surmount if they want to think of themselves as possessing at least an average degree of altruism.

It is, therefore, sensible to rely as we do on both types of incentives. At first glance – but only at first glance – extrinsic ones play only a trifling role. But what else is it that keeps employees working when the boss is not in the room? What else induces us to give street directions to strangers, etc.?

7.2.2   Whose incentives? The principal–agent problem

Firms per se do not act, only their CEOs and managers do, and these are supposed to act as the hired agents of the stockholders (called here the "principals") by maximizing the firm's profits and the value of its stock. But here as elsewhere "supposed to" and "actually do" are not the same – and these agents have an incentive to maximize their own utility instead of profits for stockholders. Let's see what difference this makes in some situations, starting with nonprofits and governments and then looking at for-profit firms.

Nonprofit organizations and governments

Consider the incentives of a manager in a nonprofit organization or government agency. Assume that neither her superiors nor any of her potential future

Box 7.1: Why Were Russian Machine Tools So Heavy under Communism?

Although there is nothing in the writings of Marx, Engels, or Lenin that suggests that machine tools should be heavy, in communist Russia they were. The reason: the difficulty of providing proper incentives. Government planners set minimum output quotas for various factories. That was relatively easy for industries with homogeneous products, like pencils, where they could specify the number of units. But machine tools come in vastly different sizes. What the planners, therefore, did was to set the quota, not in terms of the number of machine tools, but in tonnage. Since the cost per ton of making the base plate of a machine tool is much less than that of making operating parts such as cutting heads, this gave factories a strong incentive to use heavy bases.

employers can judge how efficiently she does her work. If she is trying to maximize her income, then she will not strive to run her department efficiently. Instead of minimizing her costs, she will try to maximize costs, because the bigger the budget she oversees, the higher is the salary and prestige to which she is entitled – that's how bureaucracies, both private and governmental, work. More specifically, take the case of a manager who is paid twice as much as a supervisor whose work she oversees, and who, in turn, is paid twice as much as a production-line worker. Whenever the production workers demand a wage increase, she has an incentive to agree to it. In addition, she has an incentive to award herself plentiful perks such as a luxurious office. These principal–agent problems affect not only market economies; planned economies are even more plagued by them (see box 7.1). Fortunately, the intrinsic reward of a job well done *may* override such extrinsic incentives.

Businesses

Would this problem be any less if she worked for a for-profit business instead of for a nonprofit or a government? Not at all – as long as we maintain the crucial assumption that her superiors and potential future employers cannot judge her efficiency, and also assume that she does not own stock in the company or receives incentive pay, such as a bonus. Given these assumptions, for-profits are even more likely than nonprofits to suffer from the principal–agent problem, because their managers are likely to have less intrinsic motivation for serving their principals.

Finally, the assumption made so far, that managers own no stock in the company and receive no incentive pay needs to be dropped; incentive pay is widespread and managers often own stock in their companies, not infrequently a substantial proportion of their wealth. (See box 7.2.) But unless the manager receives all earnings above a certain amount, incentive pay does not suffice to align fully the interests of principals and agents. An agent will work only up to that point where the salary plus incentive pay he obtains for the last hour he works equals the disutility of working that hour, while the principal would like him to work until he drops. Similarly, the higher the price at which a real estate agent sells a house the more she earns, but, not surprisingly, a real estate agent tends to spend more time and effort in selling her own house where she reaps all the additional money, than she does in selling her clients' houses.[3]

The principal–agent problem exists throughout the firm. Suppose you have just graduated from college and are hired by a dairy to oversee the production of its milk cartons. How much glue should you use to secure the

---

Box 7.2: Executive Compensation

Many readers will have come across numerous complaints about the excessive compensation of some CEOs. I do not want to get involved in the value judgments implicit in these arguments, so I will more or less arbitrarily assume that CEOs should be paid in accordance with their marginal productivities, and ask whether their immense pay packages might perhaps be justified that way. And it turns out that they might be. But "might be" does not mean "are."

Suppose that a company with a payroll of $5 billion per year has a choice between hiring as its CEO Mr. I. M. Adequate at a salary of $1 million or Ms. I. M. Better at $50 million. Suppose further that the latter will direct the company in a way that will make its employees 1 percent more productive than Mr. Adequate would, perhaps by being able to intuit better where the firm should spend its R&D dollars. It will then be profitable for the company to pay the $50 million it takes to hire her. And assuming no externalities, for example, the improved profitability being the result of obtaining market power or of finding a way to cover up pollution, this $50 million also represents the value to society of Ms. Better's work.

But if gigantic executive pay packages can be explained this way, how come they are a recent phenomenon, and that they were so much lower until recently? A possible answer is that one should relate the CEO's pay to the size of the corporation he or she manages, and that has risen as much as CEO compensation has. Similarly, a possible reason European CEOs are on average paid much less than American CEOs is that the typical European corporation is much smaller. Hence, while to some people it may seem morally offensive to pay a CEO say a hundred times as much as the average employee – after all they share a common humanity – that could well represent their relative contributions.

Does that *necessarily* mean that the $50 million pay package of Ms. Better is justified? Of course not. There is the controversial value judgment about what should determine pay. There is also an assumption about no externalities, and the further assumption that Ms. Better really will raise productivity by 1 percent. Perhaps the reason the company's directors voted her such a high salary is less her outstanding ability than her friendship with the directors and their felt obligation to her for selecting them to the company's board.

What increases the credibility of this explanation is the way large CEO pay packages are usually structured. To enhance the CEO's incentives much of it consists of a bonus linked to the company's stock price. But that rewards the CEO even when the company's stock rises merely because the overall market has gone up. Moreover, many CEOs are given golden parachutes that come into play, even if they are fired for incompetence or fraud. That is hard to reconcile with the notion of the directors setting the CEO's pay with only the stockholders' interests at heart. And so is the fact that many CEO contracts are so opaque that it is hard for stockholders to see how much they are paying their CEOs.

Furthermore, that so few CEOs were fired in 2007–8 when their excessive risk taking had resulted in immense losses also raises doubt about whether corporate boards are holding them properly accountable. In addition, the blunders and herding behavior of CEOs that this episode revealed do not make it seem all that likely that all their high compensation is due to their efficiency.

But keep in mind that the outsized pay packages you read about are far above the normal incomes of their recipients. Not only do these recipients spend much of their working lives on lower rungs of the corporate ladder where salaries, though large, are not that gargantuan, but also, since a large part of their compensation package consists of bonuses linked to the price of their company's stock, and hence to stockmarket fluctuations, their pay package is much lower in the average year than it is in the highest year. Moreover, a significant part of executive compensation consists of stock options. And when the CEO cashes in stock options he may have accumulated over many years, the resulting gains are counted as income in that particular year.

flaps of the cartons? The more glue, the less is the chance that a carton will accidentally open in transit, but the harder it is for the customer to get the darned thing open. If you have taken economics in college, and did not pay sufficient attention, you might see this as a problem in balancing at the margin the reduction in profits resulting from the milk spilling with the reduction in profits that results from annoyed customers no longer buying your milk. But you might also reason as follows: suppose some cartons break open. The trucker or the store will complain, and you will be blamed. But if we lose customers because they find our cartons hard to open, the dairy will not learn of this, and I will not be blamed. So, pour on the glue!

While you are considering how much glue to use, the dairy's CEO is contemplating merging with another dairy. It would cost a lot to acquire that firm, but if he does he will be the CEO of a much larger firm, and consequently have both higher earnings and enhanced prestige. Even if he intends to make the decision on the basis of what is best for the stockholders, isn't it likely that his decision will be biased? No wonder so many mergers turn out badly and reduce the value of the acquiring firm's stock. On the other hand, since a CEO who earns average profits while avoiding risky but potentially highly profitable ventures, is less likely to be fired than one who takes substantial risks, he has an incentive to take too little risk. Perhaps that is not so bad because successful people, such as CEOs, tend to overestimate their own abilities. That, too, may explain why so many mergers fail.

Everyone knows that large firms derive advantages, sometimes great advantages, from economies of scale and many people have, therefore, predicted that large firms will drive small firms out of business. In many industries, like textbook publishing and airlines, this is true. The principal–agent problem is a major reason why this hasn't happened in more industries.

The principal–agent problem raises a nasty question. How can economists assume that firms maximize profits when their assumption of self-interested behavior implies that the firm's managers do not do that? There are two answers. One is that in most situations the difference between the managers' interests and the firms' interests are not all that large, so that assuming that firms maximize profits is a useful approximation. The other is the Darwinian argument of chapter 2, that firms in which the top managers do not ride herd on their subordinates will be driven out of business.

Some principal–agent problems in the professions

The divergent incentives of principal and agent can also be a serious problem in certain professional settings where the principal is relatively ignorant, and the agent is the expert. An obvious example is medicine, where it creates a major problem for the traditional fee-for-service system. Can you trust a medical specialist who tells you that you need an expensive procedure? Even if you are convinced that he is being honest, and not just trying to extract money from you, you know that it would only be human nature for him to have an exaggerated opinion of the importance of his specialty, and hence to recommend the procedure even in cases where it is not objectively justified. More generally, it is a familiar point that professionals (such as economists) try to please not only the principals who seek their advice, but – unconsciously – also try to bolster their own self-esteem by giving sophisticated and complex advice, and hence may not give the most cost-effective advice.

Principal–agent problems can arise in a particularly nasty form in the accounting industry (see box 7.3) and also in the brokerage industry. Some investors authorize their brokers to make trades for them as opportunities arise without having to check for specific approval. Thus the broker has an incentive to undertake as many trades as she can get away with even if they are not profitable. This is called "churning" an account.

To conclude this discussion, let's look at two examples of principal–agent problems that, while not of great importance for the economy as a whole, do provide good illustrations of how difficult it can sometimes be to detect just how self-interest skews an agent's actions. First, in 2007 the legendary investor Warren Buffett decided to select a successor (since he wished to retire) to manage his mutual fund by giving three or four of the final candidates kitties of about $5 billion each, and seeing who could generate the highest return. With all due respect to Warren Buffett this is not a good strategy because it ignores the principal–agent problem. The pay-off to each competing manager comes not from maximizing the mathematically expected value of the gain to his or her fund (that is, the probability of the expected gain times the size of that gain), but from beating all the other funds. And that means taking what would otherwise be excessive risk. And the more risk people take, the greater is the likelihood that the most successful one will be, not the ablest, but the one whom Lady Luck has favored. I would not hire a CEO on the basis that in tossing coins he got five successive heads. (Note that I am assuming Mr. Buffett is looking for the highest return in this trial period. Perhaps, instead, he was looking at the risk factor of each trade and judging whether he would do the same thing.)

Second, does an economic forecaster have an incentive to provide his clients with his honest-to-goodness best forecast, or does he have an incentive to shade his prediction one way or the other? A simple view of his incentives would have him give his best prediction, because good predictions attract more

Box 7.3: Do Accounting Firms Have
the Right Incentives?

To make it less likely that firms will provide false or misleading information to investors, publicly traded corporations have to have their books audited by accounting firms. But what incentives do these auditors have to provide investors with reliable information? Why should investors give more credence to an audited balance sheet than to an unaudited one? Since it is the corporations themselves that select and pay their auditors, these auditors have an incentive to compete for business by being too permissive.

But there is a counteracting factor. The CEO of Somewhat-Shady knows that if she has Creative-Accounting audit her books it will not make any trouble about the ingenious creativity of her own accountants. But investors know that too, so its word won't mean much. Better hire Eagle-Eyed-Audits.

Accounting firms are in a similar bind. In the short run, being excessively accommodating might bring you some customers, but in the long run it loses you customers as your reputation skids. There is also the danger that, if one of your clients fails, its distraught stockholders may claim that they bought its stock only because of your misleading audit, and sue you. If they win, that could devastate not only your firm, but since many accounting firms are partnerships with unlimited liability, also the partners' personal wealth.

Auditors, therefore, have two conflicting incentives. One is to be permissive and thus get more business in the short run. The other is to be extremely, even unfairly, tough, and protect their reputation, their very existence, and their partners' wealth. In isolation, either one would generate biased results, but until recently it was widely believed that these two incentives more or less offset each other, so that accounting firms have approximately the right incentives. However, in recent years many large accounting firms began to offer consulting services to firms whose books they audited. That was logical since some of the information that auditors acquire in doing audits is also useful in providing consulting services. But it does mean that they now have a stronger incentive to acquire clients, and hence to be more permissive than they used to be. Does that mean that auditors should be barred from offering consulting services to their clients? Or will the failure of one of the big five accounting firms, Arthur Anderson, that resulted from the bankruptcy of one of its clients, Enron, be sufficient to restore proper discipline?

clients. That makes sense if he is the only forecaster in town. But suppose there are a hundred. Now his incentives are more complicated, and one can tell several different stories. One is, that while it is still true that – other things being equal – the more accurate his forecasts, the bigger his clientele, other things are not equal. If all the other forecasters predict that the stock market will go up, and he does too, then if the market goes down instead, he will be wrong, but will be in good company, and hence won't be blamed all that much. But if he predicts that the market will go down when everyone else predicts that it will go up, and it does go up, he will look incompetent. Better not get too far out of line; there is safety in numbers. Hence, evolution has seen to it that, like zebras and sheep, forecasters have a herd instinct.

Another story is that if all the other forecasters herd, a forecaster might figure out the following trick. Every year, come what may, I will forecast gloom and doom. Most CEOs will soon realize that my forecasts are unreliable, and pay no attention to them. However, I am not interested in getting their love and affection, but only in getting their subscriptions to my pricy forecasting service. And in deciding whether to subscribe CEOs have their own interests to consider. If by chance one year my gloomy forecast happens to be right, but if they, being sensible, had ignored it and have acted instead on the more optimistic consensus of other forecasters, then stockholders might indignantly ask the CEO whether she was not aware of my gloomy forecast. It may be worth it for her to pay the $1,000 a year that I charge rather than have to admit that she was not aware of the forecast of someone who is occasionally correct.[b]

7.2.3 Four examples of incentives in action

The first of these is a case were incentives work well. In the second case, we know how to set the right incentives, but doing so would interfere with other goals. The third case is one in which incentives are not what they seem to be at first glance. The final case is one where what we need to do inevitably distorts incentives.

Airline safety

Airline crashes are extremely rare despite the great number of flights every hour, the many aircraft components that could fail, and the skill required of

---

[b] However, other forecasters may have the same idea and compete away the extra profits I can earn by being the outlier, so that I may decide to join the herd after all.

pilots and mechanics. Why is that? It is because the incentives are right. Aircraft manufacturers and airlines have a strong incentive to design their planes well and keep them in tip-top shape, because crashes can be extremely costly for them both, due to lawsuits and to loss of future business. A pilot's incentive to avoid a crash is obvious. One can even make a case – but I suppose only if one is an economist – that perhaps we have too few crashes, that the money now spent on providing the last ounce of safety could be spent better lowering fares. While that would increase airline fatalities it would probably decrease total traffic fatalities by shifting travelers out of cars into planes, which have a much lower fatality rate per mile traveled.

Law enforcement

How can we best use the disincentive of punishment to reduce the social cost of crime? Perhaps one possibility would be more severe punishment. Thus one study found that the California three strikes law does lower crime overall.[4] But it also found that by adding the additional risk that some criminals incur in committing their third crime, it increases the probability that this crime will be a violent one.

Another possibility is to take the total amount of crime as a given, but to minimize its costs by fiddling with the incentives of criminals to commit one type of crime rather than another, since there are at least some criminals who are willing to switch the type of crime they commit depending on the chance of being caught and on the likely punishment. If an identity theft that yields $10,000 to the criminal imposes a greater cost on society than does a $10,000 burglary, shouldn't identity theft be punished more severely?

Sounds reasonable but let's carry this type of reasoning a bit further. Suppose for the sake of the argument that by incurring the cost of keeping a criminal in jail for an extra year we can reduce all types of crime, except murder, on which, let us assume, the length of the sentence has virtually no effect. Should we then sentence repeated shoplifters to longer jail terms than murderers? "No" says our moral intuition, the severity of punishment should conform to our sense of outrage, and not to the benefit society obtains by incurring the costs of incarceration. Which is the better approach to selecting punishment, economic efficiency or our sense of moral outrage?

Another implication of the economic approach to punishment is that, where possible, we should fine criminals rather than jail them, since incarceration is costly, while fines bring in revenue. One objection to this, that incarceration is a greater deterrent than a fine, can readily be answered by raising the fine so that it becomes as great a disincentive as incarceration, and also by pointing out that the fewer the people who are incarcerated, the greater is its social stigma, and hence the more of a disincentive it becomes in those cases where it is still used. And the greater the stigma, then the shorter, and hence less costly to the government, the sentence can be. Perhaps a better argument against fining, rather than jailing, those criminals who have the wherewithal to pay the appropriate fine, is that this is class discrimination, since the rich have the choice between paying the fine or serving time, while the poor do not.

For a sharp conflict between efficiency and fairness, remember that deterrence depends both on the severity of the punishment and on the probability of being caught. We can, therefore, get the same deterrence from spending very little on law enforcement and imposing brutal prison sentences on those few criminals we do catch. This is unfair, both with respect to those who are caught and suffer a disproportionately harsh punishment, and those who get away unpunished. But it does save money. Does that make it desirable policy? More specifically, where do we want to be along the spectrum, ranging from spending heavily on law enforcement, and then imposing a light penalty, or spending little on law enforcement, but torturing to death the few criminals we do catch.

Voting in one's economic interests

And now for an example from political economy, the branch of economics that tries to explain political behavior. The outcomes of the 2000 and 2004 elections puzzled many Democrats. Why did so many low-income evangelicals vote for President Bush? If, as economic theory tells us, people behave rationally and selfishly, don't such people have a strong incentive to vote for the party that advocates their economic interests? No, they don't. A rational poor person who acts selfishly has a strong incentive not to vote Democratic, but instead not to vote at all. Let's do a rough calculation. Suppose that your state allows you to vote by mail, so that your cost of voting is only the short time it takes you to check the right boxes, sign your name, etc., which we will value at 50 cents, plus a 41 cent stamp. Assuming that you do not have to spend any time deciding which candidate you prefer, your total cost of voting is, therefore, 91 cents. (In states where you have to vote in person the cost is, of course, considerably higher.) And what do you get for your 91 cents? That depends on whether you live in a swing state. But assuming that in this respect you are an average voter, the chance of your vote swinging a presidential election is very, very small. Let's, arbitrarily put it at 1 in 10 million. Your chance in an election for a House seat is 1 in a 100,000 votes cast.[5] I have no data for either Senate seats or for various local offices. But let's assume arbitrarily that half the economic value of an election outcome to you depends on who is elected president. Hence a rational person whose voting behavior reflects only her economic self-interest would then have to value the outcome of the presidential election at least $4.55 million to make it worthwhile spending the 91 cents on it.[c] It is hard to imagine someone doing that. Hence, if you are selfish, your economic incentive is not to vote, period. And also, for the same reason, unless you happen to find politics interesting, you have no incentive to be informed about it. When shopping for groceries, ignorance can be costly for you; when voting, its cost is an externality for you. With our great surfeit of information and entertainment it is often rational to be ignorant, or to indulge in what Bryan Caplan[6] calls "rational irrationality."

Why then do so many people vote? They must be doing it for a reason other than economic self-interest, such as a sense of civic duty, or perhaps to construct for themselves at a trivial cost a pleasing self-image along the following lines: if I believe that patriotism is an important virtue, and also that the Republican party is the more patriotic party (my own take: yes on the first, no on the second), then I can construct a pleasing self-image for myself by voting Republican. And if I believe that helping the poor is important, and that the Democrats are better at it (yes, on the first; doubtful, on the second), I can construct a self-image as a compassionate, caring person by voting Democratic. These ways of showing myself to myself in a flattering light are much cheaper than actually being patriotic by being meticulous in paying one's taxes.

There is also another problem with the argument that the poor if they would vote rationally, would vote Democratic. Look at the typical voting behavior of those who make this argument. Many of them are well-to-do people themselves, who believe that the Republican party represents the interests of the well-to-do. And yet, they themselves vote Democratic. If they do not vote in their own economic interests, why do they expect the poor to do so? Shakespeare used as his heroes and heroines aristocrats and upper-middle-class people, because it was believed at the time that only such people had the capacity to experience noble feelings, that the poor were too taken up with grubbing for a living. Is it a remnant of this belief that underlies the

---

[c]   To find the mathematical value of the prize that makes it just worth buying a lottery ticket that has only a one in ten million chance of winning, you take the price of the lottery ticket and multiply it by ten million. But be warned that this mathematical value has only a loose correspondence to the economic value of the lottery ticket, since it ignores that the marginal utility of income declines as income rises, and that people are likely to be risk averse. That is why I said "at least."

notion that "they," should vote in their own economic interests, while "we" should be noble enough not to?

Taxes and incentives

We are often told that a tax cut is beneficial because it provides an incentive to work harder. Some enthusiasts even claim that if income tax rates are cut, the greater take-home pay stimulates so much additional work that tax revenues *rise* as the effect of the expanded tax base overwhelms the effect of the lower rates imposed on that base. In principle, this could happen, but the claim that it actually does represents a victory of enthusiasm over evidence. Yet, you would expect changes in the tax base to offset *some* of the effect of changes in rates. To see why, let's look more closely at the two main ways a cut in income tax rates affects the incentive to work.

On the one hand, by increasing take-home pay it induces some people, particularly women, to enter the labor force, and also spurs those already in the labor force to work more hours. (This substitution of labor for leisure or for work at home is an example of the substitution effect discussed in appendix 6.1.) In addition, a lower tax rate induces people to take more of their total remuneration as taxable income rather than as untaxed fringe benefits, such as fancy offices. However, a tax cut also has a second effect, one that reduces work by raising after-tax income. With their after-tax incomes now being higher, people can afford to take more leisure (an example of the income effect discussed in appendix 6.1) or spend more time on non-market work, such as housekeeping, childcare or volunteer work. Which of these two effects is stronger? Economic theory alone cannot tell us. It is an empirical issue. And the empirical evidence suggests that the substitution effect is the stronger, so that a tax cut does increase work.

Tax rates also have income and substitution effects on saving. If I can earn – after tax – say 5 percent on my savings rather than only 3 percent, this gives me an incentive to substitute another dollar of saving for the marginal dollar of consumption. However, at the same time, a tax cut makes me richer, and I can now provide for given future needs while saving a smaller percentage of my income. Again, while, in principle, the net effect could go either way, there is some presumption that the substitution effect outweighs the income effect, so that raising tax rates across the board lowers the percentage of income saved.

In addition to these effects on work and savings, taxes also reduce efficiency by distorting economic decisions as people invest their funds in tax shelters, such as municipal bonds, rather than in more productive, but taxed, ways. And the capital gains tax sometimes induces them to hold on to some stocks that they would otherwise sell to invest the proceeds in stocks with better prospects. After all, if they are "lucky" enough to die before selling their stock, all their capital gains tax liability on the old stock is wiped out.

It has proved very difficult to measure the distorting effect of the federal tax system. One extensive survey of various studies that have ventured fairly comprehensive, though still incomplete estimates, has come up with costs ranging from 2 to 5 percent of GDP, though it warns that these figures are hazy. And to the costs measured by this survey one should add the costs to taxpayers of doing the paperwork, a cost that may be about 1 percent of GDP.[7] Hence, our tax system is not cheap. With federal taxes accounting for about one-fifth of GDP, these estimates suggest that the average dollar of federal tax revenue costs the economy an additional 10 to 25 cents. And some other estimates are much higher.

7.2.4   Institutions and incentives

Incentives are deeply embedded in a society's institutions. A materialistic society that admires individualism and self-made men obviously provides greater incentives for entrepreneurship than does an honor culture that admires the inherited status of an upper class and detests the newly rich. In some societies, those who "want to make something of themselves" strive to become entrepreneurs; in others, they join the military or the bureaucracy.

Property rights and the rule of law also matter a great deal. Why bother to accumulate wealth if the government can seize it at any time? Why start a business if its success will draw demands for bribes, or if rivals will be able to bribe government officials to harass it? And it is not just the danger coming from government that matters. There is also the danger of not being able to enforce property rights efficiently against other firms or customers. In a country in which courts are exceedingly slow to settle liability suits, it can be unwise to rely on certain sophisticated types of contracts despite their greater efficiency. And there is less incentive to compose songs if they can be downloaded costlessly on the internet.

Many economists think that insecurity of property rights is the main reason, or at least one major reason, for the low per capita income of third world countries. Some have argued that whether a country inherited from its former colonizer the British common law tradition or the continental statute law tradition is a significant factor in explaining its current economic development. And economic historians disagree about the extent to which the greater protection of property rights that resulted from increased democratization accounts for the rise of the West.

7.2.5   Some concluding notes

The moral of this story: yes, incentives do govern economic behavior, and changes in incentives can be used to alter behavior. Hence, when trying to predict the effects of a proposed policy it is a good idea to devote considerable thought to how it will change incentives. Do not assume automatically that it will change incentives and hence behavior in the direction desired. The next two chapters provide several examples of how policies that ignore this can go awry.

Also, do not automatically assume that the stronger the incentives, and the more closely the agent's incentives are aligned with the principal's, the better. Sometimes, incentives can be too strong, and fraud, tax evasion, and other crimes result. Sometimes even that ultimate disconnect between the principal's and agent's interests, whistle-blowing, serves a useful function. And, as discussed in the previous chapter, status rivalry and conspicuous consumption drive people to work more than they should, though here there are offsetting factors such as the disincentive effect of taxes. Moreover, people have several types of incentives that sometimes conflict. A CEO has a financial incentive to maximize his company's profits – and also an incentive from feelings of morality to treat his customers fairly. And a politician sometimes has to balance the moral incentive of loyalty to her party with the moral incentive of loyalty to her country.

To end on a personal note: many years ago I worked on a study for a presidential commission. The initial arrangement was that I would be paid my expenses plus a consulting fee. Subsequently the commission decided to save on paperwork by paying me instead a higher fee out of which I had to meet my own expenses. Although, all along I had tried hard to be conscientious and keep my expenses down, I was amazed how much lower they were when it was my own money I was spending. Incentives do work.

NOTES

1   See William Goetzmann and Roger Ibbotson, "History and the Equity Risk Premium," Yale University, School of Management Working Paper 05-04, 2005.
2   Steven Landsburg, *The Armchair Economist*, New York, Free Press, 1993, p. 3.
3   Steven Levitt and Stephen Dubner, *Freakanomics*, New York, William Morrow, 2005, pp. 8–9.

4 Radha Iyengar, "I'd Rather Be Hanged for a Sheep Than a Lamb: The Unintended Consequences of Three Strike Laws," National Bureau of Economic Research, Working Paper 13784, 2008.
5 Casey Mulligan and Charles Hunter, "The Empirical Frequency of a Pivotal Vote," National Bureau of Economic Research, Working Paper 8590, Cambridge, MA, 2001.
6 Bryan Caplan, *The Myth of the Rational Voter*, Princeton, Princeton University Press, 2007, p. 123.
7 See US Congress, General Accountability Office, *Tax Policy*, GAO-05-878, Washington, DC, 2005.

8

Looking around Corners

When Thomas Sowell, now a prominent economist, was a student at Harvard, Professor Arthur Smithies asked his opinion of a certain policy. When Sowell gave a confident answer expounding the favorable effects that this policy, Smithies asked: "And then what will happen?"

> The question caught me off guard. However, as I thought about it, it became clear that the situation I described would lead to other economic consequences, which I then began to consider and spell out. "And what will happen after that?" Professor Smithies asked. As I analyzed how the further economic reactions to the policy would unfold, I began to realize that these reactions would lead to consequences much less desirable than those at the first stage.[1]

It is such probing into what is not apparent at first glance that this and the next chapter are all about. The issues of these chapters were chosen not because they are of surpassing practical importance, many are far from it, but because they provide good illustrations of how readiness to probe beyond the "obvious" can lead to surprising results.

In many cases, such probing suffices to solve the problem – one does not need to know in great detail specific facts, such as by just how much the labor supply responds to a given change in the tax rate. In other cases one would have to know such empirical specifics to evaluate the policy. For example, many economists have criticized minimum wage laws because they increase unemployment. But recent empirical work strongly suggests that a moderate increase in minimum wages has only a quite small effect on unemployment. Hence, in many of the following examples I have had to make some assumptions (which I have tried to spell out) that are controversial.

Sometimes it is hard or impossible to get a reliable fix on the specific facts one needs to evaluate a policy. But even in these cases the type of probing I am advocating is valuable since it isolates the critical factors, and that is a necessary first step. And if no solid data are available, one just has to make what one hopes is an "educated" guess. But even when that guess is simply a wild one, the probing I am advocating often tells us something valuable: that what seemed conclusive at first glance is very much open to question. That is worth knowing.

Many of the policies I discuss are intended to help the poor or to protect the environment; in other words, they are liberal policies. That I criticize them, does not mean that I oppose these goals, or am sneering at liberalism. I do not think that liberals are any less intelligent or dedicated to the general welfare than conservatives. And if they weren't, it would not matter, because I am criticizing policies, and not their proponents. That I do not criticize an equal number of conservative proposals is largely because, with liberals, having won a predominant position in academia and among the chattering class in general, there are more of their ideas to discuss, or at least I hear more of them. I suspect, dear reader, that you do too, and, therefore, need be warned against somewhat silly ideas in the *New York Times* more than against preposterous ones on talk radio. To some readers I may come across as a Dr No since I question so many well-intentioned proposals to help our fellow human beings. But then this chapter is intended to show how to spot invalid arguments.

The problems discussed here do not call for any specialized knowledge of economics and its esoteric tools. Several do, however, use a primary device of economics and of other scientific thinking; this is, to break the problem into parts by first making some wildly unrealistic assumptions, and then, after having solved the problem, given these assumptions, seeing what difference their removal makes.

I start the discussion of most problems by stating a plausible-sounding position, and then show why it is wrong. Some of the errors are simple ones that some readers will be able to spot readily on their own; several others are much more difficult to find. Many of the latter have the annoying characteristic that after – but not before – one realizes what the answer is, it seems so obvious. To deal with these questions, ask yourself Smithies' question: "and then what happens?," and remember to take into account that those who are adversely affected by a law or some other change usually do not just sit there and take it, but try to avoid the unpleasant consequences.

8.1 Do Easier Bankruptcy Laws Help the Poor?

Off-the-Cuff Answer: Yes, of course, the poor are more likely to go bankrupt.

Problem: Ignores the effect of bankruptcy law on interest charged and credit availability.

In 2005 a Republican Congress and White House, despite vehement opposition from liberals, tightened federal bankruptcy law, making it more difficult to walk away from your debt by paying very little.[a] Although the new law has a means-test provision that treats poor debtors better than others, many opponents objected that this law was one more instance of bashing the poor to help the rich, that a better response to the rising trend of bankruptcies that the law was intended to curb, would be to restrict the unsolicited mailing of credit cards. Were they right? I don't know, but I do know, or at least think I do, what the relevant issues are.

But first a matter of definition: I define "poor" with respect to income over the long run, thus not counting as poor someone who normally earns a million dollars a year, but because he speculated with borrowed money, has had to plead bankruptcy. It is those who are poor for a long time that we should be concerned about.

Who gains or loses from a tightening of bankruptcy law? At first glance it seems obvious that it is creditors who gain. Not only will fewer borrowers plead bankruptcy, but, also, many of those who do so will now have to pay off more of their debts. Debtors obviously lose. But hold on: granted that this is "obvious" is it also true? To start with, the picture of the rich lending to the poor is overdrawn. In fact, families in the lowest fifth of the income distribution are less likely to have outstanding debts than other families, presumably because they can find few willing to lend to them.

More fundamentally, does a more restrictive bankruptcy law really benefit creditors and hurt debtors? In dealing with such problems it is sometimes useful to look at hypothetical extreme cases that bring out starkly some important aspect.[b] Let's, therefore, first look at the situation of debtors under an

---

[a] Thus the *New Republic* (Anonymous, "Primary Concern," July 4, 2005, p. 6) wrote about Senator Biden: "His vote for the bankruptcy bill is a betrayal few liberals are willing to forget."
[b] Looking at limiting cases should not be confused with the slippery-slope argument discussed in chapter 4. Limiting cases are devices to clarify one's thinking, and thus can legitimately deal with hypothetical cases that nobody expects to occur, while slippery-slope arguments make a claim about what will happen.

extraordinarily compassionate law that relies entirely on people's honesty. If a debtor declares that she cannot pay, well then, the debt is canceled. Such a law would harm, not help, people who want to borrow, because nobody would be willing to lend to them, except possibly if they are family members or good friends. At the other extreme, imposing a mandatory death sentence for bankruptcy would also prevent most people from borrowing. Thus both extremes would hurt potential debtors by making it impossible for them to become actual debtors.

With neither extreme being desirable, just how stringent should bankruptcy law be? The key insight here is that in the credit market, as in other markets, the price system is at work. Implicit in the interest rate that creditors charge is an allowance for the risk that the debtor will not ante up, and that is obviously higher if debtors can easily walk away from their debts. Tightening bankruptcy law, therefore, both hurts – and helps – debtors. Those who are prevented from declaring bankrupt, or have to pay off much more of their debt when they do, lose. But other creditors, who can now borrow cheaper, or can now borrow when they could not previously do so, gain.

How about creditors? Do they gain? Since the credit market is competitive, In the *long run* creditors earn the normal rate of profit, regardless of whether bankruptcy law is tightened, because if they earn more, other firms enter the lending industry, and drive interest rates down, while if they earn less, some firms leave the industry, and with a smaller supply of credit the interest rate rises.[c]

It may, therefore, seem tempting to argue that it does not matter to creditors whether or not bankruptcy law is tightened. That is simplistic. First, while in the long run a tighter bankruptcy law does lower the interest rate, it takes time for this to happen, and, in the meantime, debtors are unequivocally worse off and creditors better off – in particular, think of those who contracted their debts before the law was tightened. And this "meantime" is far from trivial. Indeed, one might argue that tightening bankruptcy law that applies to existing loans is to legislate a violation of contracts – a most *un*conservative thing to do. Second, tightening bankruptcy law changes the distribution of income among debtors. While the lower interest rate benefits debtors in general, those who either because of unexpected adverse circumstances, or lack of self-control, face bankruptcy and would have been able to declare bankrupt under a less stringent law but not now, are worse off. I suspect that whether one thinks of this redistribution of income as good or bad depends

---

[c]   I am assuming here that the new law does not change the supply and demand for total credit enough to affect the overall interest rate in the economy.

on whether one thinks that bankruptcy is due mainly to uncontrollable circumstances or to personal failings.[d]

In principle, a good response might be to leave it up to the market, to let creditors and debtors choose between various types of contracts, some that severely restrict the power to declare bankruptcy, and, therefore, carry a low interest rate, and some with more benign bankruptcy provisions and a higher interest rate. However, in practice, many debtors might lack the ability to make a correct choice between such contracts, particularly when expert sellers try to push them into the wrong type of contract. Besides, debtors would have an incentive to signal that they are good credit risks by opting for a stringent contract, even when a less stringent contract would be better for them.

And this brings up another point. It seems likely that many people who objected to the tightening of bankruptcy law did so, at least in part, because they think that the mass mailing of credit-card applications and other advertising induces many people to take on excessive debt. And if credit-card companies push credit on people who are bad risks, they should be the ones who bear the resulting losses. This argument has more appeal if one sees people, or at least poor people, as lacking in self-control and as helpless pawns of advertisers, than if one sees them as autonomous rational beings, like oneself. Obviously, either of these descriptions fit some people, and not others.

8.2   Should Artists Receive a Share of the Capital Gain When Their Work Is Resold?

Off-the-Cuff Answer: Getting some of the capital gain increases artists' incomes.

Problem: Ignores the effect on the initial price paid to artists.

---

[d] Opponents of the 2005 law cited data showing that a substantial majority of bankruptcy filings were not the debtor's fault, but due to adverse events, such as high medical bills or unemployment. But these data are unreliable since they were gathered by asking people why they filed for bankruptcy. People are more likely to cite a reason that puts them in a favorable than an unfavorable light. This need not require outright lying. Suppose I buy an expensive car and shortly after that am confronted with a large medical bill I cannot pay. When asked why I am pleading bankruptcy I am likely to cite the latter, not the former. As a general rule, if you ask people why they did something, or why something happened to them, don't expect a reliable answer, not so much because people generally lie, but more because causation is such a slippery concept, and people like to think well of themselves.

Suppose you are an artist who sells me a painting for $1,000. Ten years later when you have become deservedly famous, I resell it for $10,000 and have a $9,000 capital gain of which you receive nothing. To prevent such a situation, the European Union recently passed an artists' rights law requiring those who resell paintings or sculptures above a certain value to give the artist a part, albeit a small one, of the capital gain. France has had a similar law since 1920 and several other countries have also adopted such laws, as has California. That is hardly surprising, because, to many people, it does not seem fair that the buyer should pocket all the gain, particularly if he bought the picture purely for speculation.

But it turns out that, despite its noble intentions, an artists' rights law makes artists worse off, primarily because it lowers the initial price of the painting. Given such a law, the buyer, knowing that his potential capital gain is smaller, will offer less for it. To see how much less, assume that the law requires him to give the artist 20 percent of any capital gain, and that there is a 10 percent chance that he will have a $10,000 gain, and a 90 percent chance that he will not have any capital gain at all. To avoid complicating the story by having to calculate the present value of the capital gain, assume that the buyer sells the painting right away, and let's also ignore capital gains taxes, and the buyer's reluctance to take risk. Then, a 10 percent chance of a $10,000 capital gain on the picture, while worth $1,000 to the buyer in the absence of an artists' rights law is, given this law, worth only $800 to him, and he will, therefore, offer $200 less. So it may seem that it is a wash, that what an artist gains from sharing in the potential gains she loses by receiving a lower price.

But it is worse than a wash. There is inevitably a big risk that the painting will not appreciate. Without an artists' rights law, it is the buyer who assumes this entire risk, while, with such a law, the artist has to bear part of it. And the artist is usually in a worse position to bear this risk than is the buyer, since changes in the values of her human capital, as well as part of her non-human capital (canvasses she has not yet sold) are both correlated with the changes in the value of the picture she is selling. A wise, risk-averse investor will diversify her assets. Giving the artist an equity interest in pictures she is selling does exactly the opposite. Besides, if she should happen to want to invest in her own work, she does not need an artists' rights law for that. She can simply hold on to some of her pictures instead of selling them.

In addition, an artists' rights law imposes transactions costs on both the buyer, who, when selling the painting at a capital gain has to contact, perhaps after many years, the artist or her heirs, as well as on the artist who wants to make sure that she is paid. And there may be costly litigation. In addition, for practical reasons, the law has to be written in a way that allows the artist to share in the appreciation of her painting only at the time when it is resold. And that gives the buyer an incentive to hold on to it. As a result, the painting may well be held by someone who values it at less than what someone else is willing to pay for it, and that represents an economic loss.

From an overall point of view, artist's rights laws, therefore, hurt artists. Can they, all the same, be justified as helping *poor* artists, for whose benefit they were presumably intended? No, they can't. Those artists who benefit most from the rise in the value of their previous work are the ones whose reputation has risen, and they are not likely to be poor. A study of the operation of the French artists' rights law found that three-quarters of the receipts from it accrued to six wealthy families. Can artists' rights laws then be justified, even if they do hurt artists by the argument that they take away some of the ill-gotten gains of speculative buyers? No, that won't work either. As discussed in the previous chapter, risk bearing, and that is what the speculative buyer does, is a useful activity that should not be discouraged. That some speculators make immense profits is no more an argument against speculation in the art market than the fact that some buyers of lottery tickets make an immense profit on their tickets is an argument against allowing lotteries.

Finally, to bring home how one's first reaction to an artists' rights law can be misleading: consider how it depends on the way the issue is framed. Suppose it had been framed as a law requiring artists to hand over to the government 20 percent of the price of their paintings, with the government subsequently distributing this money plus interest to those artists whose reputation has risen. Such a law would be widely (and rightly) denounced. But why is it worse than a law requiring buyers to do that?

8.3   Do We Want Fewer People Exploiting the Poor?

Off-the-Cuff Answer:	The fewer exploiters there are, the better off are the poor.
Problem:	We should reduce the amount of exploitation, not the number of exploiters.

Check-cashing facilities (businesses that for a substantial fee cash payroll and other checks for people without bank accounts) have often been accused of exploiting the poor and ignorant by charging excessive fees. To ameliorate this problem in 2004 the city of Oakland (California) passed an ordinance limiting the number of such businesses permitted in the city, and allowing no more than one in each shopping center.[2] The reasoning of the city council seems clear: check-cashing facilities exploit the poor, and the fewer exploitive businesses there are, the better. A commendable sentiment, but a questionable policy, even if for the sake of the argument one grants the assumption that exploitation is systemic in this industry.

Limiting the number of check-cashing facilities, and giving a local monopoly to those located in shopping centers, reduces competition among them. This enables them to raise their charges and thus facilitates exploitation.

My point here is not just that limiting the number of check-cashing facilities is a bad policy, but that it provides a good way of demonstrating the difference in the mindset of the city council, and presumably of the voters who elected it, and the mindset of economists – and demonstrating the mindset of economists is what this book tries to do. In evaluating a policy, economists focus on how it would change the opportunities and incentives that people face. From that, they predict what the proposed policy will do, and who the gainers and losers will be. By contrast, the city council presumably saw poor people being abused and wanted to lash out at the abusers.

Granted, the judgment of economists – or at least of this economist – that limiting the number of check-cashing facilities that hurt the poor might be wrong. The more check-cashing facilities there are, the more visible they are to passers-by, and thus the more likely it is that someone for whom it is not rational to use one will be tempted to do so. It is also *possible* that any new check-cashing facility that would be established if it were not for the ordinance would collude effectively with the established ones, so that keeping them out does not hurt customers of check-cashing facilities. Neither of these possibilities seems likely to be important, but these are issues that can, at least in principle, be resolved empirically, and have nothing to do with whether the owners of check-cashing facilities are nice or nasty people.[e] Such a need to do empirical work is typical in economics. Economic theory can usually provide only a general presumption, along with a list of factors to look for in the specific case to which it is being applied. Think of economics as analogous to physics plus engineering. The physicist provides the theory and the engineer applies it to the specific problem.

---

[e]   While the firms are likely to want to collude, their actually doing so is unlikely, since each firm would have an incentive to enlarge its market share by shaving its prices below the agreed-upon level. Since price fixing is illegal other firms can't bring suit against a price cutter.

However, even if, as seems likely, the judgment of this economist turns out to be correct, and the ordinance hurts the very people it is intended to help, the issue is still not *entirely* settled, because the economists' case against the ordinance requires several value judgments, and as we saw in chapter 3, value judgments require the skills of philosophers rather than of economists. The basic value judgment that the poor and ignorant should not be exploited, is nowadays (pace Nietzsche) hardly controversial. But other implicit value judgments are at least somewhat more controversial. One is that we want to reduce the total amount of exploitation rather than the number of people who are exploiters. Someone might conceivably argue that exploiting the poor and ignorant is a sin, and public policy should reduce the number of sinners, even if it means that each of them now commits more sins. Or she might argue that check-cashing facilities earn their profits from the misery and desperation of the poor, and nobody should earn profits from that, even if by doing so they reduce the misery and desperation of the poor. (More on that later.) I don't find either of these arguments at all appealing, and suspect that almost nobody else does either, but someone *might*. (Alright, I might as well admit it, in introducing these off-beat value judgments I am being pedantic, and in the future will not hunt so relentlessly for value judgments. I did it to sensitize you to the fact that value judgments lurk even in most unlikely places.)

8.4   Cut the Gas Tax to Slow the Rise of Soaring Gas Prices?

Off-the-Cuff Answer: Yes, because it would ameliorate hardships.
Problem: Inadequate analysis of economic effects of taxes.

When gas prices rose sharply in 2005–8, protests were widespread and vehement. In response in April 2008 the presumptive Republican presidential candidate, John McCain, proposed temporarily suspending the federal gas tax for the summer driving season, while some congressional Democrats proposed reducing the federal gas tax for an indefinite period. Some congressional Republicans proposed giving every family $200 to offset the higher cost of gas. Fortunately, at least so far (June 2008) cooler heads have prevailed. More recently, French President Nicolas Sarkozy urged the European Union to cut its tax on gasoline.

The effect of cutting the gas tax is complex, so let's take it in three steps. First, think of a cut in the gas tax as equivalent to a government subsidy for each gallon sold, since to the buyer at the pump it makes no difference whether the government cuts the gas tax by, say $0.10, or pays her a subsidy of $0.10 per gallon. As the second step, temporarily make the bizarre but useful assumption that American motorists are the only users of oil, even though much oil is used for heating and in industries, such as plastics and public utilities, and about three-quarters of the world's oil production is consumed in other countries.

Then, starting with a price of $3.00 per gallon, suppose that the government pays a subsidy of $0.10. With the government now paying $0.10 of the price, consumers demand as much gas at $3.10 a gallon as they did at $3.00. Assuming that the higher price does not generate a greater supply, which is a fairly good approximation for the short run, supply and demand for oil are now equal at $3.10 instead of at $3.00. All the government has done is to make a present of $0.10 per gallon, not to American motorists, but to oil producers.

The next step is to drop the assumption that American motorists are the only users of oil. To keep the example simple (it makes no difference to the conclusion) assume that the price of oil to other users is the same as it is for US motorists. At $3.10, these other users demand less oil than they did at $3.00 (remember they do not receive the $0.10 tax reduction), and with demand being less than supply, the price of oil falls below $3.10. But it cannot fall all the way back to $3.00, because with the government now paying $0.10 of the cost, American motorists would then demand more than they did before, and that would drive the price up again. Hence, the price after the subsidy has to settle somewhere between $3.00 and $3.10. The net result of cutting the gas tax would, therefore, be to: (1) lower the after-tax price, while raising the before-tax price of gas to American motorists; (2) raise prices and reduce output in oil using industries in the United States as they have to pay the higher price of oil; (3) raise the price of oil used for heating; (4) raise gas prices and prices in oil-using industries in foreign countries; and (5) benefit oil producers. All in all, that does not sound like such a good policy.

How about the alternative of paying every family $200? This, too, is not an appealing choice. It would raise the federal budget deficit (one effect of which is to put pressure on the dollar to decline, which would then make imported oil more costly), and would provide an unwarranted benefit to people like myself who drive very little, and still leave worse off than before those who drive a lot. Besides, it would tend to establish a new entitlement precedent: that when an important price rises, the government has to compensate consumers who lose from this. That is something one would hardly expect Republicans to advocate. Besides, how many people would accept the symmetrical principle that when an important price falls, they should be taxed more?

8.5 A Costless Way to Alleviate Destitution in Third World Countries?

Off-the-Cuff Answer: Give them gold the IMF holds but does not need.
Problem: Does not distinguish between a nominal and a real transfer.

This one needs some historical background. The International Monetary Fund (IMF) was established in 1945 to stabilize foreign exchange rates by letting a country that needs more foreign currency borrow it from the IMF instead of having to obtain it by devaluing its own currency, that is, by selling it at a lower price in terms of foreign currencies. To provide the IMF with the necessary resources to make such loans, countries contributed both their own currencies and also gold, since gold could always be exchanged for any currencies the IMF needed to make loans. In the early 1970s this system of maintaining stable exchange rates broke down, and the major countries allowed the values of their currencies to fluctuate. As a result, the IMF now holds more gold than it needs. In 2005, Britain, therefore, proposed that the IMF use the profit from the sale of about $12 billion of its approximately $43 billion gold reserve to provide the money needed to write off the debts of heavily indebted, desperately poor countries. The *New York Times* wrote a strongly supportive editorial[3]:

> If you could improve the lives of hundred of millions of the world's most destitute people with a program that might – just might – temporarily reduce the profits of the global gold industry, most people would probably think it worth doing. Even most members of Congress. That's why it has been so disturbing to see gold producers strong-arm Congress and the White House into blocking just such a desperately needed measure . . . A real solution [to the problem of destitute countries] has been postponed because the wealthy countries can't agree on how to finance it. But Britain offered a good answer: have the International Monetary Fund sell about $12 billion of its gold reserves . . . That would cover debt owed the fund, which accounts for 30 percent of the interest payments owed over the next 5 to 10 years by the affected countries. [As explained earlier in the editorial these countries could use the money thus saved] to train nurses, eliminate school fees and fight AIDS . . . This is the simplest and least painful solution. It would not require new contributions or hurt lending

to middle income countries, and it is the only one that has any hope of support from rich countries. But the United States has veto power over gold decisions in the monetary fund, so this idea needs approval from Congress – and the mining industry has blocked a vote [because it is afraid that a gold sale would lower the price of gold, even though the IMF has argued that this could be avoided]. Congress needs to debate the issue, and not allow a special interest to deny help to hundreds of millions of poor people.

Once again, a great newspaper is crusading against an appalling evil. This is compelling journalism. It is also rubbish.

I have no wish to defend the gold-mining industry. If the *Times* report is accurate – that is, if the industry did not present a better case than the one the *Times* reported – then it behaved abominably. But moral outrage is not an adequate substitute for serious analysis. Perhaps, there is a genuine problem with the proposal to sell the IMF's gold, quite apart from the position taken by the gold-mining industry. That would not be surprising since the proposed gold sale seems to offer a chance to do good at no cost to anyone – and free lunches are scarce.

What the *Times* ignored is that giving aid to poor countries requires transferring, directly or indirectly, goods and services to them. And that is not costless regardless of how it is financed. Some heavily indebted countries have de facto defaulted on some of their debts, and are not making interest payments on them. Wiping out these debts by using the IMF's gold to pay them off would do little to provide these countries with additional resources. Others are making interest payments, and relieving them of some of these payments by, in effect, giving them some of the IMF's idle gold, means that they can now import more goods and services. The cost of this to the rest of the world is that it has to forego its own use of these goods and services.[f]

In real terms, the cost of giving $12 billion of aid to poor countries is essentially the same, regardless of whether it is financed by selling the IMF's

---

[f]   But can't the additional goods and services be provided by using some of the excess capacity and unemployed workers in the developed world? With the unemployment rate at the time stuck near 8 percent in France and Germany and also high in some other countries, wouldn't an increase in foreign aid have helped the rich as well as poor countries? No, it wouldn't. There are two leading explanations for the high unemployment rates in much of continental Europe. One is that labor markets are so rigid and over-regulated that an increase in demand primarily raises the inflation rate rather than employment. The other is that the European Central Bank follows a too restrictive policy because of its excessive concern about inflation. In either case, an increase in exports as poor countries increase their imports would require a reduction in domestic demand.

idle gold or by legislative appropriations in the donor countries. Arguing that selling the idle gold is a costless way to reduce poverty is no different from arguing that we can reduce poverty at home costlessly by printing additional $20 bills and giving them to the poor.

This is not an argument against providing $12 billion of additional aid to poor countries. Whether we should do that is partly an ethical issue, and partly a question of how much good it would do.[4] There is also the question of whether, if we provide additional aid, it should be allocated to heavily indebted poor countries, or to countries selected on some basis other than their having run up excessive debts, such as their willingness to reduce corruption and dysfunctional policies.[5] Finally, there is the problem of whether the ends justify the means. Using the IMF's gold is a way of hiding from the public the cost of providing aid, and, therefore, making it politically feasible to increase foreign aid. But does fostering a good cause justify evading democratic decision-making?

8.6   Ban or Fine All Speculators?

Off-the-Cuff Answers: (1) Speculators produce nothing useful; (2) they raise and also destabilize prices.

Problems: This ignores the role of risk taking and that speculators sell as well as buy.

There are few topics on which the views of the general public and of economists diverge as much as they do on speculation. The public reputation of speculators is even lower than that of economists. They are said to reap high incomes without doing any genuine work: all they do is buy something when it is cheap, and then, without having added any value to it, resell it a higher price. Moreover, they cause prices to rise (or as some other critics have it, to fall, and thus hurt producers) and are also responsible for erratic price gyrations.

These are impressive charges; are they also right? The first one is easy to dismiss. Professional speculators do have to earn their money, because trying to predict how prices will change is hard work. Some amateur speculators try to avoid this effort by following simplistic rules, such as, that if the price of a stock has risen sharply last year, it will also rise this year, or by following the advice of newsletters. But such simplistic speculators are not likely to make money, as many real estate speculators have found out. (See appendix 2.2.) Besides, as the previous chapter discussed, economic activity requires risk bearing, and what ethical rule tells us that this contribution should not be rewarded?

In bearing risk, speculators contribute to society in three ways. One is to relieve many producers and sometimes also buyers from having to bear some risks. Being able to shed some risk that way allows them, and hence the whole economy, to undertake activities that carry great inherent risk. For example, when a farmer plants wheat that he will harvest next October, he does not know what its price will then be. But what he can do to avoid the risk that the price will fall is to sell his future crop today to a speculator for delivery in October at a price set today. Similarly, a miller, who wants to tie down the price of wheat that she will buy three months from now, can buy it from a speculator at a price set today. In the first case the speculator gains if the price of wheat rises and loses if it falls, in the second case the opposite occurs.

The second way speculation benefits the economy is by providing producers and consumers with more accurate knowledge of future prices, so that they can plan their activities better. For example, it lets a farmer know whether to use some of his stock of wheat as animal feed or to hold it until later when it may – or may not – turn out to have been too valuable for that. Providing such price signals is a by-product of speculators standing ready to buy or sell commodities at an announced price for future delivery. Third, by standing ready to buy and sell at these prices, speculators also provide markets with the liquidity, that is, the ability to buy or sell large quantities, and in so doing help markets to function smoothly.

Having seen that speculators do perform useful functions, let's see what they do to prices. A common answer is that they raise prices because they buy commodities, or stocks, etc., when they become scarce, thus raising their prices even further. A converse argument, once influential among farmers, is that speculators *lower* prices, since they sell commodities they do not own – this is called selling short – and thus they artificially add to the supply. Hence, people tend to blame speculators when prices rise or fall sharply. This complaint is myopic. A speculator does not just buy; but sooner or later has to sell what she has bought. Although her purchase raises the price when she buys, her subsequent sales reduce the price.

But granted that they do not raise prices overall, don't speculators cause prices to fluctuate wildly? This could happen, but it seems unlikely. They make their money by buying low and selling high. Their buying when prices are low raises prices at that time, and their selling when prices are high then reduces prices, thus evening out price fluctuations. Are those who denounce speculation confusing high with rising and low with falling?

But that does not mean that speculators always and everywhere stabilize prices; just think of the dot.com boom and bust and the behavior of house prices since the 1990s – speculators can destabilize as well as stabilize prices. To start with, there are amateur as well as professional speculators and the amateurs can destabilize prices by buying when prices are high and selling when they are low. To be sure, they will lose money that way and eventually decide that they can do better things with their time. But, since people tend to overestimate their own abilities, and since most amateurs commit only a small part of their capital, and can, therefore, continue to take losses for some time, they may be slow to wake up from their dreams of effortless fortunes. And when some do wake up, acknowledge their mistakes, and go home, there are others ready to take their place. Moreover, if many wake up at the same time their selling will drive prices below equilibrium.

More specifically, suppose the market contains many so-called "noise traders" – that is, amateurs who form their opinion about how prices will change not by studying the fundamentals that determine supply and demand, but projecting the current trend of prices, that is, they buy when prices are rising and sell when prices are falling. If so, well-informed professional speculators, too, may act in a way that destabilizes prices, and yet make money. For example, suppose that most noise traders believe that stock prices will go up because they have risen over the last year, or because of some silly notion, such as that you can predict stock prices by looking at the length of women's skirts. (At one time some people actually believed that nonsense.) You, a professional speculator, know better. What should you do? You know that noise traders will bid up stock prices. So, the sensible thing for you is also to buy stock, and then sell it to noise traders before the bubble bursts, and they find out how silly they were. In doing so you move stock prices away from their equilibrium values, and since what goes above equilibrium has to come down again, you, and not only noise traders, are destabilizing stock prices. But since you sell your stock before the day of reckoning, you are making money, and are, therefore, happy to carry out such destabilizing speculation.

It is, therefore, not true that the market *always* rewards those who stabilize prices, and punishes those who destabilize them and drives them out. But that something is not *always* true does not mean that it is not usually true. While I know of no data on this, I suspect that in the majority of cases speculation does stabilize prices. I was, therefore, not persuaded when a *New York Times* article offered the following explanation of then recent sharp fluctuations in oil prices:[6] "to speculators volatility means the potential for big profits, so hedge funds and investment banks pile in to make big bets, bidding [oil]

Box 8.1: Ticket Scalping

One type of speculation that creates much resentment is ticket scalping. The price on the ticket says $100, and yet you are asked to pay $250 for it. What right has this scalper who bought the ticket for $100 as a speculation to ask you for $250?

First, consider the case in which the organizer of the event had sold tickets to the scalper at what she thought was the equilibrium price. If so, the scalper has the same moral right as any other speculator who takes a risk. If the event had not been sold out he would have had to sell the ticket for less than the $100 he paid for it to match the price charged by other scalpers who are also stuck with unsold tickets.

But isn't it unfair that the scalper could buy many tickets at once, and do so at a time when you could not queue up at the box office or make repeated phone calls because you were working? No it isn't, because in that respect he was acting like other middlemen by taking advantage of economies of scale and the division of labor. And in the long run, unless there is collusion among middlemen, they earn only the normal rate of return on their efforts and risk taking.

Now take the case discussed in chapter 6 in which the event organizer sells the tickets to scalpers at a below-equilibrium price. In this case, scalpers, by being able to snap up these bargains when others can't, receive an undeserved gain, a gain grounded not in some alleged characteristic that makes speculation profitable, but in a market failure, the organizers' underpricing of her tickets.

Why do we (and, yes, I have done it too) get angry at scalpers? In the case of underpriced tickets it is easy to explain. We resent paying a price that embodies the undeserved gain that the scalper receives due to the organizer's underpricing. Although, like other voluntary trades, buying a ticket from a scalper leaves both parties better off, it is only natural to resent it when the other party walks away with most of the gain; remember the dictator game from chapter 3. Another likely reason, one that applies also in the case where the tickets are not underpriced, is that we see in our mind's eye a wildly enthusiastic fan, perhaps a poverty-stricken student, who would get immense enjoyment from attending the event, but loses out to the rich person who buys the ticket from the scalper, and will not enjoy the event nearly as much. Sometimes we resent the fact that the votes which count in the marketplace are dollars.

futures up to unnatural highs and making the market even more unstable."[7] Is this statement based on a theory that speculation is always or usually, destabilizing, or else on empirical research showing that in this particular case speculation was destabilizing? Or is it merely the *New York Times* manifesting the vulgar prejudice against speculation? Unlike the *Times* I am inclined to say: "two cheers and one boo for speculation." (But see box 8.1 for what at first glance seems to be a special case.)

8.7   Is Limiting Tobacco Advertising an Effective Policy?

Off-the-Cuff Answer: Reducing tobacco advertising will lower sales and death rates.

Problem: This leaves producers more to spend in other ways that could raise sales.

There is general agreement that smoking is a major health hazard. Add the assumption that the government should reduce health hazards and you have a persuasive case for government measures to reduce smoking. But how? Smokers will not stand for an outright ban on smoking, and even if one were legislated, it would bring back the evils of prohibition. Taxing cigarettes more heavily would reduce smoking alright, but it would be a regressive tax – that is, hit the poor harder, since poor and moderate-income people spend a larger proportion of their incomes on cigarettes than do the better-off. That is not a conclusive argument against it, since other taxes could be made more progressive to balance it, but, all the same, it makes higher cigarette taxes unacceptable to many people. A more persuasive argument is that if cigarettes cost more, people smoke them further down toward their fingers, and thus inhale more dangerous particles per puff. (How is that for the law of unintended consequences?) Therefore, instead of taxing the unfortunate people who are addicted to smoking, why not go after the tobacco companies by restricting their advertising.

Seems sensible, at first glance, but why not take a second glance? To do that don't stop with the tobacco companies eliminating some type of advertising, say, TV advertising, Go on to ask what they will do with the money they save by not advertising on TV. If they use it to increase other types of advertising, cigarette sales may very well – but need not necessarily – fall. It may seem that they would have to fall, because if that other type of advertising is more effective than TV advertising, then tobacco companies would not have used TV ads in the first place. But that argument is not watertight. Who knows, perhaps TV advertising is especially effective in persuading smokers to shift from other brands towards the advertised brand rather than in increasing total cigarette sales. And that *could* be the reason why those heartless tobacco companies, who do not care about each other, used it.

Another possibility is that tobacco companies will pay out what they save by eliminating TV ads as dividends to their stockholders. If so, the ban on TV advertising will decrease cigarette sales. But there is also a third possibility: they may use the money they save to increase sales either by lowering their prices, or by improving the quality of their cigarettes. If so, something untoward might happen; the prohibition of TV advertising could, at least in principle, *increase* smoking, because the inducement of lower prices could perhaps prove stronger than the previous inducement from TV advertising. In the language of appendix 6.1, the downward movement *along* the demand curve could outweigh the downward *shift* in the demand curve as TV advertising disappears. Whether it would actually do so is a question that can only be answered by detailed econometric analysis.

8.8   Would Importing Pharmaceuticals from Canada Substantially Lower Drug Prices?

Off-the-Cuff Answer:	Importing Canadian drugs would lower drug prices.
Problem:	This ignores that drug companies would raise their Canadian prices.

Many US pharmaceutical companies sell their patented prescription drugs for substantially less in Canada than in the United States. The main reason is that Canada, which has a national healthcare system that gives it market power, sets a ceiling on drug prices. This dual price system is feasible only because the US prohibits the commercial re-import of these drugs back into the United States. Not surprisingly, consumer advocates want this law abolished. Let's see what this would do.

Because they are concerned about the safety of imported drugs, some Americans will continue to buy their drugs domestically, even if cheaper Canadian drugs are readily available. But let's assume, as seems likely, that most will not. With the demand for their drugs being so much larger in the United States than in Canada, drug companies will know that when they ship drugs to Canada they are selling these drugs largely, though indirectly, in the United States. They will, therefore, try to raise their Canadian prices toward the US level. If Canada prevents this, then they are likely to limit re-exports to the United States by reducing the amount they sell in Canada. Canada will then probably see to it that it is Canadians who get these drugs. To be sure, that will not work perfectly and some drugs will still seep to US customers, but probably not in a volume large enough to substantially reduce drug prices in the United States.

Canada is not the only country in which American drugs are cheaper than they are in the United States. The reason is that firms have an incentive to split their market into several segments corresponding to the price sensitivity of demand. They can then set a low price in the segments in which demand is price sensitive and a higher price in the segments in which it is not. Usually that means trying to sell at a higher price to the rich than to the poor. (One example of such market splitting is supermarkets placing a higher mark-up on organic food, and coffee-bars on fair-traded coffee, because buyers of these items are likely to be richer and less price sensitive than those who buy more conventional products.) Is such market splitting for pharmaceuticals bad? Not necessarily. On the one hand, it is a way of exploiting market power, and, therefore, leads to some inequities and to some misallocation of resources: if a firm succeeds in selling the same product at different prices in two markets, one price must obviously differ from marginal cost, which, as discussed in chapter 6, is inefficient. On the other hand, it does help the poor. If you wax indignant about the exploitation of consumers through market segmentation, ask yourself whether you would really want a life-saving drug to cost as much in Africa as in the United States.

Moreover, for pharmaceuticals and some other high-tech products, price discrimination can be defended by arguing that much of their costs are the fixed costs of R&D, and that it is preferable that firms cover these costs by charging higher prices to those who will not respond by substantially cutting their purchases.

8.9   An Efficient and Humane Way to Reduce Cocaine Production?

Off-the-Cuff Answer:	Pay farmers to switch to other crops.
Problems:	(1) The price of coca would rise, thus essentially restoring supply; (2) serious administrative difficulties would arise.

While it may – or may not – be wrong to call the war on drugs an obvious failure (we don't really know what would happen if drugs were decriminalized), it is certainly costly: costly to the taxpayer who has to pay for its enforcement and for a greater prison population, and to users and dealers who are caught, or are killed in drug wars. In addition, US sponsored drug eradication programs in foreign countries create ill-will towards their governments as well as to the United States. It is, therefore, not surprising that people of goodwill have searched for more efficient and humane ways to control drug use. A popular proposal is to reduce the supply of drugs by paying farmers to grow other crops instead of coca. Since these farmers earn, by American standards, very little from growing coca, it would not cost much, the argument runs, to induce them to turn to other crops.

This proposal ignores two problems. First, and more fundamentally, people respond to incentives, and the market for drugs would respond in a way that largely negates the crop-diversion policy. The price of coca in the field is just a small proportion of the street price of drugs; for the sake of the argument let's say 5 percent. Suppose that their governments offer farmers a price for an alternative crop that gives them twice the income they receive from growing coca. As farmers take advantage of this program and the supply of coca shrinks, drug lords respond by raising the price they pay for coca, so that now coca again becomes more profitable for farmers, and both the supply and use of drugs are largely back at their previous level. I say "largely" because, with coca accounting for an assumed 5 percent of the cost of street drugs a, say, doubling, of its price would raise the street price of drugs by 5 percent, and this would reduce the demand for drugs – but not by much.

It is possible to imagine a world in which this problem would not arise, and a crop-diversion policy would be not only a humane, but also a workable and efficient, way to fight the drug war. Suppose that farmers are reluctant to grow coca, and do so solely because it is the only way they can obtain the minimum income they need. Then, if offered the same income from growing another crop, they would cease to produce coca, even if they could earn a substantially higher income by continuing to produce it. But how likely is it that we do live in a world in which poor farmers would be willing to settle for a minimum income? Even if a few would, there are others who would be willing to supply the coca that these farmers no longer provide.

The second problem is how to implement a policy of inducing farmers to shift to legitimate crops. Suppose Bolivian and Colombian farmers are told that the government is willing to buy all the alternative crops they produce on the land they currently devote to growing coca, at a price that makes these alternative crops more profitable than coca. Farmers would then claim that they are growing coca on all, or nearly all, their land, and the government would have to buy up a lot of crops. If the government tries to avoid this problem by using satellite maps to show on which plots farmers had grown coca, and then buying only crops grown on those plots, farmers would switch their coca production to the plots from which the government refuses to buy their alternative crops. Moreover, suppose that this problem could somehow be solved, and we could succeed in cutting coca production. The price of coca would rise, and that would give farmers in other countries an incentive to produce more.

None of this means that offering coca farmers inducements to shift to other crops is a *total* waste of effort. It could have some small effect by ensuring that farmers do not face the choice of either risking punishment by growing coca, or extreme poverty by not doing so. But don't expect it to do *much* good.

8.10   Protecting Lives by Requiring Use of Seatbelts?

Off-the-Cuff Answer: Obviously, seatbelts save lives.
Problem: Perhaps, but it is not obvious because it ignores the response of drivers.

Do seatbelts really save lives? Maybe, but one can't be certain, because they make accidents more likely. They don't do this because of some arcane engineering principle, but by their effect on incentives. Let's look at two hypothetical extreme cases. In one, cars are built so sturdily that the probability of being killed in an accident is zero. In the other case, cars are built so flimsily that the driver will be killed even in a 10 mph collision. Even in the first case drivers have strong incentives to be careful, but they would surely drive less carefully than in the second case. Seatbelts, therefore, have two effects; they make it less likely that you will be killed if you get into an accident, but they make it more likely that you will get into one.

Can one say anything about the net effect? Having a seatbelt available gives you an additional way to reduce the probability of dying in an accident, a way some drivers find less onerous than driving slowly and more carefully, so that it reduces the cost of being safe. Drivers, therefore, "buy" more safety for themselves, and that reduces fatalities. But knowing that their seatbelts make it less likely that they will die in an accident makes them drive faster and less carefully. (This does not require a conscious decision to take more risk, but could result just from feeling less worried about having an accident.)

That makes it more likely that pedestrians and other drivers will be killed.[g] Therefore, economic theory by itself cannot tell us whether seatbelts save lives, it can only lay out the possibilities. To go from possibilities to probabilities we have to turn to the data. Unfortunately, these do not speak in unison, though, of course, nobody is arguing that the wearing of seatbelts is the dominant cause of accidents. The question is what happens on the margin.

All the same, the problem of whether seatbelts save lives, does bring out clearly the difference between the approach of engineers, who try to answer this question by using dummies in crash tests, and economists who assume that people are not dummies, and, therefore, look at incentives. Both are needed.

8.11   Do You Really Want Your Bid to Win?

Off-the-Cuff Answer: Winning bidders are better off than losing bidders.
Problem: The winner's curse.

Suppose the Interior Department opens a tract to petroleum drilling, and twenty companies enter sealed bids for the right to drill. Suppose, further, that you have a friend in the Interior Department who lets you know ahead of the official announcement that Lucky Inc. has won the bidding. Since you are unscrupulous and willing to trade on insider information, you plan to buy stock in that company and tell this to another friend, who has taken an economics course. Much to your surprise she advises you not to buy it. Her argument runs as follows: there were twenty firms which bid, and each one bid as much as it thought the drilling rights were worth. Since Lucky Inc. submitted the highest bid, this means that the other nineteen firms thought it was worth less than that. Unless you have reason to think that Lucky Inc. has smarter executives or geologists than any of these other companies you should assume that it has overpaid, and that its profits and stock price will, therefore, fall. This is called the "winner's curse."

This sounds reasonable, So you don't buy the stock – which promptly shoots up when it is announced that Lucky Inc. has won the bidding. Stupid market, or is there something wrong with your friend's argument? Well, all the firms knew about the winner's curse, and so they bid a bit less for the drilling rights than their best guess of what it is worth. Thus, even if Lucky Inc. paid more than other firms bid, it could still have paid less than the drilling rights

---

[g]   Someone has, therefore, suggested that a better way to reduce fatalities than requiring seat-belts is to require that steering wheels have a sharp six-inch spike aimed at the driver's chest.

are worth. This suggests that perhaps there is no winner's curse after all. But that's only so if all the firms behave rationally, and take the danger of a winner's curse into account. Hence, a behavioral economist – but not an economist who adheres firmly to the assumption of rational behavior – can still argue that winners are cursed after all, and that the stock market made a mistake.

The auction, to which a winner's curse could apply, need not be just a formal auction, but can be a setting where multiple businesses are "bidding" for talent or resources or another company.

8.12 Is Fast Chinese Economic Growth Bad for the United States?

Off-the-Cuff Answer: China is a US competitor, so its gain must subtract from the US total.
Problem: Economics is not a competitive sport.

Suppose the Boston Red Sox improve their pitching. That's bad news for the NY Yankees. Suppose China's GDP rises rapidly. Bad news for the United States? Many people seem to think so, perhaps because they see trade between countries through the metaphor of sports. But economics is not a sport. More importantly economics is not a zero-sum game, in which the fact that one party wins implies that the other party must lose. Those who consider it obvious that a high Chinese per capita income is bad news for the United States should ask themselves whether they also think that our high per capita income has made India worse off, and if so, how?

To see what happens to the United States when Chinese producers become more efficient, so that Chinese income rises, let's initially simplify by looking only at bilateral trade between the United States and China, and ignore for the moment that trade is conducted not by bartering goods, but by using money. Next, we have to specify just what type of goods it is that the Chinese now produce more efficiently, and, therefore, sell cheaper. Are they goods which the United States imports from China or goods which it exports to China – or at least did export before the Chinese became more efficient at producing them? Let's start with the case where they are ones the US imports.

With Chinese firms competing to sell in the United States, that these goods are now cheaper to produce means that we now get more Chinese goods for the goods that we sell to China. That does not sound like something to complain about – particularly when you consider that we are also complaining that oil exporters are making us pay too much for their oil. And while China sends us more of the goods in which we now have a comparative *dis*advantage, it also takes more of our goods in which we have a comparative advantage (such as airplanes, computer chips, and places in the classroom at elite universities). There can be no comparative disadvantage without a comparative advantage somewhere else; as increased imports destroy the jobs of some Americans, they create jobs for others. And, as chapter 3 explained, the resulting increase in trade is beneficial for the United States as a whole, in the sense that the gainers could compensate the losers and still be better off.

There are, however, two important qualifications. First, the United States and China compete not only in each others' markets, but also in third markets. And here increased Chinese productivity, by driving out US goods, can make the United States worse off. Second, in practice, compensation is unlikely to be paid to all Americans who lose their jobs, or have to settle for lower wages because of Chinese imports, and these are likely to be relatively low skilled workers.[h] Or looked at another way, if we increase our textile imports from China, consumers of textiles gain while producers of textiles lose. And even if the dollar value of the gain exceeds the dollar value of the loss, is the social value of the gain (measured in some way) greater than the social cost? Textile workers are not likely to see it as a gain. In fact, they may even come to hate all foreigners.

Now take the opposite case: China's income grows because the Chinese have become more efficient at producing those goods in which we previously had a comparative advantage, and, therefore, China no longer buys them from us. That is bad news for us because it means that to obtain Chinese goods we now have to offer China goods in which we are not as efficient as we are in the goods that we previously sold to China, so we gain less from the trade. Moreover, once we look beyond our bilateral trade with China we see that increased Chinese efficiency makes it a more effective competitor in other countries, which also reduces our gains from international trade.

Now drop the assumption that trade takes the form of barter. To retell the story just told in a much more realistic setting, we have to ask what the Chinese do with the additional dollars they receive when they export more to the United States. One possibility is that they allow the market mechanism

---

[h]   There is also the question of whether compensation should be paid. If shipyard workers in Groton lose jobs because the federal government reduces its procurement of submarines and procures more aircraft in Seattle, should workers in Seattle – or anyone else – be required to compensate the unemployed workers in Groton? If not, why should a different rule apply when the government reduces a tariff?

to work; that is, they let their exporters sell these dollars on the foreign exchange market, instead of the government intervening by buying up some of these dollars. As a result, American goods (which are priced in dollars) are now cheaper for Chinese consumers, so American exports to China increase. At the same time, the higher price of the Chinese currency, the yuan, makes Chinese goods more expensive in the United States, so that Americans import less from China. Both of these effects create jobs in the United States that offset the job losses from the increase in Chinese exports to the United States with which this story started.

But the Chinese government need not, and currently does not, allow the exchange rate to fluctuate in this way. It is highly probable that to prevent the yuan from falling to its equilibrium level, China buys up some of the dollars that exporters earn, mainly, or in large part, because it wants to keep its exports growing rapidly to help absorb the vast number of workers who are leaving the countryside and pouring into the cities. It then uses these dollars to purchase US securities. This increases liquidity, the funds available for loans to homeowners and firms, lowers interest rates in the United States, and thus stimulates US demand and thus employment, though not necessarily by enough to offset the initial effect of greater Chinese exports to the United States.

However, this policy of holding the yuan down is costly for China and it is not likely to maintain it for very long.[i] In 2007, China allowed the yuan to fall by 7 percent against the dollar, and it continued to fall in 2008. Moreover, currently, prices are rising substantially faster in China than in the United States, which also limits Chinese exports. In any case the Federal Reserve can adopt an expansionary monetary policy that offsets the reduced demand for American goods due to increased imports from China.[j]

---

[i]   One reason is that by making its goods cheaper abroad it is getting fewer foreign goods in exchange for its exports, and thus making itself poorer. Another is that by buying up dollars and other foreign currencies, which it then invests largely in American securities, China is sending abroad capital that it could probably use more profitably at home. Third, as it builds up its holdings of US securities, it increases the loss it would suffer if the dollar were to fall on the foreign exchange market – a not unlikely event. Even with its current holdings of American securities, such losses could be substantial. Fourth, when China buys dollars and other foreign currencies it pays the seller in yuan. This makes it more difficult for China to control its money supply and hence to hold its inflation in check. Finally, by holding down the value of the yuan China furnishes ammunition to those in other countries who want to raise restrictions on imports from China.

[j]   The primary target of Fed policy is the inflation rate. Hence, as Chinese goods become cheaper in the United States and as this reduces the inflation rate, the Fed almost automatically adopts a more expansionary policy by lowering interest rates, It also pays attention to unemployment, and if increased imports from China raise unemployment, that is an additional reason for it to become more expansionary.

But what about Chinese imports of oil? Won't a richer China demand an immense amount of oil and thus drive up oil prices sharply to the detriment of all other oil importers? Yes, it will, and in that way faster Chinese economic growth is bad for the United States. On the other hand, a characteristic of the Chinese economy that may prove helpful to the United States and other developed countries is that, partly as a result of its high growth rate, the Chinese are saving an extraordinarily large proportion of their incomes. The United States and other Western countries have ageing populations that have been promised substantial social security and healthcare benefits. When their governments borrow, as they are likely to, to meet these commitments, domestic savings available to finance business investment will shrink. This capital shortage will tend to reduce real wages below what they otherwise would be, because the typical employee will have less capital to work with. But it is likely that an inflow of Chinese savings will ameliorate this problem, and the faster China grows, the more savings it will have available for that.

These economic effects are not the only ways in which rapid Chinese growth can affect American well-being. To some Americans, there may be satisfaction in our per capita income being much higher than China's. Despite the teaching of moralists, many people feel better off if their neighbors are much worse off than they are. However, while I know of no data on this, I have the impression that Americans have been undisturbed by Japan and Europe closing much of the income gap that existed in, say 1960. And the same could prove to be true with respect to China.

The claim that if Chinese incomes rise then that is bad for the United States, is just one example of a common attitude that one person's gain is another person's loss, that we live in a world of so-called zero-sum games. While not denying that there are some zero-sum games and negative-sum gains, since at least 1776 economists have been busy combating the notion that they predominate. Economics – the so-called dismal science – sees both sides to a transaction as gaining, except in some unusual circumstances. The reason for this is simple: you wouldn't trade unless you saw a gain to yourself, and usually you know what you are doing. And trade here means not only the purchase of goods and services, but also financial transactions and the exchange of labor for money.

There is little doubt about how zero-sum game thinking flourishes. It is in our thinking or envy about "the other," perhaps another socio-economic class, another ethnic group, and most prominently other nations. Everyday experience tells us that shopping at the supermarket leaves us better off than not shopping, holding on to our money, and going hungry. But when thinking about foreign trade, we lack such experience; in our fears and thoughts we are in a dark jungle where the wicked "other" is all set to make us worse off. We know that if another country offers to cut its tariff if we cut ours, it does so because it stands to gain from this, and conclude that this implies that we must lose. Most people would be surprised to learn that most economists believe that if we cut our tariffs unilaterally and thus bestow a present on other countries, we would be better off too, since both sides gain from trade.

Moreover, zero-sum thinking, and the closely related attitude of seeing exploitation whenever one person or group is richer than another, flourishes among left-wingers as well as super-patriotic right-wingers. If a law is good for business, it must be bad for the average man; if some countries are rich and others poor, it must be due to the rich colonial countries having exploited their poor former colonies, and never mind that this requires some mental acrobatics to explain why Switzerland and Sweden who never had colonies are rich, while Thailand which, though forced to sign unequal treaties, was never colonized by the West, and Ethiopia, which was colonized only from 1935 to 1941, are poor.

8.13   In Emergencies Should Prices Ration Supply, Thus Letting the Rich Outbid the Poor?

Off-the-Cuff Answer: In an emergency we should not ration by price.
Problem: Perhaps, but do not ignore the costs of not rationing by price.

Suppose a snowstorm isolates a town for several days. Many people need snow shovels, but the sole hardware store has only ten in stock. Should it raise the price high enough for the market to clear, or should it sell them to the first ten customers at the old price? Most people would say the latter. Are they right?

There are three disadvantages to selling the shovels to the first ten customers. One is that over the long run it reduces the supply of snow shovels available in an emergency. If the store expects to make an unusually large profit on each shovel it sells after a bad snowstorm, it has an incentive to carry a larger inventory than it otherwise would, with the occasional large profit offsetting the costs of carrying that larger inventory. The second disadvantage is that some of the shovels go to people who have *relatively* little use for them. Suppose the price is $20. Then one of the first ten people to show up might value it at only $21, while the eleventh would-be customer values it at $40 and yet has to do without. The third disadvantage is that rationing on the first-come-first-served principle gives each would-be buyer an incentive to get to the store ahead of others, or if others are ahead of her, to wait in line. In both cases there is a nonmonetary cost without a corresponding gain to anyone.

Why then do so many people believe that the store should not raise the price? One possibility is that they are uneasy about the burden it imposes on the poor. Rationing by price, allocated the shovels in a way that gives the utility a rich person derives from having a shovel more weight than the utility that a poor person derives from it, while rationing by queue does not. Perhaps people think that to affirm our sense of community during an emergency we should treat rich and poor alike. Some people would probably object strongly if, during a flood, a privately owned helicopter were to sell the one seat it has available to the highest bidder. But, there is also another likely reason. Rightly or wrongly, it seems to offend some people's intuitive sense of how things should be if the owner of the store benefits from the plight of others. So let's turn to that question.

8.14   Is Gaining from Someone's Misfortune a Moral Wrong?

Off-the-Cuff Answer: We should not profit from other people's misery.
Problem: Profiting from misery is not the same as causing it.

Let's start by looking at several common cases and do so initially from a firm consequentialist standpoint. First, suppose you buy shoes made by workers paid less than $5 per day. Should you feel guilty? No. Your purchase increases the demand for their labor and thus raises their wages. So why guilt? Sweatshops do not cause low wages; they are the result of their workers not being able to find better jobs. But suppose there is an ample supply of labor, so that the sweatshop can increase employment without having to raise wages. In that case, too, your purchase makes poor people better off, because the newly employed workers are better off than they were before; otherwise they would not have taken the jobs. Being paid only $5.00 a day is bad, but it is better than being paid $4.00 elsewhere or being unemployed. Buying the products of sweated labor makes sweated labor *better* off.

Second, should you invest in so called real estate "vulture funds"? These are funds that buy up mortgages that are in foreclosure in the hope of selling them at a profit, so that they benefit from some people having lost their homes.

Whether you should invest in such a fund is a somewhat more difficult question, because it is not obvious whether this helps or hurts unfortunate people. On the one hand, you increase the demand for and thus the price of foreclosed houses, so that homeowners, whose mortgages amount to less than the house was sold for, are better off. On the other hand, by raising the price of foreclosed houses you encourage lenders to foreclose rather than to exercise forbearance. I suspect that the former effect is more important than the latter, but that is only a conjecture.

Third, should you let your conscience prevent you from becoming a slumlord? No, you should not, because the more people are willing to invest in slum property, the easier is it for poor people to find housing, and the lower are their rents. If a real-estate investor should feel guilty at all, it is for investing in luxury housing instead of in slums.

Fourth, consider investing in a company that behaves unethically. If you do refrain from doing so – and if just about all other investors also refrain – you would increase its cost of capital, and by that reduce its scale of operation, so that there would be less unethical behavior. But the condition that nearly all other investors act as you do is critical. Suppose that 98 percent do. Then, the company could raise its capita from the other 2 percent. It would have to offer only a slightly larger return to induce them to buy its stocks and bonds. Your good intentions would be largely – though not entirely – wasted.

Finally, suppose I have a life insurance policy on which I do not want to keep up the premiums. The "surrender value" that insurance companies offer in exchange for someone giving up a policy is usually not a good deal. Hence, there are companies that buy up life insurance policies, pay the future premiums on them, and collect when the insured person dies. Should you invest in such a company whose profits increase if people die early? Why not? Are you causing anyone to die sooner by investing that way?

Now let's vary the question somewhat. In the eighteenth century it was not uncommon, and it is still possible now, for a merchant who wanted to retire to hand over his business to someone, perhaps a relative, in exchange for an annuity. That relative now had an interest in the early death of a specific person he knew. Should the relative have been uneasy about such a deal? Perhaps he should have, because there is a possibility that this might have made him wish for the annuitant's death. That would have coarsened his mind which, in turn, might have caused him to act in a harmful way at some other occasion. Hence, even a firm consequentialist might have qualms.

Thus, with two qualifications I'll come to later, in all these above cases, except the annuity case in which you know the annuitant, you can in good conscience do what your economic interests tell you to. If, despite your consequentialist reasoning, your feelings give you any trouble when you buy shoes made in a sweatshop, you can take the money you thereby save and give it to a charity.

The first of the qualifications is that if every time you see the sweatshop shoes you feel depressed by thinking about the poor people who made them, then you should not buy them. And similarly, if getting a dividend check from a vulture fund will depress you, then you should probably invest elsewhere. The second qualification is that you may reject the underlying consequentialism, and may, for example, not invest in a tobacco company because that would make you feel complicit in what it does. All the same, I suspect that most of the objection to buying the products of sweatshops and to investing in vulture funds and similar funds – though probably not in tobacco companies – is due to a confusion of "a result of" with "results in." Buying the shoes cheaply is a result *of* low wages, but does not result *in* low wages.

8.15   Should Those Close at Hand Have a Special Responsibility to Alleviate Misery?

Off-the-Cuff Answer: Yes, as they are in a position to help.
Problem: So are others.

Suppose that while hiking on an isolated trail you come across another hiker lying near the trail with a broken leg. Should you feel responsible for helping her, or should you say that since you are no more responsible for her accident than is anyone else, you will just walk on? Of course, you should help her since you are the only one who is in a position to do so.

Now suppose you are the CEO of a pharmaceutical company that has developed a new drug against a disease that is killing many people in poor countries. Should you feel morally obligated to provide it at a low price that most of the sick people can afford, or at most at its marginal cost? It seems that many people would answer yes. But why? Others are able to see to it that sick people get this drug just as well as you can, by contributing to charities that will buy the drug from you. You are not in the situation of the hiker who knows that, if she does not help, then nobody else can. *Perhaps* one can make an argument that you should not rake off a profit from the money that others have contributed to charity, but it is not clear why not. Yes, you have a moral obligation to be charitable but why should this obligation apply with special force to you, just because you are in the business of making the needed item?

Some readers might find this argument hard to accept since they hate big pharmaceutical companies, so let me restate it in a different context: granted that the Brazilian rain forest should be preserved, should Brazil be required to bear the cost, or should the rest of the world also be required to pay for this? A more ambiguous case is that of a physician who refuses to accept patients in the Medicaid program (the government healthcare program for the poor) because it caps fees below the market level. She can argue that if many poor people are denied medical treatment it is not her but Congress and the administration that should be blamed because they have denied adequate funding for Medicaid. But, in the here and now, she knows that if she refuses to treat a particular Medicaid patient who called her for an appointment he might go untreated, and she is, therefore, to some extent in the position of the hiker who should help. If she does provide treatment she deserves praise, but, if not, does she deserve any more blame than do the rest of us who do not make equally valuable charitable contributions?

The notion that those who are closest to a misfortune are the ones who are morally obligated to help has an unfortunate practical implication: it gives businesses and professionals an incentive to provide the goods and services bought by the-well-to-do and to stay away from those bought by the poor. In particular, why invest heavily in R&D for products, such as drugs for tropical diseases, that people feel you are obligated sell at a low profit margin? Arthur Caplan, a bioethicist, has argued that: "you aren't manufacturing pantyhose when you're in healthcare. There are special moral duties attached."[7] But since these moral duties come with no rewards, the more compelling and costly they are, the fewer resources will be devoted to healthcare.

8.16   Seven Short Ones

Recently, I saw a bumper sticker informing the world that medieval peasants worked less than modern workers do. I was not outraged. Should I have been? Productivity has increased vastly since then, shouldn't workers have shared in that prosperity by enjoying more leisure time? Not necessarily. They should have shared in the great increase in productivity in one way or another. And they did. But with their increased productivity having raised their real wages so much, they may well prefer to work more hours than medieval peasants did. And, besides, did medieval peasants really work less, and if so was that a matter of free choice, or was it compelled by the seasons? Besides, your poor medieval predecessors lived, on average, a lifespan not much past thirty-five years. The fruit of increased labor is increased scientific knowledge.

Do middlemen raise prices? Generally not, because the market has already gotten rid of middlemen whose contribution does not justify the cut they take. Suppose that in an industry in which manufacturers sell directly to retailers some middlemen try to insert themselves. Unless they save either the manufacturers or the retailers more than they charge for the services they provide, such as maintaining local warehouses that permit retailers to get by with leaner inventories, they will be sent packing. Or suppose that, in an industry in which wholesalers are already well entrenched, some innovation, such as cheap airfreight, makes their services redundant. Manufacturers and retailers can now increase their profits by cutting out the middleman, and will do so. This does not mean that there is never a situation in which eliminating middlemen would not reduce prices. In the example just discussed, there is a transition period in which middlemen are no longer needed, but have not yet been sent packing. It is also possible that government regulations, perhaps instigated by the middlemen themselves, keep them in business.

To reduce crimes involving guns, some cities have instituted programs of buying up at a fixed price any handguns offered to them. Can this work? A first glance suggests that it cannot, because if the city offers less than the street price of a gun nobody will accept its offer, and, if it offers more, it will be flooded with guns by people who will buy them in other localities and turn a quick profit. But hold on, it's not *quite* that bad. Selling your gun on the street is illegal and time consuming, so that there are some people who are willing to sell their guns to the city at less than the street price. However, these are more likely to be law-abiding people who have less use for their guns than do criminals. To be sure, law-abiding people sometimes commit murder, so the program should do *some* good, but how much? New York City lowered its annual murder rate from near 2,000 around 1990 to near 500 in 2007. The police then claimed that that was as low as the rate would go, given gun availability and socio-economic conditions, because at that level, most murders are those of relatives or neighbors, usually in some great passion or emotion.

In 2006, gas prices rose sharply, and so did the profits of oil companies. Many people connected the dots and claimed that the oil companies were gouging the public. But there is another way of connecting the dots: a sharply rising demand for oil, particularly from China, raised oil prices, and that, in turn, increased the profits of oil companies. Also, the declining value of the dollar led all imports such as oil to be more expensive. Which explanation is right? The theory that the increase in profits is due to gouging has to answer a question: why did the companies *raise* prices in 2006? The answer cannot be that they have some monopoly power, because that would have resulted in prices already being high in 2006, not in prices rising that year. Thus price gouging would require an increase in monopoly power, and there is no evidence for that. But there is evidence that demand for oil rose and the dollar declined, so the price–profits connection seems more plausible than the profits–price connection.

The United Nations' *1993 Human Development Report* was concerned that in developing countries between 1960 and 1973: "GDP growth rates were fairly high, but employment growth rates were less than half this."[8] Would it have been better if employment had grown at the same rate as GDP, thus implying no increase in labor productivity?

A *New York Times* editorial complained about the difficulty that customers experience in finding clothes in sizes "outside the cookie-cutter norm," and blamed this on the stores' pursuit of "the old profit motive."[9] It did not go on to explain whether it believes that the profit motive generally results in the wrong goods being produced, or whether retail clothing is a special case in which the market mechanism malfunctions, and if so why? Since carrying odd sizes reduces inventory turnover, and since carrying inventory generates genuine costs both for the store and for the economy, it is not necessarily wrong for stores to limit their inventory of odd sizes, and make those who need such clothes bear some of the burden by having to spend more time shopping. But perhaps the *Times* is right, and the required shopping time is excessive. If so, stores should carry a wider range of sizes, and make up for the increased cost by charging higher prices for uncommon sizes. That they don't do so, suggests a *possible* market failure, a failure that could be due to customers somehow considering it unfair that they should have to pay more merely because it is more expensive to cater to them. Perhaps we are witnessing the birth of a new right, the right to obtain odd-sized clothing for the same price and with no more wasted shopping time than for regular sizes.

Here is an example that may come as something of a shocker. It is not at all obvious that we should discourage child labor in poor countries. The reason many children in these countries work is not that evil multinationals are forcing them to do so; they may want to, but how would they do it? Nor is it likely that the parents of these children don't care about the welfare of their children. It is simply that they are dreadfully poor, and, if keeping your children from working means that your family does not have enough to eat, then it may well be in the best interest of the children to have them work. When it was poor, the West, too, knew child labor. In 1860 in England, about 37 percent of 10- to 14-year-old boys were gainfully employed, in present-day Africa it is less than 30 percent.[10]

But let's look behind one more corner. If fewer children worked, then the labor supply would be smaller and wages, therefore, higher. In principle, it is possible that eliminating child labor would raise real wages so much that families whose children now no longer work would experience little decline in real income, and might even see it rise. Whether that would actually happen is an empirical question to which I do not know the answer. But, until I do have a positive answer, I am not inclined to circulate a petition to ban imports made by child labor.

8.17   On the Other Hand

This chapter has questioned many well-intentioned proposals for improving the outcomes of unregulated markets. That does *not* mean that all such proposals are wrong-headed or even that they are on average more likely to be wrong-headed than are proposals to reduce the scope of government interventions. In either case, blanket acceptance or rejection is no substitute for carefully taking into account the specifics of each case.

Chapter 6 discussed externalities and how, in their presence, individual choice in the marketplace leads to inefficiencies. Let's look at a few examples to balance the many examples of wrong-headed interventions I have given so far. An obvious one is driving. If I drive, not only do I pollute, but I also create congestion. A tax equal to the damage I thus cause will force me to internalize this cost, and thus improve matters. Many people deplore urban sprawl, but each year suburbs sprawl more and more. Why? Because potential spawlers count only the benefits of moving a bit further out, knowing that their own decision to do so will have practically no effect on the sprawl that surrounds their city, and besides it is other people who suffer from the sprawl. If I install a burglar alarm, I deflect the attention of burglars to other houses that do not have one. And if all homeowners install burglar alarms, then burglars just turn to other forms of crime while we homeowners are stuck with the fees that the alarm companies charge.

There are many such cases in which, when each individual maximizes her own welfare, the welfare of many of the others takes a hit. Yet, one should not go overboard on this. Virtually all actions have some effect on others,but if that effect is minor and the major effect is felt by the person taking the action, then there is not much of a case for regulation. Also, one might want to step back and ask whether regulating (or not regulating) in this particular instance sets a precedent that is likely to be misused in the future. Taking the potential for future misuse into account can easily degenerate into ideological dogmatism, but it can also represent principled farsightedness.

NOTES

1 Thomas Sowell, *The Vision of the Anointed*, New York, Basic Books, 2004, pp. 4–5.
2 Heather McDonald, "Oakland Curbing Check Cashers," *Oakland Tribune*, October 6, 2004, p. A 1.
3 Anonymous, "The Price of Gold," *New York Times*, June 3, 2005, p. A 26.
4 See Paul Collier, *The Bottom Billion*, Oxford, Oxford University Press, 2007; and William Easterly, *The Elusive Quest for Growth*, Cambridge, MA, MIT Press, 2002.
5 Collier *The Bottom Billion*, passim.
6 Anonymous, "Roller Coaster at the Pump," *New York Times*, October 8, 2006, p. WK 11.
7 Atul Gawande, "Doctors, Drugs and the Poor," *New York Times*, November 26, 2007, p. A 27.
8 Cited in Easterly, *The Elusive Quest*, p. 54.
9 Anonymous, "The Ends Justify the Means," *New York Times*, June 4, 2006.
10 Landsburg, Steven, *The Armchair Economist*, New York, Free Press, 1993, p. 66.

9

Natural Resources and Environmental Economics

This chapter is in some sense a continuation of the style and approach of the last chapter. That is, it uses some basic microeconomics ideas to study five additional examples of how to improve – or mess up – government policy. In particular we will be paying attention to the issues of externalities, which was introduced in chapter 6.

9.1 Running Out of Privately Owned Natural Resources

> Old Mother Hubbard
> Went to her cupboard
> To fetch her poor dog a bone
> But when she got there
> The cupboard was bare.

Older readers may remember a billboard from the 1970s. It showed a gas gauge with the needle sitting on empty, and asked what will happen when we get there? Since then, various viewers-with-alarm have tried, without much success, to pound the same message into our thick heads. Are we obtuse and short sighted, or are we showing good sense in ignoring these warnings?

At first glance it does seem obvious that the world is running out of oil and other nonrenewable resources. The earth contains only a finite amount of them, which means that at any rate of use greater than zero we will eventually run out, SUVs or no SUVs. And while, in principle, it might be possible to find additional supplies on other planets, these supplies, too, are finite, and in any case, the cost of space transport makes this science fiction story more fiction than science.

But it does not follow that we will be running out of oil in the foreseeable future. The whole notion of "running out" does not make sense because oil reserves are not a common property, but have owners. And, fortunately, these owners are greedy, and want to make as much money as possible. They will, therefore, not just sit there and hold the price of oil constant as reserves dwindle, but will keep on raising it. You may not like or approve of oil prices rising, but economists view this event differently. It creates incentives for conservation and for the discovery of new reserves, as well as for the development of substitutes. We may soon run out of relatively cheap oil, but not out of oil altogether. Expensive oil will be with us for a long time.

Let's see how the owners of oil and other nonrenewable resources determine how much they should produce each year, starting with a simplified theory which assumes that it costs nothing to extract the oil and get it to the market, and also that the owners are unconcerned about risk. We also need to make some assumption about how they expect the price of oil to change. First, suppose they expect the price to be lower in the future than it is now. If so, they will maximize their expected profits by selling right now as much oil as they can extract, and leave as little as possible for the future. Alternatively, suppose that they expect the future price of oil to be the same as it is now. In this case, too, they will produce as much as they can, because they prefer to receive a dollar this year on which they can earn interest to receiving a dollar only in the future. Finally, suppose that they expect the price of oil to rise each year at a rate that exceeds the rate of interest. If so, they will produce no oil at all this year, since oil in the ground will rise in value faster than does the money they could get by selling it and investing the proceeds in securities. Only if they expect the future price to rise at an annual rate that is just equal to the rate of interest, do they produce the same amount in future years as in the current year. In a sense, they treat oil in the ground like a saving account at a bank.

The essential point is that the current price and the future price of a storable good are linked, because its owners allocate the good between current sales and future sales in a way that maximizes their profits. Hence, we would expect the price of the good to rise at a rate equal to the rate of interest. If it rises at a slower rate, its owners would be better off increasing supply now (which would lower the current price), and if it rises at a faster rate, the owners would be better off reducing supply now (so that the current price increases) and selling more later. For example, suppose that a new substitute for oil is discovered and is expected to come on line and reduce oil prices three years from now. Oil producers increase production now, and the price of oil falls right away, not in three years.

What I have just presented sounds plausible, but is it also right? The way to find out is to look at the data – and this brings bad news. Although some support the theory, for the most part they do not. Far from rising at the rate of interest, over the long run, the relative prices of nonrenewable resources have usually not risen at all. Some have even fallen, some show no discernible trend, though this may be changing now, while still others fell in some years and then rose. Evidently, the simple theory used so far has omitted at least one important factor.

A likely culprit is extraction cost. The theory just discussed applies to the prices of oil and minerals in the ground, not to the delivered price at the buyers' gate. The latter includes substantial extraction and transporting costs, which for many raw materials have been falling, and that might account for their delivered prices falling. Moreover, even when extraction and transportation costs are constant, the price of oil at the pump rises by a smaller *percentage* than the price of oil in the ground, because the extraction, transportation, refining, distribution, and marketing costs and taxes that are such a substantial part of the pump price do not rise.

Another reason why oil prices may rise at less than the rate of interest is the unrealism of the assumption made so far that owners of oil wells are unconcerned about risk. But in actuality they face immense risk because of the prevailing mist of uncertainty regarding future demand, the discovery of additional reserves, and technological advances. It is, therefore, possible that, instead of a strategy that maximizes profits, they respond with a strategy of "take the money and run." Other factors that may limit their horizons, and hence make them pump oil at a faster rate than the profit-maximizing rate, are the need of some oil producing countries to generate sufficient revenue to keep their populations if not contented than at least docile, and the wish of the managers of oil companies to generate short-term profits that will boost the value of their stock options.

It is, therefore, not surprising that the simple model with which I started this section is, by and large, rejected by the data. All the same, this model does have an important and valid message. This is that the Mother Hubbard model of the 1970s billboard is not the way to think about nonrenewable resources. To predict the future availabilities of a nonrenewable resource, we have to do more than divide reserves by the current rate of use. We have to see what pricing strategy its owners will follow. *If* the owners try to maximize profits and *if* extraction costs and transportation costs are constant, the result of a fully anticipated scarcity of a nonrenewable resource is a relatively slow but persistent increase in its price, not a sudden, dramatic jump as reserves are exhausted.

Such jumps result only from unanticipated events. But when these events occur, they may not be reversed for a considerable time. New oil wells are not brought on line quickly. If higher gas prices convince people that they would be better off with hybrids than with SUVs, there will still be a plenitude of SUVs on the road for a long time. With both supply and demand being slow to respond to price, even small changes in supply or demand can require sharp price swings to bring them back into equality.

What does all this tell us about whether we are using up resources profligately? Even if the notion that we will suddenly run out is wrong, it is still possible that we are using them up too fast. We do not know what new deposits will be discovered and what technology will bring. Currently, known reserves are not that good a guide to scarcity. In 1865 Stanley Jevons, then one of the world's greatest economists, warned that Britain was running out of coal, and that in a few decades this would end economic progress in Britain. Yet Britain is still mining coal and progressing. For many resources there were periods when we discovered new deposits at a faster clip than we were using up known ones. There is also the problem of evaluating backstop technologies, that is, currently known technologies that will become competitive once the price of a natural resource rises beyond a certain point. Will their costs come down once we use them and gain experience with them, or will they fail to pan out? Moreover, entirely new technologies may provide us with cheap substitutes for dwindling resources. Or they may not. Technological progress might even make a nonrenewable resource scarcer. We might, for example, discover a new, much more valuable use for oil, and regret that we used so much of it in the first decades of the twenty-first century. Or, we might find a cheap substitute for oil that will make us regret that we did not use more oil in the early twenty-first century.

If we do use nonrenewable resources up too fast, are we impoverishing our grandchildren? Probably not. We are also leaving them with a larger stock of nonhuman capital than we started out with, and a vastly improved stock of technology. Hence, assuming that population will not grow much faster than is currently projected, even if they have fewer nonrenewable resources, future generations are *likely* to enjoy a higher standard of living than we do. (I say "likely," not "will," because of the potentially catastrophic effects of global warming and other possible natural disasters.)

But remember that it does not take a cataclysmic scarcity to generate substantial and, at least initially, unpleasant changes in our lifestyle. For example, if gas rises to, say, $10 a gallon, the American dream may have to change from a house in the suburbs to a condominium in a high-rise. That would not be the first time that, despite an overall rise in our living standard, we have had to cut back on something. Two hundred years ago a much larger proportion of the population had domestic servants – even though by the standards of that time we have vastly more rich people today.

All in all, reasonable people can disagree about whether we are using up too many nonrenewable resources. Our ignorance is massive. This can be used to build a case for more conservation than the market provides on its own through the profit-seeking behavior of resource owners. Given the fragility of the market's estimates of future supply and demand, we cannot rule out the possibility that the prices of some nonrenewable resources will soar to totally unexpected heights. One might counter that this possibility does not suffice to make the case for remedial action by the government, because rational resource owners in deciding on the current rate of resource exploitation do take into account the very small possibility that their resource may be immensely more valuable in, say, twenty years. But it is possible that, though they take this into account, they do not hold enough of their resource back, because they expect that if its price rises greatly the government will step in and control it, and thus deprive them of the outlandish profits that would be needed to entice them to bet on an outlandish event.

Moreover, it is possible that our theory of how resource owners operate, with its optimistic conclusion that they have a sufficient incentive to conserve the resource is just plain wrong. For instance, they might lack sufficient imagination, or be unable to obtain the financing needed to hold large enough reserves against a highly unlikely contingency.

We can, therefore, make a coherent – but not necessarily persuasive – case for government policies to reduce our consumption of nonrenewable resources. But if the government does step in and decrees conservation, what reason is there to think that it will do so to the right extent, and will not be influenced by the wishes of firms that profit from conservation efforts, or by the bumper-sticker oversimplifications that pay off well at elections? The current ethanol program seems less like a rational response to rising gas prices than a rational response to the political importance of the American farmer.

It seems likely that a stronger case for curbing our use of some nonrenewable resources can be made by arguing, not that we are running out of these resources, but that their use creates pollution. And for some other resources a strong case for curbing their use can be made because these resources, unlike the ones discussed so far, do not have legal owners. Let's now look at these.

9.2   The Tragedy of the Commons

We are over-fishing and reducing the availability of many fish species at a much faster rate than appropriate – not only from the point of view of the fish – but also from our own. At the same time, we are polluting land, sea, and air, most notably through global warming. This is an example of what is called the "tragedy of the commons" after the classic case in medieval Europe where villagers held some land in common on which each one had a right to graze his cows, even if it meant overgrazing; in other words, a situation where some property has no owner to protect it from overuse or abuse.

But the picture is not bleak everywhere. Fish farmers are not over-fishing their ponds, ranchers are not slaughtering their cattle at an unreasonable rate and, apart from smoking, few people are seriously polluting their living rooms. How come we act so reasonably in one set of circumstances and not in another. The answer is the existence of private property and the incentives it creates. If you are sensible, you take care of what is yours and do not exploit or degrade it at an uneconomic rate. But what incentive do you have to preserve what is not yours? If you limit the number of fish you catch today that will not significantly increase the number you will catch tomorrow; others will catch what you don't. So with the loss of fish that you cause being an external cost to you, you ignore it.

What can be done about this? One possibility is to "internalize" the externality by giving someone property rights over what was previously a common property. If some firm or government had the exclusive right to fish in the ocean, it would have an incentive to see to it that there will still be fish left twenty years from now. But internalizing a cost in the socially most efficient way is not so simple.

Consider a river that flows through several people's property. For those upstream it serves not only as a source of drinking water, but also, at the point where the river leaves their property, as a convenient sewer. Those who live downstream do not like this at all, and appeal to the government. The government could settle this dispute on the basis of some previously established principle, such as prior use of the river, but suppose it decides instead to use economic efficiency as its criterion. The upstreamers then tell the government that requiring them to stop polluting the river would force them to use a prohibitively expensive alternative, while the downstreamers claim that it would be prohibitively costly for them to find a new source of drinking water. The government knows better than to take either claim at face value, but it does not know which of these costs is the greater. A Solomonic solution is to auction off the right to pollute the river. If the loss from having the river polluted is greater for the downstreamers than the benefit the upstreamers gain from polluting it, then the downstreamers will buy up the right (and, of course, not use it) and if the benefit the upstreamers gain from being allowed to pollute the river exceeds the losses the downstreamers will suffer, then they will outbid the downstreamers and pollute.

But now the lawyers for both sides demand to be heard, and lo and behold, they do agree on one issue: the right to the river does not belong to the government but to their clients, they just differ on which client. Accordingly, they file suit.

From the point of view of the efficient use of the river, and never mind fairness, does it matter who wins? That depends on whether it is possible to negotiate precise, cheaply enforceable contracts. If it is – and that is a big if – then pollution will be essentially the same, regardless of who wins. Suppose the upstreamers win. They would pollute only if their gain from polluting exceeds what the downstreamers are willing to pay them for not polluting. And if the downstreamers win, they will sell the upstreamers the right to pollute if they get more for this than clean water is worth to them. Hence, if the upstream folk and the downstream folk are the only ones affected (let's assume the fish don't mind), then the right to use the river either as a drain or as clean water will go to those who value it more. The legal right to the river will only determine who pays whom.

This story of the polluters and their victims coming together and negotiating for pollution rights sounds great, at least to economists, but does not have all that much practical significance. Usually, there are many different groups of gainers and loser, and getting them all to sign on to a contract is easier said than done. Moreover, defining pollution rights precisely and enforcing them on a day-to-day basis would often be too costly for the upstream and downstream folks to reach an enforceable agreement. Then the government has to step in. It can go all the way with the upstreamers and allow unlimited pollution, or with the downstreamers and prohibit all pollution, or take a position in between by regulating or taxing upstream polluters.

What happens if there is no government able and willing to do job? Suppose we are looking at a medieval village in which all peasants had an unchallengeable right to graze their cows on the commons, and, therefore, had an incentive to over-use it. Here altruism, custom, and social pressures, along with an understanding of what is happening, might perhaps have sufficed to limit the number of cows on the commons, particularly when enforced by whoever was the strongest and toughest, who was likely to have seen to it that he got his "fair" share.

Regardless of whether or not such pressures were effective in a medieval village, in a large modern society they do not suffice, and people pollute such ownerless resources as the air and oceans, so let's see how a modern society should handle this problem of the commons.

9.3 Pollution Permits and Taxes on Pollutants

If a factory were to emit poisonous fumes that kill 10 percent of the population within a fifty mile radius, it would obviously have to be shut down. But most pollution problems are not that severe in the noticeable short run, so that they present the problem of finding the level of pollution at which the cost of further restriction outweighs the benefit of these restrictions. Does that sound as though there could be too little pollution? Yes, it does. Suppose the government were so gung-ho about controlling pollution that it requires firms to spend, say, $10 billion per year to eliminate a pollutant that causes ten people to feel uncomfortable for a day? Would that be good policy? On the other hand, it would not be good policy either to allow oil refiners to spew forth particulate matter unchecked. We have to draw the line somewhere, even if we do not know precisely where.

Once the appropriate level of pollution has been determined, how do you go about achieving it? To many people – but not to most economists – the solution is what economists call "command and control" legislation: have the government issue a regulation that orders polluting firms to switch to a specific technology that is less polluting, or else set a limit (which could be zero) on the pollutants that each firm may generate. Requiring a specific technology has the disadvantage that if left to make their own decisions about how to abate pollution, firms might find a way to cut pollution that is cheaper than the mandated technology. Remember that actual firms are not homogeneous entities depicted on a blackboard by a mathematical symbol. They vary, and each of them faces different problems and opportunities. The alternative of setting a limit on each firm's pollution, but letting it use its own way of getting there, is, therefore, better, but it still has serious problems. Suppose you decide to reduce emission of a certain pollutant from 2,000 to 1,000 tons for the entire country. How do you decide how much each particular firm has to cut back? If you require all firms to cut back by the same percentage, then those who have already achieved a low level of emission will howl, and rightly so. Moreover, firms responsible for other types of pollution that you might want to regulate in the future would get the idea that they should increase their pollution right now to establish a higher baseline from which they can then cut back easily. There would also be a lot of special pleading by firms arguing that in their particular case an exception is warranted. And some of them might even be right. Besides, how would you decide what limits to impose on new firms? But to an economist the most salient argument against a fixed percentage across-the-board cutback is that it fails to direct the cutback towards those firms that could cut back cheaply, and away from those for whom it would be expensive.

You may wonder, gentle reader, why I have hammered away at such a simple point. One reason is its great importance, since it means that, instead of issuing specific regulations for each industry or firm, the government should announce a general goal, for example, reducing carbon dioxide emission by 20 percent, and let the market decide how and where to do it. Specifically, the government should require firms that intend to emit carbon dioxide to obtain permits, and then provide such permits for only, say, 80 percent of the previous level of emissions. Firms could then trade these permits among themselves.[a]

Under this "cap and trade" system the government could provide these permits by auctioning them off to polluting firms. Alternatively, it could distribute them free to firms. Auctioning them off has two advantages. First, it would raise revenue the government could use to cut distorting taxes, such as individual and corporate income taxes, to reduce the deficit, or to finance what, let us hope, are desirable programs. Second, auctioning avoids the just discussed problem of how to distribute free permits. But selling permits also has two disadvantages. One is that it might tempt a revenue-hungry government (and these are hardly uncommon) to restrict pollution too much. In addition, one might argue that, given the great political power of some industries, the only way sufficiently strong environmental legislation can be passed is if its cost to business is reduced by the government giving away instead of selling the required permits.

---

[a]   Alternatively, the government could impose a fee on emissions, with the fee set at the level that it *expects* to be just high enough to cause a 20 percent reduction in emission. In the former case (permits), the government knows exactly the maximum level of pollution that will occur; in the latter case it does not, because it cannot know exactly how many of the polluting firms will want to emit at the set fee. That is not necessarily bad, because if, at a certain fee, firms want to pollute more than the government expected, that must be due either to the demand for the polluting firms' output having grown faster than the government had foreseen, or else to the cost of cutting back on pollutants being greater than the government had anticipated. Both are reasons to stop and reconsider whether the initial goal was perhaps too ambitious. Or conversely, if firms want to pollute less than expected at the set fee, this suggests that the burden of reducing pollution is not all that great, and that a larger cutback might, therefore, be appropriate.

Irrespective of whether firms are required to buy permits or get them free, it is important that they can buy and sell these permits. That ensures that pollution is reduced where the cost of doing so is least, because if permits are issued free, firms that can cut pollution at a low cost will sell some of their permits to firms that can cut their pollution only at a high cost, while if permits are auctioned off, the firms that find it most expensive to reduce pollution will be the ones buying them. Trading in permits also gives firms an incentive to find less polluting ways of production, since if successful, they can then sell their excess permits or buy fewer. And as they develop a less polluting technology, that will justify issuing fewer permits in future years.

Compared to permits, pollution taxes also have a big disadvantage: people hate them. Partly, this seems due to a rigid (I am tempted to say hysterical) dogma of "no more taxes." Partly, it is due to a naive belief that if firms are required to buy pollution permits, this just takes money away from greedy corporations, while pollution taxes would be paid for by consumers. Actually, we would expect firms to pass on a pollution tax and the cost of pollution permits to the same extent. With respect to that poster for pollution taxes, a carbon tax, there are additional problems. They are regressive (though this could be offset by devoting some of the revenue to programs that help the poor), they hit certain people especially hard: some of whom would find it very difficult to adjust, so that they are considered unfair (see box 9. 1) and many people behave as though they believe that cheap gas is an inherent human right.

The second reason I have spent so much time on what is basically the straightforward point that either permits or taxes are superior to command and control, is that its economic logic runs into strong emotional resistance. This resistance has four major sources: sources that often bubble below the surface rather than being expressed explicitly. One, is a feeling that we cannot trust the market to do the right thing, that every opportunity to substitute government regulation for market processes should be eagerly grasped. The banner of environmentalism does seem to attract some people who would advocate socialism if they thought it had any political traction. (That, however, should not be held against environmentalism per se, and besides, on the other side of the fence, much opposition to reasonable environmental measures also has a hidden agenda: upholding a rigid ideology or serving the advocate's self-interest.) Moreover, we can readily make a strong case for moderate environmentalism also on conservative grounds: if I pollute the air that drifts over your property, I am violating your property rights, and protection of property rights is an important conservative principle.

Another source of opposition to permits is a feeling that providing them is morally wrong because it legitimizes "the right to pollute." In the words

Box 9.1: Pollution Permits Would Let the Rich Pollute as Much as They Want

The typical economist does not find this objection to pollution permits persuasive. Suppose we accept the existence of income inequality and also treat pollution as a negative good, the same way one might think of having to do an hour's work as a negative good, or put differently, we treat the enjoyment of unpolluted air, etc., like any other good. Then, as long as the rich pay for it, there is no reason to object to them polluting more than the poor do, any more than there is reason to object to them buying more jewelry. Imagine a world with only two people, one who wants to buy something owned by other, and is willing to pay enough to make the second person willing to sell. Why should this trade be unacceptable just because the "something" is clean air? That is the way economists see things. End of story?

Not quite. Those who argue that the rich should not be allowed to pollute more than the poor treat pollution, not as a negative good, but as an immoral act, and argue that selling an indulgence that allows a person to perform an immoral act is inherently wrong. Hence, the argument turns on the ethical assumption underlying the economist's view, that pollution is just a negative good and not immoral per se, and there is no reason to give the economist's ethical assumptions precedence over other people's. End of Story?

Not quite: there is still the insuperable (?) problem of how to implement a rule that the rich are not allowed to pollute more. When we talk about selling pollution permits we are talking entirely, or almost entirely, about selling permits to firms, not to individual families, though firms will largely pass the cost of buying these permits on to consumers. And most polluting industries sell to rich and poor alike. End of story?

of former Senator Muskie (the 1968 Democratic vice-presidential candidate): "We cannot give anyone the right to pollute for a fee."[1] Mike Huckabee, a former Arkansas Governor and candidate for the 2008 Republican presidential nomination, compared pollution permits to the Catholic Church's sales of indulgences. Both ignored that command and control regulations also legitimize pollution. Saying that a firm must use the best available technology for curbing carbon dioxide emission still lets it emit some carbon dioxide. And if we have to allow *some* pollution, what is immoral about charging a fee for it? (See box 9.2.) Moreover, we do impose "sin taxes" on alcohol, tobacco, etc., thus selling the right to indulge in those sins.

Third, there is the claim that people have a *right* to live their lives without being subject to pollution. And this being an *inherent* right, it cannot be traded away by selling permits to pollute. I have already discussed the assertion of rights in general, in chapter 4, but let's ask where this particular right is supposed to come from. It is surely not part of people's "ancient rights." In medieval Europe, people were subject to much more pollution than we are now: raw human sewage was dumped into rivers, drinking water was not purified, and wood and peat fires polluted huts that had little ventilation because heat had to be conserved. Anyone who thinks that the automobile has led to an increase in pollution should read descriptions of nineteenth-century city streets awash in horse excrement. Here is an eye-witness report from just one city: "Much of the muck followed from the still-unavoidable reliance on horses – forty thousand of them who each working day generated some five hundred tons of manure, twenty thousand gallons of urine, and almost two hundred carcasses."[2]

Fourth, there is what might be called "emotive environmentalism." This belief system rejects the economists' consequentialism, with its attempt to balance costs and benefits. To an emotive environmentalist, pollution is *inherently* evil: we should inhabit the earth with as small a footprint as possible. Central to this claim, are issues which are beyond economics, and I will, therefore, not discuss it, except to note that it is very much a minority position, and that in its denunciation of consumerism it reminds me of the sects of flagellants so prominent in the Middle Ages and in the Renaissance. The left, too, has its fundamentalists.

While I am, therefore, unpersuaded by the arguments against pollution permits, I recognize that much of my disagreement with their opponents is based on differences in value judgments, not on disagreements about economics. Moreover, to be an effective policy, pollution permits have to be administered with a firm hand: the number of permits issued has to be kept sufficiently low, and there should be no special favors shown to particular firms or industries. (Despite its support of the Kyoto Treaty, the European Union has done poorly on that score.) And I do concede that there are some special cases in which command-and-control regulation is appropriate. Where we cannot measure the emission of pollutants, such as groundwater contamination, permits and taxes are not feasible, and instead we have to order firms to use particular technologies that minimize the damage. Moreover, in sudden health emergencies, such as extremely bad smog, a permit system might take too long to install. In 2008 at the Beijing Olympics, the Chinese authorities banned, a couple of weeks before the start, major economic, trucking and other activities to ensure clean air for the athletes. Whether this was the right decision, or whether they should have used a pollution tax I do not know.

In addition, in those cases in which the effects of pollution are very severe and are heavily concentrated in a particular area, we may want to require special permits for polluting these areas. Similarly, in an area of great scenic or historical interest we might want to set the price of permits so high that nobody buys any, thus, in effect using a command and control system.

9.4   Tail-pipe Pollution

Enough of these generalities. Let's now look at a particular type of regulation, the way the government controls automobile pollution by imposing a "corporate average fuel economy" standard (CAFE) that sets an average mileage requirement each car maker must meet. In other words, each one is implicitly given a pollution permit for every car it produces and can allocate these implicit permits among its cars in any way it pleases.

While this is certainly better than imposing a specific standard on each car, it would be still more efficient to extend this flexibility by allowing automobile makers to trade these implicit permits among themselves. Then those who find it particularly costly to meet the CAFE standard could buy permits from those who find it least costly. Suppose Ford develops a light car that proves highly popular. It can, therefore, meet and even exceed its CAFE requirement without doing anything else, so that the CAFE regulation gives it no incentive to adopt even very low-cost ways of raising its gas mileage. Suppose, further, that GM, which has experienced a surge of demand for its large cars, is forced to adopt extraordinarily expensive technologies to meet its CAFE requirements. If it were, instead, allowed to buy Ford's excess permits, the total cost of controlling pollution would be lower. To be sure, pollution would increase since Ford's previously unused permits would now be used. But that increase could be offset by raising the CAFE standard applicable to both firms, since the cost of meeting a given CAFE standard would now be lower.

We can do even better. Why not let GM also buy the right to produce more gas guzzlers from firms in other industries that agree to cut back on their own or on their customers' emission of greenhouse gases?

Or better yet, why not impose an across-the-board carbon tax, instead of going just after the automobile industry? That would shift the cost of reducing pollution to wherever in the economy its cost is least. But, environmentalists might reply that imposing a carbon tax is not politically feasible, and since a CAFE standard is the best we can get, that is the policy we should support. And they may well be right.

9.5 Protecting Endangered Species

A problem akin to controlling pollution is to protect endangered species. Let's take the case of elephants. One way elephants have been protected has been an international ban on the sale of ivory, a ban that applies not only to ivory from newly slaughtered elephants, but also to old ivory, such as nineteenth-century ivory carvings. But it is not clear whether the ban on old ivory is appropriate. On the one hand, it makes the ban on new ivory easier to enforce, both because new ivory could be disguised as old ivory, and also because it creates a social stigma to buying and displaying any ivory objects. (However, it is now possible by means of DNA to trace ivory to its source, and that may help to distinguish new ivory from old.) On the other hand, prohibiting the sale of old ivory also increases the pay-off to poaching. Suppose that for some reason I am desperate to acquire an ivory statute of Buddha, while you, who own one, would be willing to sell it to me if that were legal. If I cannot buy it from you, I will have to buy it from a poacher, and thus raise the demand for and the price of ivory and thus the incentive to poach.

Apart from banning ivory sales, another way to protect elephants would be to encourage privately owned elephant reservations. Their owners – the people who live there – would be paid for every elephant spotted on their reservation. Along these lines, China, which has banned the sale of tiger parts, is currently considering establishing tiger farms that would be permitted to sell tiger parts. But this has been criticized for sending the wrong signal to consumers. Moreover, elephant and tiger farmers would also have to deal with poachers. However, those living in the area are likely to find it easier to spot poachers than it is for the typically underfinanced government officials. Establishing privately owned conservation areas has worked well in Africa.

Another possibility is to give local people a stake in conservation by encouraging eco-tourism. A further possibility might be to flood the market with fakes. For example, a certain Mexican turtle species is endangered because its eggs are considered an aphrodisiac. It might be possible to produce realistic-looking fakes and sell them on the black market. The price of these eggs would then fall, not only because the supply is larger, but also because demand would be less when potential buyers have to consider that they may be buying a fake.

NOTES

1   http://www.economist.com/finance/displaystory.cfm?story_id=9, 6/21/2007.
2   Edwin Burrows and Mike Wallace, *Gotham: A History of New York City: To 1898*, New York, Oxford University Press, 1999, cited in Thomas Sowell, *Economic Facts and Fallacies*, New York, Basic Books, 2008, p. 20.

PART IV
LOOKING AT DATA

10

Empirical Economics

Although the previous chapters did speak of empirical evidence, their main focus was on deductive reasoning. But many of the spurious arguments that you come across in economics are not primarily deductive arguments, but claims about what "the facts," that is, the data, show.[a] This and the following chapters, therefore, teach you to protect yourself against such claims. They will also give you a better idea of what economics is about. Since it is an empirical science, economists devote considerable time to measuring the magnitude of predicted effects, as well as to testing theories against observations. A recent survey of up-and-coming young American economists as represented by assistant professors in the top ten American economics departments found that about half of them do mainly empirical work and almost a third do mainly a mixture of theoretical and empirical work.[1] The idea of economics as "just a bunch of theory" is a prejudice fostered by the fact that introductory economics courses focus on chains of deductive reasoning.

10.1 Role of Empirical Work in Economics

One reason why empirical work is so important in economics is that all that economic theory can usually give you are essentially qualitative, not

---

[a] Trying to draw a sharp distinction between "theory" and "facts" or "data" or "observations" is naive. Any theory in the empirical sciences must embody some observations, otherwise we would not know what to theorize about, and every observation requires some "theory," if only to allow the brain to interpret the signals it receives from the senses. (Mathematics, which is not an empirical science, is different; it simply assumes its axioms.)

quantitative, results. While it can tell you that if x happens, prices will rise, and if y happens, output will fall, etc., it cannot tell you by how much. Yet it is the "how much" question that is often the important one. If theory tells you that a rise in interest rates will temporarily cause unemployment to increase, that does not give you enough information to decide whether to favor or oppose a rise in interest rates. For that, most people will also want to know by how *much* and for how *long* unemployment will increase. And only empirical evidence can settle that issue.

Another reason for the emphasis on empirical work is that it is not just some lowly servant who fills in the details that lordly theory has left unexplored. It is also the master or judge, a sort of St Peter who welcomes some theories into the canon, and sends others to rot in the underworld of the disconfirmed, and, therefore, abandoned. (Admittedly, this is something of an idealization: some theories survive unperturbedly for a long time, despite a heavy pounding from disconfirming evidence. But not forever.)

All that deductions can do is to bring out the implications that are contained in their premises. If economists have applied the rules of logic correctly, then their conclusions are also correct. But what about the assumptions? As discussed in appendix 2.1, what matters is not the truth of an assumption in some absolute sense, but whether it is sufficiently accurate for the purpose at hand. And that can be established only by seeing whether the theory that is built on it is consistent with the empirical evidence.

10.2   Types of Empirical Evidence

There are several types of empirical evidence that can be used to estimate the magnitude of an effect and to test theories.

10.2.1   Anecdotes

We are all familiar with that old standby of the media and everyday conversation, the anecdote. It is colorful, entertaining, does not tax the listener's mental energy – and can be used to "prove" just about anything. If Helen Hardnosed argues that welfare recipients are a bunch of loafers because she knows someone who quit her job to go on welfare, and Sybil Softheart responds that she knows someone who is looking for a job but cannot find one and would starve were it not for welfare, they are both right in what they are saying, and wrong in treating it as it though mattered. All they are showing is that there is at least one person on welfare who is a loafer, and at least one person who is deserving.

Whoever denied that? Arguments from a single case can cause much damage; and not only in economics. That Chamberlains' appeasement of Hitler in the late 1930s was wrong does not mean that all efforts to avoid a war are wrong.

10.2.2   Dramatic events

Closely related to the anecdote is the dramatic event. Like many anecdotes, it relies on a single instance, but the instance is a spectacular event, for example, the Great Depression of the 1930s. It has two advantages over the usual anecdote. First, any theory that tries to explain a certain category of events fails dramatically if it cannot explain a spectacular event encompassed in that category. Second, though, in principle, a dramatic event need not have a dramatic cause (a snowball may start an avalanche), in many cases the main causal factor of a dramatic event will often be something that shouts out to us from the data, and not something that murmurs so quietly that we can hardly hear it over the background noise. Hence, although the dramatic event may often be described in terms of numbers, i.e., statistics, it can frequently tell its message without the aid of elaborate statistical techniques.

Hence, although reports about spectacular events are actually anecdotes, at least on the heuristic level, they have more to teach us than the usual anecdote. And one can make a good case that economists are strongly, perhaps excessively, influenced by them when they occur. But the problem is in "when they occur." They are by definition rare events, and, therefore, economists must usually look for something else.

10.2.3   Statistics

As a saying has it: "anecdote" is the singular for "data." If Helen Hardnosed had cited not just one case of a welfare cheat, but a thousand, and if these thousand cases were a representative sample, then she would have had a strong argument. To make valid generalizations, we need to look at many cases, and while in principle we could just rattle off each individual case, one after the other, that would not only be extremely time consuming but probably also overtax the listener's memory and certainly her patience. So we need to summarize these cases in some way. Sometimes we can do this without recourse to numbers, e,g., you might say "people tend to live in family settings." But if you want to be more precise you need to quantify; for example, to cite the percentage of people who are living in a family setting, that is, to use statistics.

Allowing us to describe the data in compact form is one important use of statistics, but not the only one. Another, is to dig beneath what is readily observable and to infer underlying relationships: for instance whether the difference in income between a sample of New Yorkers and a sample of Chicagoans is likely to be due merely to the idiosyncrasies of the samples or to an actual difference in incomes, and whether changes in one variable, say the federal deficit, generate changes in another, such as GDP. The purpose of this book is to teach you how to spot and reject incorrect arguments. Accordingly, you will read about the many ways that statistics can be used to bamboozle you. From this, you may conclude that it is not worth bothering with statistics at all. But this is wrong. An even moderately thorough list of all that can go wrong when you go shopping, from slipping while getting into the car to dropping the groceries on your toes while putting them away, may also make it seem that you are better off staying home and starving.

To explain how to read and evaluate statistics I need to combat three perverse attitudes. One is that statistics provide some kind of "scientific" authentification; that citing statistics that support you is a definitive way to put an end to an argument. This is nonsense. Often, "looking at the data" is just the first step of a serious analysis. Sometimes we have to ask how they were compiled, how well the definitions used correspond to what we want to measure, what alternative data show, etc. The second attitude is that all statistics are untrustworthy, and should be ignored, that while figures don't lie, liars figure. But that, too, is nonsense. Used thoughtfully, statistics provide a thoroughfare to truth. The correct response to the existence of dishonest and unreliable statistics is to be a skeptical, but not a cynical, reader, that is, to treat numerical information as you would purely verbal information. The third is the belief that when confronted with statistics you cannot understand what is going on unless you know a great deal of math. As mentioned in chapter 1, these statistical chapters assume no knowledge of math beyond the elementary school level. Here neither the wide jaws of the summation sign, Σ, nor the embrace of the integral sign, $\int$ threaten you. Box 10.1 explains the little bit of math beyond the grade-school level that is needed. The content of these chapters is, therefore, more akin to everyday applied verbal logic than to mathematics. To those who refuse to read something that contains any algebra my advice is just to ignore the very few pages that use it.

10.3   What to Watch Out for in Statistics: Some General Problems

Before dealing with specific statistical measures and their potential misuse, we need to look at some reasons for being cautious about statistics in general.

Box 10.1: A Whiff of Mathematics

This box deals with three items: raising a number to a power, finding a root, and logarithms. One can write any number as some other number multiplied by itself a certain number of times. For example, 1,000 can be written as $10 \times 10 \times 10$, or more conveniently as 10^3. The superscript, 3, called the "exponent" or "power," tells you how many times you have to multiply the number by itself; it is one less than the exponent; 10^1 is just 10, 10^2 is 10×10, etc. Similarly, 2^4 equals 16. What goes up also comes down. The square root of a number (N) is that number which, when multiplied by itself gives you N. For example, the square root of 9 is 3. You can think of finding a square root as "unsquaring."

Finally, there is a useful device called logarithms or logs. You first select a base number, let's say 10, and can then express any other number, N, as the power to which 10 has to be raised to equal N. For example, you have to raise 10 to the second power to get 100, so the log of 100 to the base 10 is 2. Since exponents need not be round numbers you can express every number as the log of 10. There is, however, one complication: we generally use as the base not 10, but a number called e which is one of the fundamental constants of mathematics, and is approximately 2.178. This has the advantage that logs then correspond to percentage changes and hence growth rates; for instance on a chart that has a log scale a 1-inch distance measures the same percentage change regardless of where it is on the scale, rather than the same absolute change, as it does in a conventional chart.

10.3.1 The narrowness of focus

The condensation of information that statistics provides is a great benefit – but also a great detriment – of statistics. By shining a powerful searchlight on one particular aspect of a situation it seduces us into neglecting its other aspects, and thereby washes out what could be important differences among our observations. To a statistician bent on measuring how much people weigh, a 140-lb, 25-year-old male investment banker in New York and 140-lb, 60-year-old destitute woman in Haiti are identical. The only thing about people that matters is their weight. Contrast this with the practice of a journalist who interviews, say, five Iraqis and reports the result as though it represents Iraqi public opinion. Nonsense, says the statistician, her sample is much too small and is not representative, since these five people were probably selected because they were willing to talk to an American reporter, and perhaps also because they speak English. Instead, do a statistical survey with an adequate, randomly chosen, sample. The reporter can reply that though her report is statistically flawed it trumps a statistical survey, because, by letting these people speak in their own words it provides a nuanced understanding that mere numbers cannot. As Arthur Koestler (the author of the great political novel, *Darkness at Noon*) once remarked: "Statistics don't bleed." And what statisticians wash out when they present an average can be important. At his retirement party, a defense lawyer is supposed to have said: "I got off some clients who I know were guilty, while some other clients who I know were innocent were convicted. Well, on average, justice was done."

Moreover, since measurement is so important there is a strong temptation to believe that anything that cannot be measured cannot be important, or at least to deemphasize what cannot be measured. For example, in explaining the savings ratio, that is, the percentage of their income that families save, economists can readily measure several explanatory variables, such as a family's size, its income, and its wealth. What they usually cannot measure is its foresightfulness. So, they usually assume that this is essentially the same for all families, and can, therefore, be ignored when trying to explain differences in the savings ratios of different types of families. Sometimes, when you do this and ignore a factor because you cannot measure it, the data rap you on the knuckles: you find you can explain only a small proportion of the variation that you are trying to explain. But suppose, as seems likely, that foresightfulness is correlated with wealth. Then your analysis may give a good fit to the data, but will overstate the importance of wealth because wealth is, in part, standing in for foresightfulness, and also you will have missed entirely the importance of differences in foresightfulness.

10.3.2   Hand-me-down data

Generating raw statistical data from surveys is often excruciatingly expensive, and also omits those who don't bother to answer. (Appendix 10.1 discusses additional problems with survey data.) Since the government has deep pockets, and since it can compel answers, economists largely rely on statistics generated by the government. However, the government does not generate these data to please academic economists, but for its own use. Sometimes, what the government measures corresponds fairly closely to what economists would like to have measured, but at other times the government's measures have only a tenuous link to the variables used in economic theory, so that using these data to test the theory is sometimes a precarious business. At times, if the data disagree with the theory, it is more reasonable to throw out the data as inappropriate than to throw out the theory.

10.3.3   Errors in the data

Another major problem is the quality of our data. While some, such as data on stock prices and exchange rates, are excellent, most are poor to varying degrees. One obvious reason is that gathering data is expensive, and even though unreliable data can result in harmful policy decisions, proposing to spend more money on economic statistics is not a sure way to fire up voters. A second reason is that some people have an incentive not to provide the needed data, or to falsify them. Thus there are many people working in what is called the "underground economy," that is, working without their earnings and employment being reported to the IRS and other government agencies. The resulting understatement of GDP is hard to measure, and the available estimates vary widely, but for the United States something like 10 percent of GDP does not seem unreasonable. In many other countries, particularly in less developed countries, it is substantially larger.[2]

A third, more subtle, reason is the disconnect between what we would like our data to measure and what they actually do measure because of the difficulty of measuring the former. For example, in principle, the work that people do in cooking meals and in other housework is output and production, just like the work they do in factories and offices. But we lack adequate data on housework, so we do not include it GDP. And, as discussed in appendix 10.2, that is only one of several differences between what we would like to include in GDP and what we can include. Many other data sets have their own specific problems; appendix 10.2 discusses in addition to GDP also price indexes, and the measurement of employment and poverty.

Fourth, data derived as small residuals from differences among large numbers, and expressed as percentages, for example, the savings rate, are prone to large errors.

Then there are computational and copying errors. At one time they polluted a surprisingly large number of papers in academic economics journals, and perhaps still do.[3] While in most cases they probably do not change a paper's overall results, in some they may.[4] When you are dealing with a large mass of data, copying errors, such as transposing digits, are likely to occur. (I have twice found serious errors in a widely used data base.) In my own work I have found that some errors survived even painstaking checking. The use of computers has not eliminated this problem.[b] Moreover, even if the data are keyed in correctly, in complex calculations different computer programs can yield significantly different results, and, at most, one of these can be correct.

10.3.4   Accuracy and errors

Do not be taken in by the apparent precision of economic statistics. In most cases it is pretense.[5] For example, the 2008 *Economic Report of the President* shows GDP in 2007 as $13,970.5 billion.[6] We can consider ourselves fortunate if the third number of this figure is off by no more than 1.

Preliminary estimates are subject to substantial revisions, and, therefore, do not deserve much attention. The first estimate of the growth of hourly employee compensation in the second quarter of 1966 had it growing at a 6.6 percent rate. The first revision brought this estimate down to −1.2 percent. Economists know this and are not fooled by such spurious claims to precision, but others may be.

10.3.5   Compositional problems

In the third quarter of 2006 the median price of a house in the United States *fell* by 1.7 percent. Yet, the data also show that in all the four regions of the country the median price *rose*: by 19.3 percent in the Northeast, by 4.0 percent in the Midwest, by 0.7 percent in the South, and by 1.6 percent in the West. What is going on here? The answer is that the regional composition, and hence the weights of the various regions in the national average, changed. The number of homes sold in the South rose from 49 percent of the national total in the previous quarter to 55 percent in third quarter of 2006. Since the median home in the South is much cheaper, the greater weight of Southern homes in the average pulled down the national average.[7] Here is another example. A university was accused of sex discrimination in admitting graduate students because it admitted a smaller proportion of female applicants. Since graduate admissions are handled by individual departments, the university checked and found there was no discrimination at the departmental level. However, the departments that had the largest proportion of female applicants accepted a smaller proportion of both male and female applicants than did other departments.[8] Arguing from what happened to a total to what happened

---

[b]   Moreover, if you make a mistake, such as multiplying when you should be dividing, then if you are carrying out the laborious calculations with a desk calculator you are more likely to notice it, than if you simply make a keystroke that instructs the computer program to multiply.

to its components is dangerous. If you have to investigate why something went up or went down, you may save yourself time by first looking at what happened to each of its components.

10.3.6 Intellectual commitment and data mining

Another problem is excessive intellectual commitment. An economist who has done several studies of the same controversial question is likely to come up in his subsequent work with an answer similar to what he obtained in his previous work. We all have a strong motive to see our new data confirm or at least not refute what our previous work has shown. It is good for one's feelings of self-satisfaction – who wants to admit a mistake? Often, it is also good for one's career. In academia, as elsewhere, leadership usually requires hewing to a consistent line. Besides, who wants to disappoint their intellectual allies? Another, but I think less important, reason is that we want our research results to harmonize with our political and ideological convictions.

Intellectual commitment does not necessarily imply dishonesty. We not only believe what we see, but also see what we believe. Here is a simple example. Suppose I undertake a statistical test and get a result that is wildly out of line with what I expected. My first reaction is that I must have made a key-punch error. So I check, and indeed that is what happened. Fine and good. It would have been irresponsible to publish a result that could well be due to a key-punch error. But suppose I had made a key-punch error that supported my hypothesis. Then I would not have double-checked. Such disparate treatment, while reasonable, does bias my statistical results in favor of my hypothesis.

As you can see, the word "bias" often has a somewhat different meaning in economics and statistics than it does ordinarily. It does not necessarily, or even usually, imply dishonesty and special pleading, but normally refers to an unavoidable problem. Bias denotes a moral failing of the researcher only if it could have been avoided, or if she kept an inevitable bias hidden from the reader, or else if she hid results because they would support the "other side."

A more complex – and ambiguous – version of throwing out tests that reject one's hypothesis is the following: suppose you believe that changes in the growth rate of money are the main factor explaining changes in the inflation rate. You look at the data on the growth rate of money and at the inflation rate and, alas, the data do not bear you out. What can you do? Well, you might ask yourself whether you have perhaps not allowed sufficiently for the length of time required for changes in the growth rate of money to do their work. So you redo your analysis, this time allowing for a longer lag. If that works, fine and good. If not, you might ask yourself whether the measure of money that you have selected for the test out of the several that are more or less plausible is perhaps not the correct one, and, again, redo your analysis. If that does not work, you could add an allowance for supply shocks, such as sharp increases in oil prices. By exercising your imagination, you can probably dredge up a few more ways to modify your test. Then, when one of these variants finally does support your hypothesis, you can proudly proclaim: "the data support my hypothesis." This process of torturing the data until they confess has many names, among them "data mining," "data snooping," and "fishing." Despite many raised eyebrows, it is practiced extensively.

One reason for this is that often the hypothesis being tested uses concepts, such as "money," that do not have clear and unambiguous counterparts in the available data; money can be measured as narrowly as currency in circulation plus checkable deposits, or broadly enough to include time deposits and shares in mutual money market funds. Moreover, our theory usually does not specify how long it takes until the predicted effects occur, and what other variables have to be taken into account. (More on that in chapter 13.) Hence, if on the first try you don't succeed, it is entirely reasonable to put the blame not on your hypothesis, but on the particular variables and time lags you have used, or on the specifics of your statistical technique, such as converting the data into logs. You can never test any hypothesis in isolation: the test always includes subsidiary hypotheses, such as the correct way to measure certain variables, or the length of certain lags. Since we cannot specify these with much confidence at the outset, we just have to try several variants. The ideal situation would be to have two or more sets of data, and use one of them to find the correct measures, lags, etc., and then to use this information to test the hypothesis with the other data set. But often, only one data set is available.

This problem is not unique to economics. That hypotheses have to be tested jointly is also true in the natural sciences. Nor is the practice of presenting only your best results unique to economics. When some pharmaceutical companies test new drugs and get a negative result, they test them again and again, in the hope that eventually they will get a positive result that they then can make public.

A reasonable response is not to take a result reached by any single study all that seriously, whether in economics or in other fields, but to wait until it has been confirmed by other studies using different data or methods. This would also help with respect to the previously discussed problem of data errors. But advocating such patience is often unrealistic advice. Many studies are not replicated because their results are not considered important enough to make it worth someone's while; or if they are, and the replications reach the same results as the original study, journal editors are likely to consider them not worth publishing since they are not sufficiently original – which reduces the incentive to undertake them in the first place. Moreover, there may only be a single set of data available, so that a replication shares some of the problems of the original study.

10.3.7 Lying and spinning

As long as there are people who are impressed by numbers because numbers are precise, mathematical, and, therefore, "scientific," there will be a ready supply of sham statistics, some of them outright lies. But one does not have to lie outright to leave the wrong impression. Spinning will do. An example of misinforming with technically correct statements is to say "as much as," or "as little as." A store is not lying when it claims that it has cut prices by "as much as 50 percent," even though only a single one of the 3,000 items on sale has been cut by more than 5 percent. And customers are more likely to remember the "50 percent" than the "as much as."

Retailers and advertisers are not the only villains. Government officials are also accomplished spinners, both because being caught in an outright lie would be most embarrassing for them, and because an outright lie, such as falsifying the unemployment rate, would be known to many potential whistleblowers in the bureaucracy. So they have to be cautious in misinforming the public. But they do what they can. For example, since the labor force is growing, it is possible for the number of people employed to rise even though the unemployment rate is rising. If that happens, a White House news release is likely to stress the employment figure, and ignore the unemployment rate, while if the opposite happens it is likely to stress the decline in the unemployment rate. Moreover, definitions can be adjusted to suit needs. For example, when President Eisenhower faced the prospect of a small, but symbolic, deficit in the federal budget, the Federal Reserve (which was not on-budget) was persuaded to give some funds to the Treasury, so that the budget seemed balanced, even though all that happened was a meaningless transfer from one pocket of the government to another. Subsequently, to reduce the published, but not the true, deficit, President Johnson brought the social security trust fund into the budget. And in 2006, when the federal deficit was less than in the preceding year, the White House announced that this showed the success of President Bush's fiscal policy. It did not add that budget projections showed that the deficit would rise sharply in subsequent years. The press release did not lie; it was just economical with the truth. The projections for future years,

as well as the "adjustments" made by the Eisenhower and Johnson adminis-
trations were available public information, so the government cannot even
be blamed for excessive secrecy.

Lower levels of government are also adept at spinning. David Cowles[9]
found the following delightful example: the Minnesota Department of Natural
Resources stated that the National Safety Council reported that there were
fewer people seeking emergency room treatment for sports injuries per
100,000 participants for hunting than for football, baseball, billiards, and
ping-pong. As he points out, this ignores the seriousness of the injuries, as
well as the number of people who instead of landing up in an emergency
room, land up in a morgue, and also makes no allowance for the amount of
time people spend in hunting and in pursuing other sports.

Social activists, too, can spin a fine web. Thus the Save Darfur Coalition
published an advertisement that gave a death toll of 400,000 "innocent men,
women and children," when, as far as one can tell, the actual toll was half
that. As Joel Best remarked:[10] "the press asks the activists for statistics . . .
Knowing that big numbers indicate big problems and knowing that it will be
hard to get action unless people can be convinced a big problem exists (and
sincerely believing that there is a big problem) the activists produce a big
estimate." Should one blame them for this? Imagine you are an activist for
the homeless. You are certain that homelessness is a much bigger problem
than most people think. Shortly before being interviewed on TV you come
across two estimates of the number of homeless children, one twice as large
as the other. You have no way of checking which one is right. What should
you do? If you mention both and stay neutral between them, you will appear
ill informed, and thus reduce the effectiveness of your message. Is it fair to
upbraid you for dishonesty if you cite only the higher estimate? My own answer
is, yes. I can understand why others may disagree, but they should beware
of a slippery slope. The next point on this slope is to use the higher estimate
even if you think that the lower estimate is more likely to be correct, and
soon you are at the point where you use the higher estimate even though you
know it is wrong. Politicians are particularly subject to this temptation, as
are radio and TV personalities.

If you think that sliding much of the way down the slope is most unlikely,
then consider the following. A survey in 1991 reported that 11.5 million American children were at risk of going hungry. That sounds terrible, particularly
if one confuses being "at risk" of hunger with actually going hungry, as an
inattentive reader is likely to do. But this survey treated a child as being at risk
of hunger if its parent answered yes to any one of a set of questions, one of
which was: "Did you ever rely on a limited number of foods to feed your

children because you were running out of money to buy food for a meal?"[11] – hardly a good definition of "hungry." In another example, Thomas Sowell relates that when it was shown that the claims made about how much money would ultimately be saved by providing better prenatal care were unjustified, the chair of the prenatal and fetal health department at the Harvard School of Public Health responded that "justification of these services on a cost–benefit analysis is a weak reed," but justified it, because "people were reduced to this sort of effort," since politicians are "reluctant to spend money on services for the poor."[12] In other words, distorting is alright when done for a good cause. And this from an academic!

Sometimes it is hard to tell what is spin and what is true. Suppose income taxes are cut 10 percent across the board. Moderates might say that taxes were cut proportionately, liberals that the tax bill of a rich person fell much more than that of a poor person, and conservatives might say that the major part of the tax cut went to middle-income people. All three are right, so who is spinning?

10.3.8 Carelessness and ignorance

While intentionally twisting the facts is reprehensible, honest but thoughtless errors also generate much misinformation. Sometimes it is not the producer of the data but the reader who is at fault. Suppose a news report states "as many as fifty people died." If questioned the moment after they have read that, a number of readers may get it right, and say they do not know exactly how many people died, only that it was no more than fifty. But I suspect that if asked an hour later most would reply "fifty" or perhaps "about fifty." Numbers tend to stay in our heads, qualifications don't. But the carelessness of readers does not absolve the media from blame. A headline in the *New York Times* read "70 Taliban Killed in Night Battle, NATO Force Says," while the article itself reports that "NATO and Afghan forces . . . *might* have killed *as many as* . . ."[13] David Murray, Joel Schwartz, and Robert Lichter[14] provide numerous examples of how the media misinterpret the results of scientific studies. Joel Best cites an article in the 1995 volume of an unnamed journal claiming that "every year since 1950 the number of American children gunned down has doubled."[15] The author had garbled the information given by his source, a 1994 report saying that *since 1950* the number of children killed each year by guns had doubled – which is far different from the number doubling *each year.*

John Harwood wrote in the *Wall Street Journal* that "Sentencing data signal judges haven't gone soft since the Supreme Court made [sentencing] guidance's voluntary, not mandatory . . . [J]udges are staying within the guidance in 62.6 percent of the cases, with many more-lenient sentences resulting from prosecutor requests. Sentences were more severe than guidance's in 2.2 percent of cases."[16]

With 62.6 percent being within the guidance's and 2.2 percent being more severe, it follows that in 35.2 percent of the cases judges were more lenient than they were previously when all sentences had to be within the guidance's. When the Census Bureau published a report of a survey undertaken in mid-2004 showing that less than half of all marriages contracted between 1975 and the end of 1979 had lasted until their 25th anniversary, there was a great outcry that the American family was in crisis, and that something should be done about it. What should have been done is to notice that marriages undertaken in late 1979 had not yet had a chance to reach their 25th anniversary, and that when adjusted for that, the report showed that the divorce rate was not rising.[17]

10.3.9   Garbage in – garbage out

Computer scientists coined this phrase, often abbreviated to GIGO, to deal with situations where computers are supposed to make silk purses out of sows' ears. The same problem arises in statistics. Statistics can answer many questions – as long as you don't care whether the answer is correct. And since some people don't, you should watch out for "answers" to unanswerable questions. For instance, precise information about intimate personal matters, such as sexual behavior, or potentially embarrassing matters, such as drug taking and drunkenness, should be treated skeptically. So should responses to questions on which the respondent lacks the required information. For example, questions asking about the change in income from the previous year produce garbage: people don't remember. And so does the question "how much did you save last year"; this question has to be phrased much more precisely. And do not trust data from surveys where the respondents have an incentive to manipulate the results. Many years ago the California state legislature became concerned about the lack of emphasis on teaching at the University of California and asked it to undertake a survey of how its faculty spent its time. Accordingly, the University told its faculty to keep a time-use diary for a week, Not only was there no way of verifying whether they told the truth, but also professors can easily shift the work they do from one week to next, for example, spending more time this week on teaching by preparing lecture notes they need for subsequent weeks, and shifting their research into these subsequent weeks. It is, therefore, hard to take the results of this survey seriously.

10.3.10   Some other problems

Another problem is establishing the domain to which the hypothesis that has been tested applies. Suppose the data show that an additional year of schooling raises one's lifespan by one and a half years. Does that mean that by spending an additional twenty years in school (four or five Ph.D.s?) people can on average raise their lifespans by thirty years? Of course not: the data come from observations of people with more or less normal levels of schooling, and there is no reason to assume that they apply to cases way outside this range. Indeed, even within the range of years of schooling actually observed in the sample, the overall good fit to the data may perhaps be due entirely to the more heavily populated part of the range.

Some of the most important techniques in statistics were developed in the context of agricultural experiments where the experimenter could assure himself of a random sample simply by applying the treatment whose effects he was investigating to random plots of land. But in macroeconomics, and sometimes in microeconomics, too, much of the data we use are supplied not by an experimenter but by history, so that individual observations are not random. For example, GDP in the third quarter of 2008 and in the fourth quarter are not independent observations; what happens in the former affects the latter, while a variable, such as monetary policy, which affects GDP in one-quarter, also affects it the next quarter.

One final warning: watch out for data that seem to float in the air without any conceivable tether to a source. If someone tells you that in an average year 21,134 Americans trip over a cat, you might wonder who could possibly have counted.

The problems listed so far are not the only ones that bedevil the often grubby task of inferring correct information from the available data. Box 10.2 gives some other examples. One additional problem, avoiding the regression fallacy, requires an understanding of sampling, so I will defer it until the next chapter, and another problem, inferring causation from observed correlations, will have to wait until chapter 13, which deals with measuring the correlation of data. However, the problems discussed so far should suffice to demonstrate that when evaluating statistical evidence, salt is healthy. But then the same is true for purely verbal evidence. Caveat lector.

Box 10.2: Some More Examples of Statistical Traps

1   "Those with medical insurance visit physicians more frequently than do the uninsured. This proves that insurance improves medical care." That does not follow. Perhaps sick people are more likely to buy medical insurance. Moral: don't ignore other plausible explanations.

2   "This year 342,598 people visited this museum." No, all you know is there were 342,598 museum visits, but surely, some people visited the museum more than once. Moral: Ask yourself how the data were obtained.

3   "Data on the average age at death in various occupations show that students on average die at a younger age than others. Studying is dangerous." Hold on, since students are young, when students do happen to die you would expect them to be young. Moral: Before drawing conclusions ask whether the groups being contrasted are indeed comparable.

4   "Ninety percent of the students in this class know another student who cheated. That proves that there is much cheating." Once, again, no. Suppose of the hundred students in the class one cheated, and ninety students know him. Moral: saying "that proves" doesn't prove anything.

APPENDIX 10.1

Survey Data

Many of our data come from surveys of firms or households. For example, surveys of firms provide some of the data used to estimate GDP, while surveys of consumer expenditures tell us the relative importance of various goods and services in the consumers' price index.

A widespread, though by no means unanimous, attitude among academic economists is that evidence from questioning families and firms is unreliable, particularly if it aims to tell us *why* firms or families behave the way they do. A cynic might respond that asking households and firms why they do something is a technique that competes with the economist's theorizing, and a competitor's ware is never as good as one's own. A less cynical person would attribute economists' dislike of survey evidence to some serious problems with such evidence (discussed below), to many past examples of badly designed surveys in economics, and also to many economists being unaware of the sophisticated literature that sociologists have produced on how to undertake surveys, and, therefore, not being aware of the great skill with which surveys can be conducted.

A serious problem with surveys done by academic economists, who lack the government's power to enforce compliance, is the low response rate. A one-third response rate is usually considered quite good. If the characteristic you are studying is uncorrelated with the willingness to participate in the survey that problem can be cured – albeit at some expense – by increasing the size of the sample. But there are many cases where the willingness to respond is correlated with what you are trying to measure, and then non-response can bias your results. For example, if highly educated people are more willing to respond to a survey about their education, then the responses you receive will overstate the number of years of education completed by the population you are sampling. Similarly, a telephone survey of elderly people asking about their health would generate biased responses. Those who are seriously sick are less likely to answer the phone than those who are healthy.

Another problem is that even slight variations in how a question is worded, as well as the order of the questions, can have substantial effects on the results. And it is often very hard, or even impossible, to phrase a certain question unambiguously. For example, a government survey of firms that planned to increase their capital equipment asked whether the intended purchase was a building or a machine. Seems a straightforward question. But not for firms intending to buy ships. In my own work, I have spent, on average, several hours per question, and even so I have landed up with some real clinkers. In general, questions regarding factual issues about which the respondent is well informed, such as, what make of car she drives, can elicit useful answers – but only when well formulated and not intrusive, and when an honest answer would not threaten the respondent's self-image. But questions that ask much of a respondent's memory, such as his income three years ago, are likely to generate garbage. And so are questions about motives. Not only may people not really know why they did something, such as dropping out of college, but they may be reluctant to reveal their motives, even to themselves. Hypothetical questions, such as: "If your tax liability were cut by 10 percent what would you do with the extra money?" are also useless, because people lack the incentive to give much thought to how they would act in a hypothetical situation. Moreover, with questions about intentions or motives there is often a serious danger that respondents will misunderstand the question because they do not think in terms of the particular abstractions in which the question is worded. For example, suppose you ask someone: "Does inflation, by reducing the real value of your assets, reduce your consumption?" She is likely to say "no," because she does not think in such terms when deciding whether she can afford a new car. And yet inflation does reduce some people's wealth, and if people feel less wealthy, they are less likely to buy a new car.

My own take on survey evidence is that it can be highly useful, but only if the survey is carefully done – and limited to certain types of questions. Many, probably most, economists are less well disposed to survey evidence than this, but I think that is changing – albeit slowly.

APPENDIX 10.2

Measuring GDP, Savings Rates, Price Indexes, Employment, and Poverty

Many people treat government data as unproblematic. And indeed most are not, as are so many data presented by interest and advocacy groups, intended to "make a case." Even so, there are serious problems. To illustrate this let's look at four data sets: GDP, price indexes, saving, and employment.

GROSS DOMESTIC PRODUCT

GDP is intended to be as comprehensive a measure of a country's output of final goods and services as we can obtain. "Final" here means that, to avoid counting an item more than once, it excludes intermediate output, that is, output that becomes embodied in some other output, for example, the iron ore that is used to make to steel. "Gross" in GDP means that it does not subtract for the wear and tear of capital equipment used to produce this output, because our data on that are poor. "D" stands for "domestic" because it counts production within the country, including production by foreign firms, but excludes what domestic firms produce in other countries.

GDP has three faces. One is the volume of final goods and services that is produced, another is total expenditures since all of these goods and services are ultimately bought by someone, and the third is total income because what is spent by one person is received by someone else.[c] GDP is only one of several related output measures that the US Department of Commerce publishes. Another is "personal income," which is the income received by

---

[c]   What happens when some output is not sold? We treat it as "bought" by its producer, and hence as income received in non-money form. Seems a bit silly, but it is needed to keep the books straight.

persons, thus excluding undistributed corporate profits, but including the income of nonprofit institutions serving households. "Disposable personal income" then measures this personal income after personal taxes, primarily the personal income tax.

Although GDP is our broadest measure of production, it ignores several major items. Thus, it does not explicitly subtract for the costs of the pollution generated along with output, because of the difficulty of measuring these costs. Suppose that the index of air quality improves slightly and greenhouse gas emissions are reduced by 2 percent, while the index of water pollution worsens significantly, and five hundred more species become endangered. Question: in what direction – and by how much in dollar terms – should GDP be adjusted for these changes? There is, therefore, good reason for GDP accountants to omit such factors, even though this has the following paradoxical effect: a regulation that costs polluters $1 billion, while saving families $5 billion dollars in clean-up expenses reduced GDP by $1 billion.

The value of unpaid housework or the food grown in one's own garden is also excluded from GDP, even though a study for Britain found that it was roughly as large as measured GDP, because of the difficulty of measuring it and its year-to-year variations.[18] Similarly, the value of most government services cannot be measured directly. Imagine, for example, trying to attach a (positive or negative?) dollar value to the work of the Secretary of Defense. Hence, for many government services GDP measures, instead of the value of output, the value of inputs, such as the salaries of government employees. That implicitly assumes that the productivity of a dollar paid for these government services is the same in every year, that there are no gains in productivity over time. That may well be true in some cases, but not in all.

Moreover, GDP excludes important types of investment from its measure of investment and often from GDP itself. The cost of installing a new computer system consists not only of the required hardware and software, but also of the retraining of those who will use it. Yet the latter is lumped in with the costs of producing the firm's output, so that it does not appear as investment, or as an increase in GDP. The same is true for much R&D.

In addition, GDP is measured initially in nominal, that is, current dollar, terms. A price index, called "the GDP deflator," is then used to turn the nominal estimates into real ones. But price indexes are subject to a host of problems discussed below. These are by no means the only problems in estimating GDP.

Fortunately, there is an important ameliorating factor. This is, that the most common use made of the GDP data is to compare GDP in different periods, such as seeing whether GDP this calendar quarter is growing faster or slower than in the last quarter. For that, it does not matter very much that GDP does not take into account pollution or housework, etc., because these omissions impart approximately the same bias to the data in every period. Unfortunately, that is not so for many straight measurement errors. Because businesses as well as others want to know economic developments right away, the Commerce Department publishes preliminary data long before it has all the information it will subsequently use to generate more reliable data. Preliminary quarterly GDP data are released only one month from the end of the calendar quarter. Two months afterwards, they are revised. In July of each of the following three years they are revised again, and they receive a final revision every five years or so. Since these revisions can be substantial we should treat the preliminary figures with great caution. For example, on February 28, 2007, the real GDP growth rate for fourth quarter 2006 was revised downward from 3.5 to 2.2 percent.

International comparisons of GDP or per capita GDP have additional problems. Saudi Arabia, for example, is credited with a high per capita GDP because its oil production is treated as net output, rather than mostly as the running down of a natural resource, and hence as a reduction of capital rather than as income. A widely cited figure closely related to per capita GDP, the number of people living on less than a dollar a year, is also defective. These people earn their incomes in their local currencies, which the UN data then translate into dollars at the prevailing exchange rate. But exchange rates reflect, and inaccurately at that, only the prices of internationally traded goods, and not the prices of all goods and services, and also ignore that basic necessities are cheaper (and some luxury goods more expensive) in low-income countries than in the United States. A World Bank study[19] cites China's estimate of its 1992 per capita GDP as $390. By making an adjustment for differences in prices, as well as some other relatively minor adjustments, it raises that figure to $1,910, though it admits that this figure "is subject to wide margins of error that probably impart an upward bias."

The savings rate

The personal savings rate, that is, the percent of disposable personal income saved, was about 8 percent in the 1950s. It then rose to over 11 percent in 1982, and fell to 7 percent in 1990, before dropping precipitously to little over 2 percent in 2000, and to 0.4 percent in 2006. Does this mean that individuals are not saving enough for retirement, and that the nation as a whole has become much too dependent on foreign capital to finance its investment?

The answer depends – in part – on how income and saving are defined. For instance, an alternative measure of saving that, along with some other adjustments, treats the purchase of consumer durables as saving and treats only their depreciation as consumption, tells a very different story. Now, the decline in the savings rate from 1990 to 2000 is only about 0.6 percentage points, not as under the more common definition, 4.7 percentage points.[d] And even if consumer durable purchases are not counted as saving, the other adjustments reduce the decline in the savings ratio to only approximately 1.4 percentage points.[20] This does not necessarily mean that the fall in the savings rate is not a serious problem. For most purposes, the conventional way of measuring the personal savings rate may well be appropriate. But it does show how our perception of a problem may depend largely on the technical details of how we define certain measures.

PRICE INDEXES

As described in the next chapter, when dealing with a single, homogeneous good, making up a price index is straightforward. But what if there are many, heterogeneous goods as, for example, in making up a price index for consumer expenditures? A simple average of the prices of various goods and services that gives them all the same importance will not do. Most people are worse off if the price of gas rises by $2 per gallon while the price of ballet tickets falls by $2. If you want a price index that can be used to gauge changes in consumers' welfare or in the purchasing power of the consumers' dollar, you have to weigh each of the price changes by the percentage of consumer expenditures on that item.

And that creates a problem: how should we weigh the various goods? Consumers are not mindlessly passive. They react to price signals. If the price of beef goes up while the price of pork falls, they respond by buying more pork and less beef. Hence, if we weigh the prices of beef and pork by expenditures on them in the initial year, we overstate the loss that consumers have suffered. But if we weigh them by expenditures in the current year, we understate the loss, because consumers are worse off if they have had to switch from beef to pork to keep costs down. Fortunately, partial solutions to this

---

[d]   The other adjustments are in the inclusion of capital gains in income and saving, in the treatment of claims on pension funds, and the use of the real instead of the nominal interest rate in calculating consumer interest payments (interest paid on personal debt is treated in the GDP accounts as consumption expenditures.)

problem exist, but they require data on consumer expenditures on various items in every year, and that makes them expensive.

Changes in the quality of goods and services create a more important and even nastier problem. You may now pay $1,500 for a PC, just as you did in 1985, but you now get vastly more computing power for your money. You hear constant complaints about the cost of medical care rising much faster than inflation. But has it really done so? If now one visit to a physician who charges $80 clears up a problem that took three $40 visits five years ago, then in this instance, the cost of medical care has not doubled, but has fallen by one-third. And there has been a significant increase in life expectancy.

The introduction of new goods creates a similar problem. Suppose that per capita income since 1950 had risen as much as it did, but that the increase had consisted entirely of more of the same goods and services that were available in 1950: no personal computers, internet access, jet planes, disk players, new medical treatments, answering machines, etc. Wouldn't we be much worse off? And even among old goods, we now have access to a much greater variety, such as restaurants serving various types of ethnic foods. Yes, globalization has resulted in a greater choice, and not in homogeneity.

To drive home the importance of quality changes and of new goods, let me try to play a trick on you. Suppose you win a lottery and can choose between a $500 gift certificate for goods from the 1960 Sears-Roebuck catalog with all items at their 1960 prices, or else a $500 gift certificate for goods from the current catalogue at current prices. Which would you choose? If you choose the former, or if you hesitate between the two, then this suggests that there has been no inflation since 1960; that a dollar has just as much, or even more, value now than it did in 1960, even though the consumers' price index was seven times as high in 2007 as in 1960. Admittedly, the question just posed is unfair. Had the choice been between $500 gift certificates at produce stores, you would obviously have preferred the 1950 certificate. Moreover, at least some of your preference for current goods over 1950 goods is just a matter of fashion. All the same, this trick question does bring out the importance of quality changes and new goods.

Price indexes do try to take account of quality changes and of new goods. But they cannot do so completely. For instance, typically, when new goods appear, they do so at a high price, and are bought by few people. By the time they are in sufficiently widespread use to be included in the index, their prices have fallen substantially. The index misses that decline. In 1996 a government commission, the Boskin Commission, estimated that the upward bias in the consumers' price index was 1.1 percentage points per year, with a plausible range of 0.8 to 1.6 percentage points.[21] By no means everyone accepts this estimate, and, since it was made, the Bureau of Labor Statistics has improved the way it compiles this index. All the same, it tells us that the index has some serious problems.

To conclude, here is a question related to index numbers that is so difficult that I see no way of resolving it. Do present-day blue-collar workers have a higher or lower standard of living than Henry VIII of England? They certainly lack his army of domestic servants, and castles, but they have a lot of goods he didn't. Who is better off?

EMPLOYMENT

The government measures the number of people employed in two ways, with results that sometimes diverge significantly. One way, a survey of households, shows that by July 2004 employment had risen by about 1.5 percent over its March 2001 level. The other way, a survey of employers' payrolls, shows employment to have fallen by about 1 percent in this period. Hence, in the 2004 election campaign Democrats charged that during George W. Bush's presidency employment had fallen, while Republicans claimed that it had risen. Admittedly, the difference is usually not as great as that. And over the long run such differences tend to iron out.

Several factors account for the difference. One is that while the payroll survey counts the number of jobs, so that a person with two jobs is counted twice, the household survey counts such a person only once. Second, the payroll survey excludes the self-employed, agricultural workers, household workers, unpaid family workers, and workers on unpaid leave, but unlike the household survey does include workers under sixteen years old. All, seemingly technical details, but they can make a big difference.

THE POVERTY RATE

What is poverty is in the eyes of the beholder. But the eyes of most beholders do not differ all that much, so we want to measure it at least roughly. In the United States it is measured by using one available piece of relatively objective information. The US Department of Agriculture calculates the minimum cost of a nutritionally adequate diet for various types of families, "designed for temporary or emergency use when funds are low."[22] The threshold for poverty is then calculated by dividing these food costs by the proportion of their incomes that families spend on food, e.g., if these families spend one-third of their income on food, the poverty line is set at three times the cost of an adequate diet. The figure that is usually cited is the average thus calculated for various types of families, and is adjusted each year for inflation. In August 2005 it was $19,806 for a family of four, which defined 12.6 percent of Americans as poor.

This procedure is not without its critics. Some think that it is set too low, that with rising incomes we should adjust our measure of poverty to take into account rising standards of living. Others object that, in estimating the number of families living in poverty, we should include in family income, as we do not do now, the value of in-kind receipts from the government, such as Medicare and food stamps, and also the "free rent" that homeowners receive. Moreover, they point out that many families classified as poor are simply suffering a low income temporarily, and, therefore, can consume more than their current incomes. Also disturbing, is the fact that the recorded poverty rate was about the same in 2006 as thirty years earlier. This is counter-intuitive given the large increase in per capita income, the growth of anti-poverty programs, as well as data on consumer expenditures that show large increases in the expenditures of the poorest 20 percent of the population, and the strong evidence for the improved nutrition, health and housing of the poor. A possible explanation that has been suggested is that the year-to-year variability of income has increased, so that more people spend some time at an income level well below their normal one.

NOTES

1 Andrew Oswald and Hilda Ralsmark, "Some Evidence on the Future of Economics," www.andrewoswald.com (2007 papers).
2 See Friedrich Schneider and Dominik Ernste, *The Shadow Economy*, Cambridge, Cambridge University Press, 2002.
3 See W. Dewald, J. Thursby, and R. Anderson, "Replication in Empirical Economics," *American Economic Review*, September, 1986, pp. 587–603.
4 T. He Ling and Joseph McGarrity, "Data Errors in Small Data Sets Can Determine Empirical Findings," *Atlantic Economic Journal*, June, 2004, pp. 89–99.
5 Andrew Kamark, *Economics and the Real World*, Oxford, Blackwell, 1983.
6 Executive Office of the President, Washington, DC, 2008.
7 James Hamilton and Menzie Chin, "Intertemporal Measures of Housing Prices," www.econbrowzer, October 27, 2006.
8 Robert Hooke, *How to Tell the Liars from the Statisticians*, New York, Marcel Dekker, 1983, p. 26.
9 David Cowles, "Safer Than Ping-pong?," *New Republic*, February 27, 2006, p. 8.

10   *Damned Lies and Statistics*, Berkeley, University of California Press, 2001, p. 21.

11   Stats, 2004, www.stats.org/record.jsp?type=news&ID=412.

12   Thomas Sowell, *The Vision of the Anointed*, New York, Basic Books, 1995, p. 33.

13   Abdul Wafa, "70 Taliban Killed in Night Battle, NATO Force Says," *New York Times*, October 30, 2006, p. A11 (italic added.).

14   D. Murray, J. Schwartz, and S. Lichter, *It Ain't Necessarily So*, Oxford, Rowman and Littlefield, 2001.

15   Ibid., pp. 1–2.

16   Anonymous, "Washington Wire," *Wall Street Journal*, March 25, 2004, p. A4.

17   Betsey Stevenson and Justin Wolfers, "Divorced from Reality," *New York Times*, September 29, 2007.

18   Diane Coyle, *The Soulful Science*, Princeton, Princeton University Press, 2007, p. 105.

19   World Bank, *China*, Washington, DC, World Bank, 1995, p. 3.

20   Marshall Reinsdorf, "Alternative Measures of Personal Saving," *Survey of Current Business*, September 2004, pp. 17–27.

21   Advisory Commission to Study the Consumer Price Index (Boskin Commission), *Towards a More Accurate Measure of the Cost of Living, Final Report*, Washington, DC, 1996.

22   Gordon Fisher, "The Development and History of the US Poverty Threshold: A Brief Overview," http://aspec.os.dhh.gov.poverty/papers/hptgssiv.htm, 2006.

11

Some Simple (?) Ways of Presenting Data: Percentages, Figures, and Graphs

The previous chapter was a grand tour of some general problems encountered in reading economic statistics. By contrast, this short chapter looks at some nitty-gritty of two common and seemingly unproblematic ways of presenting statistics.

11.1 Percentages

Percentages may seem innocuous: doesn't everyone understands percentages? No, they don't. Percentages can be tricky, very tricky. Fortunately, there is an easy way to avoid being confused by them. This is to remember always that "percent" is Latin for "per hundred." That will induce you to ask "per hundred of what?", and thereby protect yourself against some pitfalls. That sounds simple, but doing so consistently takes practice, so as a form of drill let's work through ten examples, before looking at two other potential sources of confusion.

11.1.1 Examples of the misuse of percentages

One straightforward example of misstating a percentage is when a store advertises that it has cut a price by 100 percent. That is nonsense. Price cuts should be stated as a percent of the original price, so that a 100 percent price cut implies that the price is now zero.

A second, more subtle, example is if a price is cut by, say, 25 percent and then raised again by 25 percent, so that it *seems* to be back to where it was. No, it isn't. Suppose it was $1 initially, so that after being cut 25 percent it is now \$0.75. Raising it by 25 percent of 75 cents then brings it to only \$0.94.

Here is a third example: Suppose that public-sector employment and private-sector employments both rise by 5 percent. Does this mean that the government sector and the private sector each generated the same number of additional jobs? No: equal percentages translate into equal numbers only if the bases from which the percentages are calculated are equal. If government employment rose by 5 percent, that is, 5 percent of what *it* was before, and, similarly, if private employment rose by 5 percent, that too is 5 percent of what *it* previously was. Hence, unless government and private employment happen to be initially equal, they rose by different amounts.

Fourth, here is something I once found in a college textbook. (I have replaced the actual numbers the book gives by hypothetical ones, but that does not change the principle.) The careless author stated that in 1930 industrial production fell by 25 percent, in 1931 it fell by a further 20 percent, and in 1932 it fell again by 10 percent, so that in the 1930–2 period it declined by 55 (= 25 + 20 + 10) percent. What is wrong? The same thing as before. The 1930, 1931, and 1932 declines are all stated as percentages from different bases, and, therefore, cannot be directly added together. When the fall in employment is restated, as it should be, as a percentage declines from its level at the beginning of 1930 it amounts to 46 (= 25 + 15 + 6) percent, not 55 percent.

For a fifth example, suppose that a school has a program to reward its most effective teachers. It finds that 60 percent of these outstanding teachers are women and 40 percent are men. Does this mean that at least in this school a woman is more likely to be an outstanding teacher than a man? Not necessarily. Suppose that 90 percent of the teachers are female. In that case the data suggest that, if anything, men are more likely to be outstanding teachers. Again, the trick is to relate the percentage to its base.

Sixth, suppose you are a CEO of a bank and want to impress your stockholders with how high your profits are, while impressing your consumerist critics with how low they are. Without lying, you can readily accomplish this miracle. Tell your stockholders that you earned a 20 percent profit, and the consumerists that you earned a measly 2 percent profit. Both statements are correct. The trick is to switch the bases of the percentages. The 2 percent is the dollar amount of your profit expressed as a percentage of your bank's total assets. But since (let's assume) your bank's total assets are 10 times as large as your bank's capital (deposits make up most of the difference), a 2 percent return on total assets is equivalent to a 20 percent return on capital. A similar thing applies when profits are expressed as a percentage of sales. A company may only earn 1 percent profit on sales, but if its annual sales happen to equal 30 times its invested capital, that amounts to a 30 percent profit on its capital.

Seventh, assume that a corporation's profits this year are 500 percent of what they were last year. Lucky stockholders? Perhaps not, profits last year may have been only 0.1 percent of net assets, so that this year they amount to a measly 0.5 percent.

Eighth, assume that the prospectus of a mutual fund tells you that the fund charges an annual 0.8 percent management fee. Sounds fine. But it isn't. The 0.8 percent cited is not the percentage of the annual earnings of the fund, but 0.8 percent of the amount invested. Thus if the fund earns, say 8 percent a year the fee swallows up one-tenth of your earnings.

Ninth, suppose that last year teenagers accounted for 20 percent of all people arrested, while in the previous year they accounted only for 19 percent. Does that mean that last year more teenagers were arrested than in the previous year? Once again, no. The increase in the percentage tells you only what has happened to the frequency of teenager arrests *relative* to adult arrests. If adult arrests fell, then perhaps fewer teenagers were arrested last year than in the year before.

Finally, a smaller percentage of traffic accidents occur between 2 a.m. and 3 a.m. than between 8 a.m. and 9 a.m., but that does not mean that it is safer to drive at night. The moral of all these stories: knowing that something amounts to a certain percentage tells you nothing unless you know what it a percentage is of.

11.1.2   Some concerns about wording

Now let's look at two questions relating to correct English. First, if a price rises from $1 to $3 by what percentage has it risen? By 200 percent, not 300 percent. It is now 300 percent of what it was before, so that it has *increased* by 200 percent. Second, if profits rise from 10 percent to 12 percent of sales, how should you describe this increase? One way, is as a 20 percent increase; another, is as a 2 *percentage point* increase. Both ways are correct as long as you do not mix up percent with percentage points.

Another way percentages can be confusing is by hiding the number of actual cases. It is reputed that when Johns Hopkins University first admitted female students, an opponent of this assault on the very foundations of western civilization complained that one-third of these students had married their professors. He was right: one of the three women had.

Before leaving percentages, an aside on a related measure, index numbers. To calculate an index number of, say, prices, you select some particular year, as the "base year" and express prices in all the years in your sample as a percent of prices in that year. You then eliminate the percentage sign. That's all that's to it. Just be sure to remember that the value of the index in any one year depends on the particular base year you chose. If a price was $100 in 2001, $110 in 2005, and $111 in 2008, expressed as an index number with a 2001 base year it is 110 in 2005 and 111 in 2008. But if the base year is 2005 then in 2008 it is only 101.

11.2 Figures and Graphs

Much information about the economy comes in the form of figures and graphs. While they make it easy for the harried reader to grasp the data at a glance, they can also be confusing.

11.2.1 Types of graphs

The most common type of graph is the line graph which shows one or more statistical series as lines, while other graphs, such as a pie chart, provide pretty pictures.[a]

An important type of graph is a scatter diagram such as figure 11.1. This plots the linked values of two variables, so that you can see their co-movements, if any. For example, the horizontal axis might show industrial production and the vertical axis employment, with each point relating to a certain year,

---

[a] A special type of line graph, called a "semi-log" graph (but sometimes miscalled a "log graph"), has the vertical axis (or occasionally the horizontal axis) scaled, not in natural numbers, but in the logarithms of natural (that is, everyday) numbers. Still another type of graph, a genuine log graph, has both axes scaled in logs. You can quickly tell whether a graph is a conventional graph or a semi-log or a log graph by noting its scale. An axis scaled in logs looks like a reflection in a distorting mirror, e.g. the distance between 2 and 3 is equal to the distance between 20 and 30, and also the distance between 200 and 300, etc. Fortunately, you do not have to know anything about logs to read such a graph. Just remember that in the natural-numbers graph everywhere along the vertical axis going up by, say, one inch, measures equal absolute changes in the variable being graphed. Suppose, for example, that the scale is drawn so that going up a distance of one inch represents a move from $1 to $10. Going up the scale a further inch then represents a move from $10 to $20, and so on. By contrast, in a graph that has a logarithmic scale, equal distances mark off equal *percentage* changes. For instance, if the first inch denotes a move from $1 to $10, i.e. a nine-fold increase, the second inch also denotes a nine-fold increase, that is, a move from $100 to $1,000. As a result, on such a graph a constant percentage change shows up as a straight line, and not, as it does on a natural numbers graph, as a line with a slope that grows steeper and steeper.

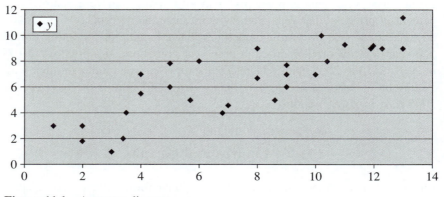

Figure 11.1   A scatter diagram

or else each point may show education and annual earnings for a hundred families, with each point representing one of the families. When, as in the case of industrial production and employment, each of the observations comes from a different year, the plotted points need not be, and usually are not, in a temporal sequence. Going in a westerly direction on such a graph, the first point might come from 1998, the second from 2005, the third from 2001, etc. Occasionally the date for each of the points is written next to the point, or a line is drawn connecting the points in a temporal sequence. Sometimes a straight line is drawn through a scatter diagram to represent an average relationship between the two variables.

11.2.2   How graphs can trick you

While graphs are easy to read they are also easy to misread. A quick glance at figures 11.2(a) and 11.2(b) suggests that profits are growing at a much faster rate in figure 11.2(b). But they are not. Both figures plot exactly the same numbers. Why then do they give such different impressions? The reason is that the vertical scale in figure 11.2(a) has been drawn all the way down to the zero line, while in figure 11.2(b) it has been truncated at 10. As a result, the same dollar change in profits looks like a much larger percentage change in figure 11.2(b) than it does in figure 11.2(a). Such a cut-off is quite common because it saves space, and despite giving a distorted impression of the percentage change, it does give the dollar amount of the change correctly. Always look whether the vertical scale has been cut off.

Also do look at the units marked on the scale. A $20 billion increase will show up as a much steeper rise if the vertical scale is such that one inch

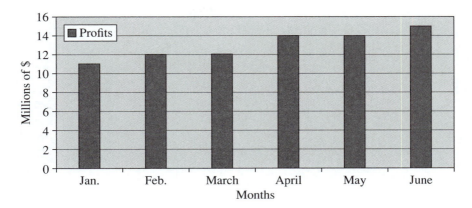

Figure 11.2(a) Profits

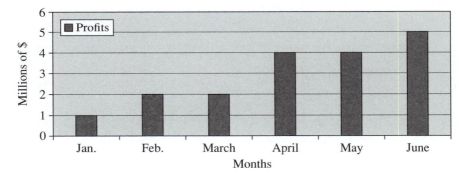

Figure 11.2(b) Profits, truncated

represents $10 billion, than if one inch represents $50 billion. And there is still another optical illusion you need to beware of. A quick glance at figure 11.3 might suggest that it shows two variables that are closely correlated. But a closer look will show that this is an illusion produced by a single dramatic point where the correlation is indeed close. In the rest of the figure, the two variables go their merry ways independently of each other.

Also watch for tricks with regard to the starting and ending dates. In figure 11.4 (based on hypothetical not real data) if one were to start the graph with 1992 it would show that real wages have risen. But if one were to start it with 1996 it would show them falling. Choosing starting or ending dates that support your argument is an easy way to bamboozle readers. And it occurs not

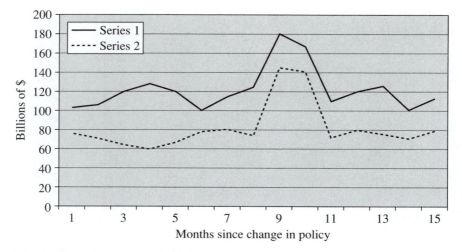

Figure 11.3   A spurious correlation

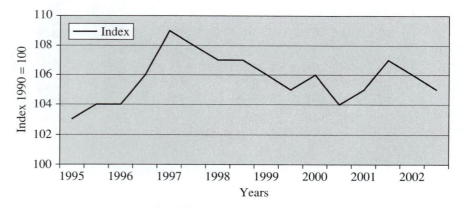

Figure 11.4   Index of real wages, widget manufacturing

only in graphs, but also in tables and in statements such as: "Since 2007 we
have raised our price by only 2 percent." Yes, but if you had looked back to
2006 you would have had to say that you had raised them by 20 percent.

    More generally, one should also be on the look-out for overly favorable (and
even totally wrong) verbal descriptions of what a graph shows. For example,
if I am convinced that the data will show that a certain variable is rising
(or am eager to convince you that it is) then, even if I do not play any tricks
when plotting the data, I will tend to interpret the graph as showing that the

variable is rising, even when, as in figure 11.4, to an objective observer, it is far from clear that it actually is. Here, as elsewhere, believing can be seeing. So, when you read that a certain figure or table shows something, look at it, and see if it really does. You may be surprised by how often it does not.

So much for time-series graphs: that is, graphs that show the behavior of a variable over time. Scatter diagrams present different problems. One is that they are hard to interpret. What looks to the eye like a random scatter, i.e., as no relation between the two variables, upon statistical analysis (as described in chapter 13) could turn out to exhibit a significant and important relationship. Moreover, it is easy for the eye to be distracted by a few extreme points, or to fail to notice that while the points plotted in one area of the scatter diagram suggest a positive relation between the two variables, those in another part suggest no relation, or perhaps even a negative relation. More on this problem in chapter 13.

12

Samples and Their Problems

Most of the data that economists use come from samples. Only occasionally do we have data on what statisticians rather grandiloquently call "the universe," that is, on all relevant cases. One reason is that gathering data is expensive, so that we try to make do with as few observations as we reasonably can. Another is that, when testing most theories, it would be impossible to avoid taking a sample, because most theories are general statements, such as "when the growth rate of the money supply increases substantially, the inflation rate rises," statements that are intended to apply to a wide range of past, present, and *future* circumstances.

This prevalence of samples raises two big issues that need to be addressed. First, was the sample derived in a way that is likely to make it representative of the universe, and, second, could the results it shows be due merely to random sampling error. The second of these questions (see below) requires a more abstract discussion than does the material discussed so far in this chapter, or for that matter most of the previous material, but it is only a few pages, and it is needed to understand the regression diagnostics discussed in the next chapter.

12.1   Selecting a Representative Sample

A representative sample is one that is typical of the universe with respect to the characteristics you are interested in. For instance, if you want to estimate the proportion of people in your suburb who go to a movie on a Saturday night, don't select your sample by standing in front of the parking lot of a cinema on Saturday night and asking passers-by whether they go to a movie on Saturday night. But calling the first name on each page of the telephone directory will give you a sufficiently random sample, as long as you don't call on a Saturday night.[a]

When economists work with hand-me-down data as they so often have to, the samples they work with will frequently not be completely random. But if the unrepresentativeness is minor it should not distort the results enough to matter. And even when the distortion is large, an unrepresentative sample – usually called "a biased sample" – might sometimes still provide useful information. Suppose that your sample is biased against the theory you are testing. If despite this, your theory survives the test, this test strengthens it more than an unbiased test would have. All the same, the question whether a sample is seriously biased, and if so in which direction, does need attention.

12.2 Watching for Inappropriate Samples

A bias in the sense of unrepresentativeness is not the only thing that may be wrong with a sample. Another is that the sample may not be related closely enough to what the author is claiming. A good illustration is the argument that the Fed should keep the inflation rate low, say, below 3 percent, because the data show that inflation reduces economic growth. If you take a sample of countries with a wide variety of inflation rates you do find that, other things being equal, there is a negative relation between the inflation rate and economic growth. But this negative relation is all due to countries that have a high inflation rate, and, therefore, does not provide an argument against, say, a 2 percent inflation rate. (This is not to deny that even low inflation has some bad effects, but that is no excuse for misused statistics.)

Another example is an ed-op article that supported gay marriages, because "social science research has established *beyond reasonable doubt* that marriage, on average, makes people healthier, happier, and financially better off."[1] Quite apart from the question whether causation runs from marriage to health, etc., or in the reverse direction, there is the problem that existing social-science research has looked only at heterosexual marriages, since those were the only marriages existing at the time. Maybe these results do carry over to same-sex marriages, I suspect that they do, but maybe they don't. The matter is not "beyond reasonable doubt."

---

[a] Purists might object that this sample, too, would not be completely random because people who frequently go to movies on Saturday nights might perhaps be less likely to be at home even when you call at other times. You might, therefore, want to choose your sample by using a table of random numbers. But that seems pedantic.

Following the publication of Richard's Herrnstein and Charles Murray's *The Bell Curve* there has been much discussion about whether the observed difference in the mean IQ scores of blacks and whites is due in part to genetic factors, as that book claims.[2] (Actually, one cannot properly separate environment from genetic factors, but let that pass.) One argument has been that within the population in general, environmental differences among individuals account for x points on an IQ test, so that if the black–white gap is, say, $2x$, then genetic factors must account for half of it. Here the error is that if on average the difference in environment factors between blacks and whites is greater than is the average difference in environmental factors in the population in general, as seems highly plausible, then one would expect the difference in environmental factors to contribute more than x points to the difference in mean black–white IQ scores. In other words, the difference in environmental factors among the population in general is the wrong sample for discussing the differences between blacks and whites.

12.3 The Regression Fallacy: Building a Bias into the Sample

A different type of trap in arguments based on what a sample shows, the regression fallacy, requires more attention because it is subtle, insidious, and hard to detect. So let's look at eight examples. The classic example, the one that gave it its name, was committed by the great geneticist Sir Francis Galton (1833–1911). He took a sample of men of great achievements and found that, on average, their sons had achieved less than their fathers had; they had *regressed* toward the mean of the population. From that, he drew the pessimistic conclusion that ability was declining from generation to generation. He was wrong. Why? Well, since the fathers were all high achievers, their sons could at most – that is, if all of them were also high achievers – make it seem that ability is constant from one generation to the next. And even if only a few of them were not high achievers, then Galton's test would necessarily show a decline in ability. But had Galton looked at the *fathers* of men of high achievements – some of whom were not high achievers themselves – he would have found that ability had *increased* from one generation to the next because all the sons in the second generation were high achievers, otherwise they would not have been included in the sample.

Suppose a study shows that some industries that were highly competitive twenty years ago have become less competitive since then, and concludes from this that competition has decreased in the American economy. This is wrong, because had the study looked at a sample of industries that were monopolistic twenty years ago, it would have found just the opposite. Some of them have become more competitive since then, so that it would have found that competition has increased.

Suppose a school district considers a new method of teaching reading. To evaluate this method, it takes all the students with readings skills in the lowest quartile, tries the new method on them, and finds that they have improved. It, therefore, switches to the new method. Next year, average reading scores drop. How could that be? The sample of students on which the new method was tried consisted entirely of those who did not learn well with the old method, and it paid no attention to those for whom the old method was better suited than the new.

There have been many studies comparing the performance of managed mutual funds with what investors would have earned had they just bought a representative sample of stocks and hung on to them.[b] Some of the earlier studies did what comes naturally: they selected a representative sample from a list of currently existing mutual funds. But that created a bias, called the "survivorship bias," because mutual funds that did badly are more likely to have disappeared than more successful ones. What they should have done is to select a sample of mutual funds that existed at the beginning of the period covered by the study.

Assume that you take a representative sample of people who are currently unemployed, and ask them for how long they have been unemployed. From their responses, you conclude that the mean unemployment spell is, say 6 months. That is incorrect. A person who is unemployed for, say, 12 months is 12 times as likely to be unemployed in the particular month in which you happen to take the survey than is someone who is unemployed only one month. She is, therefore, 12 times as likely to be included in your sample, so that your estimate of the average length of an unemployment spell has an upward bias.

Here is a personal example. Many years ago the National Gallery in Washington was crowded and I was bothered by the noise of people talking. Having heard several people speaking German, I thought: "Germans do talk a lot in museums." This was wrong. There could have been many silent Germans present, and I would not have known it.

---

[b] One reason why professionally managed mutual funds perform on average less well than the market as a whole, and hence less well than a random sample of stocks, is in part that, as explained in appendix 2.1, financial markets tend to be efficient, and in part that mutual funds charge their stockholders a far from trivial fee for their services.

Finally, it is part of folk wisdom that if something starts to go better for you and you tell people about it without saying "touch wood" it will get worse again. What's the experience behind this? Think of what is going better for you as obtaining heads when you toss a coin, and you have just gotten five heads in a row. There is a 50 percent chance that on the next toss your good luck will end. Since it is likely that you will not have remarked on your good luck until after you got several heads in a row, it is not surprising that after you talked about it your good luck ends. Your sample of cases in which things turned out badly after you talked about them is not a representative sample of cases, but is a sample of cases in which you have been lucky at first, and it is in the nature of luck that you cannot expect it to continue.

12.4   Sample Size and Coincidence

Suppose that you have avoided the snares of the regression fallacy, and your sample is a representative one. You still have to worry about whether it is large enough. A common mistake in casual discussions about economics is to use too small a sample; by and large, we tend to make too little allowance for coincidence. Perhaps this stems in part from our wish to see the world as a predictable place – which also helps to explain why astrology still flourishes alongside of science – and in part from our failure to consider the vast number of cases in which a coincidence could have occurred, but did not. If the chance of something happening is 1 in 100,000, then don't be surprised when it does happen once in 100,000 times. And we all experience many thousands of events every week. It may seem that 3 planes crashing at the same airport within a week cannot be a coincidence, but there are 7,300 days in a 20-year sample period, and lots of airports with many flights each day, so don't insist on a "deep cause" when once every 20 years you hear about such an event. That does not mean, of course, that you should not look for a common cause, but it does mean that you should not insist that there must be one.

Here is an exercise: look at figure 12.1 and see if you can find a pattern, or make out what the mysterious y that it charts is. If you can't, don't be disappointed. What it shows is a sequence of numbers from a table of random numbers.[c] Much money has been lost by investors who thought they saw patterns in stock prices. Yes, in the past, every time the event x occurred, the

---

[c]   No, I did not cheat by trying various sets of random numbers until I got one that looked like a pattern. The data shown in figure 12.1 are the only set of random numbers that I tried.

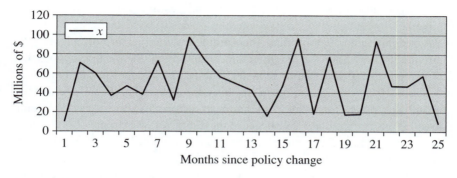

Figure 12.1   A mystery series

stock market went up. But with thousands of potential x's out there, it would be surprising if, in the past, one or more of them were not correlated with stock prices purely by coincidence, and hence offer no guide to what will happen in the future.

12.5   Sampling Error, Confidence Intervals, and Significance

Just as in tossing a hundred pennies one would not expect to get exactly fifty heads, so one would not expect the mean of the sample to be exactly equal to the mean of the universe. This and similar differences between the universe and the sample are what economists and statisticians mean when they talk about sampling error: an inevitable error, not a human error.

We cannot be certain how large this error is. But what we can do is estimate the *probability* that is no greater than a certain number. This why public opinion polls after giving you the president's approval rating as shown by their sample mean tell you that this figure is accurate within a range of, say, plus or minus 3 percent. Such a 6 percent range around the mean is called the "confidence interval."

What does this confidence interval depend on and how is it calculated? One factor is the size of the sample. Suppose you estimate the mean of the universe from a sample of only 10 observations. Then, the inclusion of a single extreme observation, say one that is 5 times as large as the mean, would have a strong influence on the estimated sample mean. But with a sample of 1,000, those observations that differ greatly from the mean of the universe in either direction largely offset each other; the good old "law of large numbers" takes over, and the sample mean is a reliable estimate of the mean of the universe.[d]

A second factor determining the confidence interval is how closely the individual observations in the universe cluster around the mean. Suppose that 99 percent of the observations cluster within a band equal to the mean plus or minus 10 percent of the mean. In this case, the probability of the sample mean being pulled *far* away from the mean of the universe by a few extreme observations is extremely low, because there are so few extreme observations. By contrast, if only 5 percent lie within plus or minus 10 percent of the mean, while 20 percent lie far from the mean, then the probability that a few large observations will distort the sample and give you a false estimate of the mean of the universe is much greater.

A simple measure of how closely clustered the observations are around the mean is the "mean deviation." To calculate this, you take the difference between each of the observations and the mean, ignore the signs of these differences, add them, and divide this total by the number of observations.[e] A more important, but a bit more complex, measure is the "standard deviation," often abbreviated by the Greek letter sigma (written as σ). To calculate it, you obtain the deviations from the mean as you do for the mean deviation, but before adding them you square them, and then divide the total of these squared deviations, by the number of observations. Then take the square root,[f] and that's your standard deviation.

Fortunately, for many distributions of the data, or "frequency distributions" as statisticians call them, once you have calculated the standard deviation you can tell what the confidence limits of your mean are. For the familiar bell curve distribution, also called the "normal distribution" or the "Gaussian distribution," approximately two-thirds of the observations lie within one standard deviation either side of the mean, 95 percent lie within two standard deviations, and approximately 99 percent lie within three standard deviations either side of the mean. Suppose, for instance, that in a random sample of men's heights taken from a normally distributed universe the mean height is 5 feet, 10 inches, and the standard deviation is 1 inch. then if you say that

---

[d] However, the accuracy of a sample does not change in proportion to the increase in the size of the sample. To cut the sampling error in half, you have to quadruple the size of the sample.

[e] Adding pluses and minus is a legitimate mathematical operation. It gives you a sum that is expressed neither as a positive nor a negative number, but as an "absolute number," and that is appropriate when talking about a difference.

[f] No, squaring the deviations, taking their mean, and then taking the square root of this mean, does not give the same answer as not squaring the deviations, and then not taking the square root. If you don't believe me, try it.

the mean height in the universe from which you have taken your sample is somewhere between 5 feet 8 inches and 6 feet, despite the existence of a sample error, if you do this often enough, you will be right in 95 percent of the cases.

Here is another application. Suppose you have a sample of students who have taken a test, and use this sample to see whether students who got special coaching did better on it. You find that the ones who got coaching had a mean score of 102, while other students had a mean of 97. Is such a 5-point difference likely to be due just to sampling error? If the standard deviation is 2, so that the difference between the two groups is equal to two and a half times the standard deviation, then (assuming that student scores are normally distributed), if you say that the difference between the coached students and other students is statistically significant and not just the product of sampling error, you will be right in 95 percent of the cases.

This can be described as saying that the coefficient of the coaching variable is 5 and its standard deviation – which in these situations is usually called its "standard error" – is 2. For easy comparison, the coefficient is often divided by its standard error, and the resulting ratio is called the coefficient's "t ratio" or just its "t."

How large must the t value be before can you say that the results are meaningful and not just due to sampling error? This question has no definitive answer. The lower you set the standard for the t value at which you say that your results are meaningful, the more false results, that is, results that are merely due to sampling error, you will unknowingly accept, and the higher you set the standard for the t value the more true results you will reject in the belief that they may just be due to sampling error. It's a trade-off. And since there is no definitive answer, we rely on a convention. This is, to accept a result obtained from the sample as meaningful only if the probability of it being due merely to sampling error is less than 5 percent, that is, if its t value is 2 or greater. Sometimes, however, a result is given limited credence even though it is significant only at the 10 percent level.

Why 5 percent, why not 6 percent, or 4.498 percent? Well, as the old saying has it: "there is no reason for it, it's just our policy." Five percent is a reasonable number. It is low because science traditionally, and rightly, puts the burden of proof on a new hypothesis. You have to make a strong case for it before it is accepted as part of our knowledge base.

But don't blindly follow the 5 percent convention in deciding what to do. Suppose you are on a panel evaluating drug safety. If there is a 6 percent probability that a certain drug that is intended to whiten your teeth will turn your toe nails slightly yellow, you may consider the drug safe, but you would not do so if there is a 4 percent chance that it will cause heart failure. Whether you accept and act on a hypothesis should depend not only on the probability that the hypothesis is correct, but also on the gains and losses that occur if you accept the hypothesis when it is actually false, or reject it when it is true. It's the old story; after having made a lot of calculations you still have to make a judgment.

12.6   Some Warnings about Significance Tests

A significance test is a powerful tool with which to penetrate the fog emitted by sampling errors. But it has its limitations. One is that looking at the *t* values protects you only against the danger of errors that are random, such as sampling errors and certain types of errors in gathering and keypunching the data, and not against anything else, such as use of a biased sample. Sampling errors get considerable attention because they are measurable, and if you are too strenuously trying to be "scientific," you tend to concentrate excessively on what you can measure at the expense of what you can't. Moreover, papers with sickly *t* statistics are usually not publishable, so that researchers have an incentive to mine their data until their *t* values look good. This undermines the rationale of significance tests. It is a bit like tossing 60 pennies 5 times and then being surprised if one of these pennies comes up heads five times.

A second problem is that you must ask not only whether a coefficient is significant in the sense that it is unlikely to be merely the result of sampling error, but also whether it is important and hence "significant" in a substantive sense? Suppose you have an immense sample, so that your standard error is very, very small. Then, a coefficient, or the difference between the means of a sample of males and a sample of females, could be statistically significant at the 5 percent level, without being substantively – and hence practically – significant. Suppose you find that the probability of having an automobile accident is 0.00001 percent greater for male than for female drivers, and that this result is statistically significant at the 5 percent level. So what? Who cares about such a trivial difference? To be meaningful, a difference must be significant in both the statistical and the substantive senses.

Now let's look at the opposite case: suppose you find that, as your hypothesis predicts, *x* has a strong effect on *y*, but that in your sample this effect is not statistically significant at the 5 percent level. You are disappointed. Can you console yourself by saying "well, at least I have demonstrated that the hypothesis is false, and that, too, is a contribution to knowledge"? No, you can't even do that. The low *t* statistic does not tell you that the hypothesis is false. Perhaps it is low only because your sample is too small. I cannot confirm that it will rain on January 18, 2027, but that does not entitle me to say that it will *not* rain that day. A jury's decision that the suspect's guilt has not been proven beyond reasonable doubt does not mean that the jurors are convinced of her innocence. This point is worth stressing, because, at times, even sophisticated economists have ignored it.

APPENDIX 12.1

The Normal Distribution

Assume that the value of a variable, *y*, depends on many factors, some raising it, and some lowering it. Assume further that they all have approximately the same strength, and also, that they are independent of each other. Given these conditions, if you have a large sample of *y*'s they will tend to follow a normal distribution. (You need about 50 observations before you can feel comfortable in assuming that you have a normal distribution.) Here is why: it would take an unusual coincidence for all of them, or even for most of them, to change *y* in the same direction at the same time. Hence, it is more likely that *y* will be closer to its average value than that it will be close to one of the extreme values which it would have if all the factors were pushing it in the same direction. Suppose you toss two coins. The possible outcomes are HH, HT, TH, and TT, that is, one case of zero heads, one case of two heads, but two cases of one head and one tail, so that the mean value of the number of heads is more frequent than is either extreme. If we toss enough coins to smooth out random fluctuations, we get the smooth bell-shaped curve shown in figure 12.2.

The normal curve describes well the distribution of many variables. Men's height is the classic example. But "many" does not mean "all." Do not let yourself be taken in by the label "normal." An interesting case occurs when the effect that various factors have on *y* is proportionately greater for large values of *y* than for small values of *y*. Then you tend to get a so-called "log-normal distribution": that is, a distribution in which the logarithms of the observations are normally distributed. Here is an example: imagine that you set up a separate trust fund lasting twenty years for each of thirty people, with each year's earnings and capital gains to be reinvested in a large sample of securities that differ among the trust funds. After twenty years, will the values of these trust funds be normally distributed? No they won't. Those funds

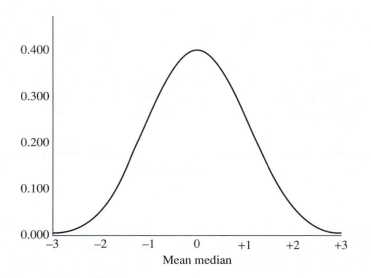

Figure 12.2   The normal distribution

that do well in the first year will have more money to invest in the second year, and, therefore, can be expected to have higher earnings (in dollar terms, though not in percentage terms) in the second year, and so on for the rest of the twenty years. Many variables, for instance, the distribution of income, the number of books written by an author, the number of ships sunk by different German submarine commanders in World War II, have approximately this "log-normal" distribution. It is just as "normal" in the ordinary sense of the term as is the normal distribution of natural numbers.

Although many data sets can be approximated by either normal or log-normal distributions others can not. For some of these there are other distributions that can be used, but not for others. All the same, economists usually assume that their data are normally or log-normally distributed, a rather questionable practice (mea culpa), and hence a further reason for being less than entirely convinced by *t* tests.[g]

---

[g]   Economists often test whether their data are normally distributed, but accept the hypothesis that they are, unless a *t* test rejects this hypothesis at the 5 percent level. This is unconvincing: the fact that you cannot reject a hypothesis at the 5 percent level does not allow you to say that it is likely to be true.

NOTES

1   Jonathan Rauch, "Imperfect Unions," *New York Times*, August 15, 2004, section 4, p. 11, italic added.
2   Richard Herrnstein and Charles Murray, *The Bell Curve*, New York, Free Press, 1994, ch. 13.

13

Regressions: The Workhorse of Empirical Economics

[J]udgment causes one to be wary of statistical relationships, regardless of statistical significance level. Significance of results can be determined only by having a deep understanding of all aspects of the issue. One must have knowledge of all the relevant theory relating to the subject, knowledge of the broader literature on that subject, and knowledge of the institutions that are central to the issue being looked at.
(David Colander, *The Making of an Economist: Redux*, p. 243)

The main statistical tool used in economics is regression analysis. This is a way of seeing whether two or more statistical series move consistently in either the same or in opposite directions, and if so, by how much one series changes when the other one does: in other words, seeing how they are *co-related*, and how precise this co-relationship is. Suppose we want to explain or predict sales of tweezers. We call sales the "dependent variable," since we want to find out what variables it depends on. We then rely on economic theory or on ordinary common sense to tell us what these determining variables – called the "independent variables," or more frequently the "regressors" – are. They are called "independent variables" because, while they affect the sale of tweezers, we assume that the sale of tweezers does not, in turn, affect them.[a] (More later on what happens if, as is frequently the case, this condition is not met.)

In the natural sciences two variables often have an exact relation that can be stated as a scientific law. For example, one variable y is always exactly

---

[a] It is also possible to solve a set of regression equations simultaneously where the dependent variable in one equation becomes the independent variable in another one.

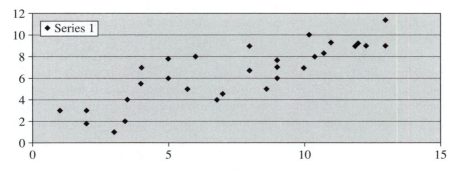

Figure 13.1 Relation between two variables

b times as large as another variable, x. In that case, we do not need regression analysis. All we have to do is to look at the values of any pair of x's and y's and we can calculate from this the value of b. But this does not work if x is not the only variable affecting y, so that, as in figure 13.1, the relation between x and y is not exact. Given their position on the horizontal axis, some points are at too high a position on the vertical axis, and vice versa. One way to think of regression analysis is to imagine that there *is* an exact underlying relationship between x and y, such as y equals $3x$, but that before you are given the data someone has sprinkled some positive and some negative random numbers on the y's. Your task is to dig out the true relations of x and y from the polluted observations that you are given. Specifically, it is to: (1) determine the size of the effect on y of a unit change in x; (2) to ascertain whether this effect is statistically significant; and (3) to estimate what proportion of the change in y that we observe is accounted for by changes in x.

13.1   The Regression Coefficient

For simplicity let's assume that the relation between x and y can be depicted by a straight line. The equation for a straight line with just a single independent variable is $y = a + bx$, where a and b are constants, that is, numbers that do not vary, say 34 and 8. Then b tells you that if x changes by 1 unit, y changes by 8 units. It is like a gearing ratio transferring changes from x to y.

What a regression of y on x then does is to select the particular values for a and b that give the best prediction of y you can get from knowing the value of x. More precisely, the computer selects those values for a and b that minimize the squared differences between the values of y that the regression predicts and the actual values of *y*. To simplify, forget for the moment about the squaring and also about the constant, *a*, and think how you would describe a situation where – as a general rule – *y* increases by 3 whenever *x* increases by 1, but sometimes increases by a bit more and sometimes by a bit less. Wouldn't it make sense to say: *y* equals 3*x* plus or minus a fudge factor? This fudge factor is called the "error term." Insofar as it results from random sampling errors it will, in a large enough sample, be normally distributed. And with positive and negative numbers tending to cancel out, its mean will approach zero as the sample gets larger and larger. Insofar as the fudge factor is due to the influence of some additional independent variables that we omitted, but should have included, we also assume, or to be more honest, we hope, that these errors, too, will be normally distributed, and hence more or less cancel out.

Suppose the computer calculates that *a* is, say, 10 and *b* is 3. Due to sampling and other errors (i.e., the fudge factor) this does not allow us to say that *y* must be 13 whenever *x* is 1. But insofar as these errors are random, we do know from the previous chapter what to do about this. We look at the standard errors (i.e., the standard deviations) to get the range within which we can reasonably expect *a* and *b* to fall, usually going out plus and minus two standard errors to get to the 5 percent probability level. Or, if we just want to know whether there is a less than 5 percent probability that in the universe either *a* or *b* are actually zero, we check if their values, called "point estimates," differ from zero by more than two standard errors, that is, if their *t* values are 2 or greater.

What do these *a*'s and *b*'s really measure? Since *a* is a constant, that is, the same regardless of what *x* is, it can be interpreted as the value of *y* when *x* is zero. And it can be positive, negative, or zero.[b] Since we are primarily concerned with how *x* affects *y*, and not with what *y* is when *x* equals zero, this constant term is normally of little interest. Instead, what we are interested in is the coefficient *b*, called the "regression coefficient." Graphically, it is the slope of the regression line, that is, the line drawn through the cluster of the points (observations), so that it minimizes the squares of the deviations

---

[b]   The value of the constant can be intrepreted in two ways. One is, as above, as the value of *y* when *x* is zero. However, this is often not the best way to think of it, because in many cases, for example, in the relation of income to education, a zero value for either variable is seldom, if ever, observed. In most cases, a better way of interpreting the constant is as a term that is added to the regression equation to avoid having the computer choose a value for *b* so that *y* is zero when *x* is zero. This allows it to pick a value for *b* that gives the best fit over the range that the data actually inhabit.

of the points from the line, and in that sense is the best representation of the observations.

So far, I have assumed that the relation between x and y can be described by a straight line. Strictly speaking, there is no reason why this should be so, but usually it is a close enough approximation so that we can use it.[c] And when the data are not well described by a straight line in natural numbers their logs may be. If so, we fit the regression to their logs. Using logs has the advantage that the changes in both the dependent and the independent variables can then be read off as percentage changes.

Until now, we have worked with just one regressor. But usually, things are more complicated because the behavior of y depends on many factors; for example, the demand for cars depends not just on the price of cars, but also on the price of gas and of public transportation, the prices of competing goods, on incomes, and on people's fondness for cars. Hence, we often need to include many regressors: if, say five independent variables have a substantial effect on the dependent variable we need to write the regression equation as: $y = a + bx_1 + cx_2 + dx_3 + ex_4 + fx_5 + e$, where the subscripts of the various x's denote different regressors, and e is the error term. One can include many independent variables in a regression, provided that there are enough observations. Most regressions now use more than one regressor, but to keep the discussion simple let's for the time being talk about a single regressor.

13.2 How Well Does the Regression Fit the Data?

Suppose your computer tells you that car sales decrease by 5 percent when the interest rate on automobile loans rises by one percentage point. That is useful information if you work in the marketing department of an automobile company. But it does not tell you to what extent changes in car sales that you observe are explained by changes in interest rates, rather than by other factors, such as changes in consumer incomes. It is possible that the prediction that each percentage point change in the interest rate lowers car sales by 5 percent is highly accurate, and yet most of the actually observed changes in car sales could be explained by factors other than changes in interest rates.

Economists and statisticians measure how well the regression equation fits the data, that is, how well you can predict y (car sales) just from knowing x

---

[c] It is also possible to use regression equations that have nonlinear regressors, such as x^2 but that sometimes causes the computer program to hang up.

Box 13.1: The Coefficient of Determination

To calculate R^2 you compare two guesses about the values of each of the y's. One is the guess you would make if you did not have any knowledge at all about the relation of x and y, and the other is the guess you make when you have the regression equation linking x to y available, and know the values of each of the x's. For example, if you want to guess the annual consumption expenditures of a particular family you know nothing about, the best you could do is to use the mean for all families. Now suppose you are told the family's income, and also the regression equation: consumption expenditures = $20,000 + 0.8 income. You could then use this information to estimate the family's consumption.

In this case, as well as in the case where you did not have the regression equation available and just used the mean consumption expenditures of all families, your estimate will contain some error. And the relative size of the errors in these two cases tells you by how much having the regression equation has improved your estimate. You can, therefore, express the error when you have the equation as a ratio to the error when you don't. If the equation would give a perfect fit your error when you use it would be zero, and hence the ratio would also be zero, while if the equation does not help you at all the two errors will be the same and their ratio will be 1. But it's a bit inconvenient to use as your measure of how well your regression equation fits the data a ratio that is lower the better is your equation, so let's use a trick, and that is to express the measure of correlation not as the above ratio, but as 1 minus that ratio. That turns it the right away round: now the better the correlation, the higher is the measure of the correlation.

One more step is needed. For technical reasons it is better not to compare the mean errors you get with and without use of the equation, but to compare instead the means of the squared errors. And this is what R^2 measures.

(interest rates), by the coefficient of correlation, R, or more usually by its cousin, R^2, the coefficient of determination. R and R^2 lie in the range of 0 to 1 and, subject to important qualifications discussed below, it measures the proportion of the variation in y – or more precisely the proportion of the squared variation in y – that is explained by variations in x.[d] (For a further discussion of R^2 see box 13.1.)

---

[d] Although R^2 cannot be negative since squaring a natural number cannot yield a negative number, it is sometimes sloppily reported as negative to remind the reader that the relation between x and y is negative.

Hence, other things being equal, if you want to find the factors that best explain the observed changes in your dependent variable you should choose a regression equation that has a R^2 of, say 0.8 over a regression equation that has an R^2 of only 0.5. But don't overdo this: a small difference in R^2, such as between, say, 0.834 and 0.830, is meaningless, and might even be reversed had you used a different computer program. And besides, other things are often not equal.

13.3   What Should You Look at in a Regression?

Which is the important measure, R^2, the size of the regression coefficient, or its t value? The answer is: "all of the above." All three are important because they answer different questions. Suppose you ask how well your regressors explain or predict the behavior of y. Then, as just discussed, R^2 is the relevant measure. But if your question is whether a one-unit variation in the regressor has a sizeable effect on the dependent variable, then you have to look first at the t value of its coefficient to guard against the danger of ascribing important-ance to the result of mere sampling error. And you also have to look at the substantive significance of the coefficient to see if the effect is large enough to matter. Here you need to pay attention to the units in which x and y are measured. For example, if in estimating the determinants of the interest rate the regression coefficient of the federal deficit is, say, 0.001, it does make a difference whether this means that the interest rate rises by 0.001 percent when the deficit increases by a million dollars or by a billion dollars.

Attention to the units of measurement is necessary, but not sufficient, to establish whether the coefficient is "large" or is too small to matter. Here there is no mechanical rule like the 5 percent convention of statistical significance. What is needed is *your* judgment, not the computer's.

When looking at the coefficient of a regressor you should also be careful not to confuse its size or its t value with its importance in explaining the observed changes in y. For explaining these changes, what matters is not only the size of the regression coefficient, but also how much the regressor itself changes. Even if the regression coefficient of x_1 is much larger than the regression coefficient of x_2, if x_2 varies much more than x_1 does, then variations in x_2 could perhaps account for a larger proportion of the observed changes in y. Suppose that in a regression explaining the percentage of income saved by families you include a regressor, x_8, for whether the family had a child that year. The regression coefficient for this regressor is likely to be large, but it will not explain much of the variation in the percentage of income saved by the families in your sample, since in any particular year for most families x_8 will be zero.

Even if you are interested only in how well your regression explains and predicts the dependent variable you should look not only at R^2, but also at the individual regression coefficients and their t values. Suppose you regress the sale of Christmas cards on the unemployment rate and, to take account of seasonality, also on an additional regressor, a so-called "dummy variable," that in this case takes a value of 1 in December and 0 in other months. You get a high R^2. But that does not tell you that changes in unemployment have much effect on Christmas card sales – you would also get a high R^2 even if you had used instead of the unemployment rate, the number of kittens born that month, because it is the seasonal dummy, not the unemployment rate that does the work. ("It's the dummy, dummy.") There is a story about a peddler who came to a village, announced that he had a special stone for sale out of which you could make a wonderful soup, and offered to demonstrate it. As he was boiling the stone he told the villagers that stone soup was delicious, but would taste even better if some carrots were added. So they put some carrots into the pot. As it came to boil he told them that adding some onions would make it even better. And after adding the onions he told them that to get the very best stone soup they should add some meat!

Finally, suppose you are interested only in the effect that a certain regressor has on y, and not in explaining what determines most of the changes in y. Even so, you should also look at R^2 to see whether the regression explains enough of the variation in y to be meaningful. If a regression leaves 98 percent of the variation in y unexplained you cannot put much trust in it.

How large then must R^2 be for the regression coefficients to be meaningful? A good question, but one that has no good answer. It depends, in part, on how high an R^2 rival regressions have obtained. It also depends on the specifics of the dependent variable.[e] Some studies with an R^2 of 0.2 or less have been published in highly reputable journals, though I, myself, find such low R^2's somewhat disturbing. At the other extreme, an R^2 of, say, 0.998, is also disturbing, because it is too good to be true, and might be due to both variables having the same time trend, or y having a common component with x.

---

[e] For example, suppose you are trying to explain the saving rate of families. If your dependent variable is the saving rate of individual families you will get a low R^2, since many idiosyncratic factors, which are not in your regression equation, such as job loss, receipt of a large gift, etc., will affect the saving ratio of particular families. But if your data are the average saving rates of families grouped into various income classes, these idiosyncratic factors will essentially cancel out, so that you should set the bar higher for R^2.

13.4   A Summing Up

This has been a complex discussion, so let's review it. Suppose you are writing an article on whether the government should aid the residential construction industry during a recession. The industry's website argues that, as goes residential construction, so goes the nation's economy, buttressing its argument with a regression relating the quarterly level of GDP (the dependent variable) to the previous quarter's GDP and to that quarter's residential construction. R^2 is 0.91. Leaving aside the issue of causality should you be impressed? Not really. Since GDP in any one quarter is highly correlated with the previous quarter's GDP, you might get that high a R^2 even if you had used temperature fluctuations in India instead of residential construction. So, you look also at the regression coefficient of residential construction, and find that it is substantively significant; a dollar spent on residential construction raises GDP by $4. Seems a bit implausible, so you look at the t value of this coefficient, and it is only 0.5. You rightly reject the industry's argument.

   Now let's add a complication. Suppose the t value had been 1.9, what then? You could be hardnosed and say that since there is a greater than 5 percent chance that the true value of the coefficient is zero, you will not accept the industry's argument. Or you could say that, while the industry has not met the scientific standard of proof, there is a substantial probability that the true value of the coefficient is greater than zero. Hence, you might tentatively accept the industry's argument. In fact, you *should* do so if you think the loss from accepting this evidence for the industry's position when it is actually wrong is no greater than the loss from not accepting it when it is actually correct.

13.5   Looking the Workhorse in the Mouth

Regression analysis is powerful tool, used in many fields and for many purposes – see, for instance, boxes 13.2 and 13.3, and chapter 14 – but it also has the potential to mislead. Four important traps are the danger of projecting past relationships into the future, the need to include the correct control variables, the possibility of being misled by one or several extreme observations, and the danger of inferring causation from correlation.

   As you read about these dangers, you might get the impression that what I am saying is that regression analysis, and hence most of empirical economic analysis plus much of other social science research is worthless, that we might as well rely on our intuition, feelings and prejudice. This is not so; decidedly

Box 13.2: Measuring Trends

One common use of regressions is to find the trend of a series, such as GDP. All you have to do is to assign consecutive numbers, e.g., 1, 2, 3 . . . n, to each of your consecutive (say annual) observations, and then regress your y variable on these numbers. Measuring trends is useful not only for prediction, but also for showing how the change in a variable during a particular period compares to its usual change. For example, it is easier to make sense of a report that "employment grew last month by slightly more than its trend," than to interpret a report that "it grew by 110,000." The reader does not know whether 110,000 is a "large" or a "small" increase.

Another way to hear the quiet but steadfast voice of long-run change through the incessant chatter of short-run fluctuations is to fit a moving average to the data. The basic idea is that you get a better fix on some data, say stock prices, if you look not just at their current value, but at their average value over some time. So you pick a period of a certain length (often a more or less arbitrary choice), say five years, take the mean for these five years, and plot this mean at the middle year of the five-year period. You then drop the first year and add a year at the end, and plot this as the point for the next year, and so on. Such a moving average irons out much of period-to-period fluctuation, but is not as rigid as a straight-line trend.

Here are two warnings about trends. First, the value of the trend coefficient can sometimes be manipulated by choosing a particular starting or ending date. If you start with a year when the variable was unusually low you will get a faster growth rate than if you start with a year when it was high. Second, trend is not destiny. Do not heed either the warnings of prophets of doom, or the rash promises of the starry-eyed, when they project current trends far into the future. If the stock market has risen by 30 percent per year for the last three years, it will surely not continue to do so for the next ten years. Sorry about that.

Unfortunately, while predicting what will happen by analyzing the underlying factors is difficult, projecting a trend is easy, and often leads to dramatic and hence newsworthy conclusion, particularly if readers forget the proviso: "*if* current trends continue." The proper response to trend enthusiasts is to say that long before the time when their predictions will be put to a test all of us will be dead, swallowed up by a gigantic cat. There is a kitten in our neighborhood that is now twice as large as it was a week ago. Projecting this trend for five years . . .

Box 13.3: Using Regressions to Detect Gender Discrimination

A standard way of detecting job discrimination is to use regression analysis to determine whether a person's race or gender helps to explain his or her salary relative to the salary of other employees with similar qualifications. Let's see how you would do that to test for discrimination against female professors. First, you would think of all the variables that may determine of a professor's salary. You might then write the following equation: $y = a + bx_1 + cx_2 + dx_3 + ex_4 + fx_5 + gx_6 + hx_7$. Here y is the salary of every professor in the sample, a is a constant, x_1 is a measure of the quality of the university where the professor received his or her Ph.D., x_2 is years since receipt of the Ph.D., x_3 the professor's field, x_4 his or her teaching evaluations, x_5 an index of publications, x_6 gender, and x_7 all the other variables that should be included but must be ignored because they are not known or cannot be measured. The significance, both statistically and substantively, of g will then tell you whether there is gender discrimination and how large it is.

When fitting this equation to the data, the mystery variable, x_7, must, of course, be excluded. If – but only if – it is not correlated either positively or negatively with x_6, the gender variable, or if x_7 has little if any effect on a professor's salary will g be an an unbiased estimate of the extent of gender discrimination. Perhaps this suggests to you that these studies are not highly reliable. But are there any better ways of answering the question?

not. Such an impression would be about as accurate as the idea you get when you read a book on diseases: that you are suffering from a vast number of ailments. As someone spent much of his life working hard at empirical economic research, including lots of regression equations, I certainly don't think that they are useless.

13.5.1 The past is not the future

Obviously, unless you are clairvoyant, all the data you have come from the past, and, if you are only trying to explain past events, that is fine. But, more often, you are interested in the future, and the assumption that the future will be just like the past can be a somewhat uncomfortable one. For example, regressions run in the 1960s and 1970s found a stable relation between changes in the money supply and in nominal GDP. For shorter-run changes, this relationship almost disappeared in the 1980s as financial innovations, deregulation of financial markets, and high interest rates changed the way firms and households made their payments (credit cards are one example), and the way they managed their financial assets. A similar problem arose in 2007–8 when economists tried to predict whether a recession was imminent, and if so, whether it would be a deep one. Due to losses on mortgage-backed and other asset-backed securities, the financial system had become much more fragile than at any time since the Great Depression. The regression-based econometric models fitted to post-World War II data could, therefore, tell us little about how such financial fragility would affect the economy. Similarly, after a stock market crash, the regression equation that gave you such a good fit to the previous run-up in stock prices may now have revealed itself to be not a trustworthy friend, but a treacherous foe.

A special case in which regression coefficients are unstable arises when the government changes its policy. Suppose it has previously cut taxes only when it intended to maintain the lower level for a long time. An economist then runs a regression to measure the effect of a tax cut on consumption. She finds a large and highly significant coefficient. This encourages the government to adopt a new policy. From now on, it will cut taxes during recessions to boost consumption, and then raise them again when the economy recovers.

But after some time, people catch on, and know that when their taxes are cut they will soon be raised again. Now, when their taxes are cut they do not increase consumption by nearly as much as before. Thus, the adoption of a new policy can outdate the regression coefficients on which the new policy is itself based. This is known as the "Lucas critique," after Nobel laureate Robert Lucas. While everyone agrees that, in principle, Lucas is right, and that a change in policy can outdate the previous regression coefficients, there is much disagreement about the quantitative significance of this. Many economists, while acknowledging the logical validity of the Lucas critique, treat it as relatively unimportant for most day-to-day practical problems, because they expect the public to change its expectations about government policy only slowly. Others think that the Lucas critique invalidates most of the previously standard predictions of the effect of changes in government policy. The Lucas critique is probably much more important for some policy changes than for others, but, on the whole, the jury is still out.

Unstable coefficients are a problem not only for studies using time-series data, but also for ones using cross-section data, that is, data taken at one specific moment, such as surveys of current unemployment. For example, now that people are much more aware of the dangers of smoking, a regression equation that explained differences in cigarette consumption well in the 1950s may no longer do so.

13.5.2 Choosing the control variables

Suppose you regress sales of BMWs on their price. You would expect a negative regression coefficient, since obviously at a higher price, fewer are bought. But your computer may instead deliver a positive coefficient. Here is why. At those times when incomes are rising rapidly, more BMWs are bought, and this is also the time when dealers are likely to raise prices. (In terms of the supply and demand diagram in appendix 6.1, the demand curve shifted up and now intersects the supply curve at a higher price.) But you have not told the computer anything about the rise in income, and, not surprisingly, it interprets all observations that show that both prices and sales are rising as a positive relation between price and sales. To be sure, it also has some observations where the price of BMWs rose and sales fell (a movement along the demand curve) and it interprets these correctly as a negative relation between price and sales. But it can give you only a single regression coefficient that covers both cases. So it throws at you a coefficient that is a meaningless mishmash, and could be either positive or negative.

As another example, suppose you regress income on education. In doing so you have left something out. People with more education tend to have higher IQs, and also for each level of education, those with high IQs tend to have a higher income. But since you have not told the computer anything about IQs, all it can do is to attribute to education the entire difference in the incomes of people with varying levels of education. In doing so, it serves up a regression coefficient that is too high, because it includes the effect of differences in IQ along with differences in education.

Here is a third example: in some areas in the Balkans, the number of births in a village is positively correlated with the number of storks. The reason is that large villages have more births, and also more chimneys for storks to roost in. Still another example, is the correlation between the size of the feet of grade-school students and their reading scores. Older students have larger feet.

To avoid such confusion, or let me be more honest, to minimize it, you usually need to include in your regression some additional regressors, called "conditioning variables" or "control variables," which are of no inherent interest to you, just so that these variables will not pollute the coefficients and *t* values of the variables you *are* interested in. Thus, in the above example, by including IQ as a control variable, you allow the computer to keep the effects of IQ away from the coefficient it computes for the effect of education on income.

Deciding what control variables to include is often difficult. Economic theory tells you that – ceteris paribus – if x occurs y will result, but often does not tell you enough about what is impounded in the ceteris paribus clause, and should, therefore, be treated as a potential control variable. Or, if it does specify some of these variables, it usually does so only in general terms, such as "income." Does that mean only current income or also past income, and if so how far back? And what about expected future income?

The solution may seem obvious: include all the potentially relevant and important control variables. But that advice brings several problems with it. One, is that some of these variables cannot be included because they cannot be measured. For instance, in the previous example of education and income, a person's ambition should be included as a control variable, but usually the data provide no measure of that.

Moreover, if a control variable has a strong positive correlation with the regressor you are interested in, then, *in a small sample*, including it could substantially reduce the t value of that regressor, because the computer could attribute to the control variable some of the effects of the regressor you are interested in. To ameliorate this problem, many economists after running a regression with numerous control variables, eliminate all the ones that are not statistically significant at the 5 percent level, rerun the regression, and report only this second, cleansed regression.

Another problem is that experimenting with combinations of various control variables opens the door to experimentation until you find a set of variables that yields results that support your hypothesis – remember the discussion of data mining in chapter 10.

A wrong guess about which control variables to include may be fatal. Even when choosing only among seemingly reasonable control variables, the size of the coefficient that you are interested in may depend strongly on which control variables you include. Sometimes even the sign of the coefficient may change when different ones are included. A classic example is the question of whether the death penalty deters murder. Many studies have regressed the homicide rate in various states on a dummy variable that measures whether or not the state imposes the death penalty, along with several control variables. Their results have varied all the way from the death penalty strongly deterring homicide to it having no effect, or even a positive effect, on the homicide rate.[1]

When using time-series data it is particularly easy to be tripped up by a missing control variable. Many time series, e.g. the population of India, the

GDP of Belgium, and the number of visitors to the Uffizi gallery in Florence, etc., have an upward trend and are, therefore, correlated. Fortunately, regressing the year-to-year changes, instead of the levels of the variables, often suffices to eliminate the common time trend.

While all this is certainly troublesome, it does not mean that one should throw up one's hands in post-modernist despair and proclaim that it is equally "true" that the death penalty deters murder and that it does not, or for that matter that storks do and do not bring babies. But it does mean that one has to worry about which control variables should, and which should not, be included. A helpful procedure is to try several sets of regressions that include different control variables to see how robust your results are to some more or less arbitrary choices of control variables. Only if all of these "robustness tests" yield broadly similar results can you feel confident about your conclusions.

13.5.3 The rickety bridge from post hoc to propter hoc

Much confusion could be avoided if the spelling and pronunciation of "correlation" were changed to "co-relation." This would clarify that all that correlation means is that two or more variables are found in a particular relation, such as y being consistently high when x is high. Most philosophers (and philosophers are the guardians of our concept of causality) and economists (who think of causality more casually than philosophers do) agree that something more than such co-relation is needed to establish that x and y are causally linked. Determining exactly what is needed, is a deep and excruciatingly difficult philosophical problem. Let us pass it by, and work instead with the everyday use of the term in all its vagueness and ambiguity. This nebulous concept suffices, because all I want to do is to bolster your power to resist the widespread claims of having demonstrated some causal relationship, merely by showing that a correlation exists.

If the data show that x and y are correlated that could be due to: (1) x causing y as claimed; (2) coincidence, or put another way, the sample being too small; (3) failure to include the correct control variables; and (4) y causing x, so-called "reverse causation." The first case, x actually causing y as claimed raises no problems and, therefore, does not need discussion. The second case, coincidence, can be disposed of quickly by pointing out that if one uses a 5 percent significant level, and *if* the data are normally distributed, then in up to 5 percent of the cases one should expect to find a statistically significant – but spurious – relation between x and y. I have already dealt with the third case, the absence of correct control variables; if z causes both x and y, then regressing y just on x may result in a spurious correlation.

The fourth case, reverse causation, is a ubiquitous problem. Again and again, the media carry reports such as that people who exercise are healthier. Hardly surprising: it may indicate that exercise keeps you healthy, *or* that many sick people cannot exercise. Married men earn more than single men, so marriage makes you richer. Yes, it seems plausible. But it is also plausible that women are less likely to marry men who earn little. Countries that provide strong protection for property rights have higher per capita incomes than those which don't. Does that mean that countries with weak property rights can increase their incomes by strengthening these rights, or does it mean that being rich induces a country to protect property rights? Or is it perhaps a bit of both? If the candidate who received the larger campaign contributions is usually elected, does this mean that campaign contributions determine elections, or that candidates who are more likely to be elected receive larger campaign contributions? The data show that religious people are happier. Does that mean that religious belief makes people happy, or that being happy makes you more disposed to believe in the existence of a benign god? Is the golden rule that he who has the gold rules, or that he who rules gets the gold? When confronted with a reported correlation it should be routine to ask: "which, if either, is cause and which effect?"

How can one tell whether a correlation carries a valid causal message? It is easy in cases where we ourselves have intervened to bring about changes in one of the variables, for example, by heating a chemical to see if it will explode, and that is a major reason the laboratory method has made the natural sciences so effective. And we also know which is cause and which effect when the intervention, though not our own doing, is by some factor that could not possibly be the result of the variable that we treat as the dependent one. The roof collapses because of the hurricane: the collapsing roof did not cause the hurricane. In economics such clearly exogenous interventions, while not entirely absent, are scarce. But where they can be found they can resolve the reverse-causation problem far better than any other method. For example, there is a clear correlation between number of years of schooling and health, but it could be due to education inducing people to adopt a healthier lifestyle, or to healthy students staying in school longer than sickly ones. The solution: look at states that intervened by raising the age at which children could leave school, and see if health improved. It did.

Other ways of establishing causation are more complex. One answer, which has often been tried, is to rely on the principle that cause precedes effect. Suppose that changes in the money supply and in the price level are correlated, and that changes in the money supply precede changes in the price level. Then, the straightforward interpretation is that changes in the money supply are the cause.

But straightforward does not always mean correct. One problem is that for such a timing test to be valid the variables must be defined correctly. For example, economic theory tells us, or rather seems to tell us, that when the Fed raises the federal funds rate (a short-term interest rate that it controls) other interest rates should rise too. But suppose you observe that these other rates rise before the federal funds rate does. Does this mean that their rise caused the Fed to change the funds rate? No, a more likely explanation is that the market anticipated what the Fed was going to do, and raised interest rates right then and there. The variable we should have looked at is not the Fed's action, but the market's anticipation of it.

Or suppose you observe that the money supply does not rise ahead of output, but rises around the same time. Does that mean that output is largely unaffected by monetary policy? Again, not necessarily, because what could be affecting output is not the *level* of the money supply, but its rate of change. And the rate of change of a smoothly moving series has its peaks and troughs before the level of the series does. Such problems can be tricky.

Another problem with a simple timing test is that even if the peaks and troughs of each series are clearly delineated, as in figure 13.2, it is often hard to see whether a particular peak in one series should be matched with the preceding, or with the subsequent peak in the other series. This problem would largely disappear if we knew that it takes one variable, say, six months, to affect the other. But our theory is usually not that specific. It may even suggest that the lag is likely to vary substantially from case to case. If so, while it is then not quite correct to say that in matching peaks or troughs in two series anything goes, a lot more goes than one would like. All the same, a simple look at the sequences of peaks and troughs is probably used frequently (and rightly so) as a rough and ready first approximation. But rough it is.

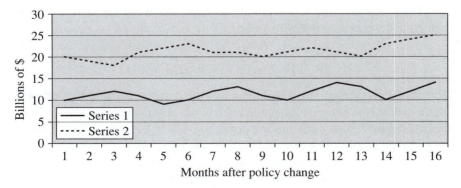

Figure 13.2 Comparing cycles in two series

A sophisticated response to the causality problem is the "Granger causality test" (after Nobel laureate Clive Granger). This treats one event, x, as a cause of another, y, if the occurrence of x makes it more probable that subsequently y will also occur, while, at the same time, the occurrence of y does *not* make it more probable that x will occur. More specifically, the factors determining the behavior of an economic variable are usually more or less persistent from one quarterly (or even yearly) period to the next, so that regressing a variable on its own past values often allows you to predict much of its observed behavior in the next quarter. Now, suppose that when you regress, say, the inflation rate on its own values in several previous quarters, as well as on the previous period's growth rate of money, you get a significant and substantial regression coefficient for the growth rate of money. But when you regress the growth rate of money on its own past values and on the past inflation rate, the coefficient of the inflation rate is not significant or has the wrong sign. The first of these findings, Granger would argue, is consistent with the hypothesis that changes in the growth rate of money cause changes in the inflation rate, while the second is inconsistent with the hypothesis that changes in the inflation rate cause changes in the growth rate of money. Hence, the observed correlation of the rate of money growth and the inflation rate should be interpreted as the former causing the latter. However, the validity of this interpretation of causation is still controversial.[2] Moreover, successful application of the Granger test requires that lagged x is significant in one regression, while lagged y is not significant with the right sign in the other regression. If not, then no Granger test.

Granger causality tests, like other timing tests, face the problem that many of our data series are not specific enough. Although we have hourly data on changes in stock prices and could get minute-by-minute data on exchange rates, some other series, such as industrial production and unemployment are available only monthly, and GDP data are published only quarterly. Hence, sometimes we cannot tell which variable moved first.

13.5.4   Three other problems

Here are three lesser, but still important problems: one is that the squaring of the deviations between the predicted and the actual values of y that occurs in calculating R^2 enhances the importance of a few large deviations relative to many small ones. For example, a deviation of 5 and a deviation of 7 have a mean of 6, as do deviations of 2 and of 10. But the square root of the mean squared deviations is 6.1 in the first case, and 7.2 in the second. To illustrate the effect that a single outlying observation can have, figure 13.3 adds one outlier to the 29 observations in figure 13.1 (see southwest corner). R^2 falls

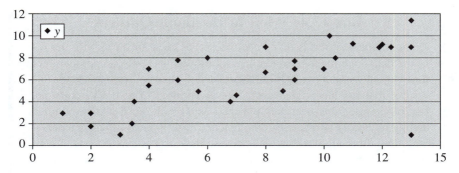

Figure 13.3 Adding one outlier to figure 13.1

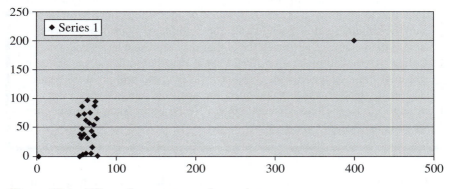

Figure 13.4 Effect of two extreme observations

from 0.68 to 0.40. In figure 13.4 (based on a different set of 30 observations) R^2 is 0.47, the regression coefficient is 0.46 with a t value of 5.2, but the entire correlation results from two outliers (see southeast and northwest corners). Without them, R^2 falls to 0.00. Box 13.4 discusses what to do about them.

Second, here is a tricky point: in figure 13.3 the first five points in the southeast corner show a negative relation between x and y instead of the positive relation shown in figure 13.3 taken as a whole. Is this just due to sampling error – with only five observations it may well be – or are the data telling us that the positive relation between x and y does not hold for low values of x and y? You can't say without further investigation. But one thing is clear: it helps to look carefully at the scatter diagram.

Third, one of the most frustrating problems in economics is that models that fit past data very well often fail to provide good forecasts. The reason is not just that, as already discussed, the past is not the future, but also that the good fit obtained from past data may be the result of data mining.

Box 13.4: What to Do about Outliers

One extreme position is that since the outlier does not fit in with the rest of the data there must be something wrong with it, and you can, therefore, throw it out without even telling the reader. To make a strong case for this, assume that you have a data set of hourly earnings of textile workers, and one observation has been key-punched as $1 million. But many outliers are not obviously garbage, and the practice of dropping outliers can degenerate into dropping observations because they do not support one's hypothesis. If there is the least doubt about the justification for dropping an outlier, readers should be told that it was dropped and why.

The other extreme is to say "well, that's what the data show, and that's that." But this is unrealistic. When you have an outlier you rightly feel impelled to examine it. After all, it *could be* just a key-punch error. Or, it may be genuine, but a special case. For example, if your dependent variable is the volume of air travel, the outlier may represent a strike at a major airline. If you can make a reasonable case that the outlier is special case you may want to report your regression results both with, and without it. There are mathematical techniques for spotting outliers, but even so, where to draw the line is sometimes a delicate issue. Such a dependence on judgment is not "unscientific."

Finally, do not automatically assume that the explanation (i.e., theory) offered by the regression equation with the highest R^2 and best t value is necessarily the best explanation. Good fit is only one of several criteria for selecting among theories. Generality, fruitfulness, tractability, and relatedness to other theories matter too. Assume, for example, that you can predict future wage increases better from a regression equation that uses as its regressors wage increases in eight prior calendar quarters, than from one that uses the unemployment rate. The latter is surely a deeper and more meaningful explanation than is the former.

13.6   In Conclusion

A large part of this and the previous three chapters have dealt with what to watch for when reading an argument based on economic statistics. Fortunately, such a critical reading usually does not require any great knowledge of economics and statistics. What it does require is adopting a critical attitude instead of sheepishly kowtowing before the proffered statistics. The media may tell you that there is a correlation, but have neither the space, nor presumably the inclination, to discuss such "details" as the control variables that were used. There is nothing that one can do about that, unless one has the time to go to the original source. But one can ask whether the proffered correlation should be read as causal, and if so in which direction causality runs.

In general, given the incomplete information that the media provide about the details of the statistical studies they cite, it is reasonable to place at least some weight on human factors: what biases are the authors likely to have, what sanctions, if any, in terms of lost reputation (which can be serious for academics and the staff of better think-tanks) do they face if caught in error? Do you know of any misleading or careless statements the authors have made in the past? Did the study appear in a peer refereed journal?

Sometimes, the only solution is to admit ignorance and treat the available information as tentative, not as a "fact" merely because it takes the form of a number. The statement that the budget deficit five years from now will be \$301.3 billion is less, not more, "scientific" than the statement that it will be large.

To foster such a skeptical attitude, these last chapters have covered so many potential pitfalls that some readers may get the impression that, in economics, statistical results should never be taken seriously. That is wrong. The alternatives to relying on economic statistics are unappetizing: relying on mere assertions, anecdotes, the lessons of one or a few scarce major events, or on untested theorizing.

Besides, questionable statistics are not unknown in the natural sciences either, and yet these sciences make astounding progress. Moreover, as the next chapter will illustrate with specific examples, despite the numerous problems discussed in this and the preceding chapters, econometric analysis can provide us with valuable knowledge. Finally, a critical discussion of verbal reasoning and its rhetorical tricks could also leave the impression that it should not be taken seriously. "Caveat lector" applies everywhere, not just to econometric work. But what this phrase means is "Reader beware," not "Stop reading."

NOTES

1 For a summary of recent studies of the effect of the death penalty on the homicide rate, see Adam Liptak, "Does the Death Penalty Save Lives? A New Debate," *New York Times*, November 18, 2007, pp. A1 and 24.
2 See Kevin Hoover, *Causality in Economics*, New York, Cambridge University Press, 2001.

14

The Workhorse in Action: Some Examples of Empirical Economics

The last chapter's discussion of potential errors in regression analysis may have left the impression that in empirical testing in economics just about everything may go wrong, and nothing is ever likely to go right. This chapter provides some examples of hypothesis testing that *did* go right. It starts with an overall look at a topic, explaining and predicting the savings ratio and its complement, the percentage of income consumed, and shows how the interaction of theory and regression analysis has enhanced our understanding of this subject. It then looks in more detail at three specific papers, one on mutual funds, one on African economic history, and one on fiscal policy, that have successfully used regression analysis.

I have used these three papers, in part because they illustrate some of the problems and techniques used in the previous chapter, and in part because they seem, to me at least, both interesting and highly competent. This does not necessarily mean that they are the three most important and best such papers written in recent years; I do not pretend to second-guess the Nobel committee. Besides, I had to choose papers that could be taken up without lengthy and elaborate background discussions. I have also allowed some play to my prejudice in favor of papers that spend much effort in deriving and cleansing the data rather than in applying the latest elaborate statistical techniques to readily available data, as well as to my prejudice in favor of papers that, like two of these papers, make use of findings that do not come from mainstream economics. While this is now less rare than before, it is still uncommon. In describing these three papers I have concentrated on issues raised in the previous chapter, and to save space have slighted some issues discussed at considerable length in these papers.

14.1 Consumption and Saving

The proportion of their income that people save has interested economists for a long time, since, by raising the capital stock, saving is a major contributor to economic growth. During the Great Depression of the 1930s it attracted further attention for a very different reason. Saving no longer looked so socially desirable when firms were firing workers because there was insufficient demand for their output. For about two decades, the issue of "excessive" savings became a standard problem of economics. Even the wording changed, and we thought and still think, in terms of the alternative to saving, consumption, and thus we have theories of the "consumption function." Let's look at a few.

14.1.1 The absolute income theory

In his path-breaking 1936 book, *The General Theory of Employment, Interest and Money*,[1] Keynes argued on the basis of little more than casual observation and introspection, i.e., common sense – economics was then much less formal and rigorous than it is now – that the main determinant of a person's saving was his income. Not only does a rich person save a larger dollar amount than a poor person, but he usually saves a larger proportion of his income. And the statistical evidence seemed to confirm this so-called "absolute income theory." Other factors, such as the rewards for saving, that is, the interest rate and the lure of capital gains, the wish to be prepared for a rainy day, etc., do play their roles in the savings decision, but they are only supporting actors.

This theory implies that the savings ratio will be higher at the top of a cyclical peak than at a trough of a recession when income is lower. And the data confirm this implication. But it also has another – and disturbing – implication. Technological innovation and a rising capital stock continually raise potential income. But unless the expenditures that offset saving, that is, investment, exports, and government expenditures are rising at a sufficiently high rate, we will sooner or later reach a point at which so much will be saved that the demand for consumer goods will be insufficient to keep the labor force fully employed, and the unemployment rate will keep on rising.[a]

---

[a]   In principle, the increased saving could lower the interest rate enough, so that investment expands sufficiently to fill the ever-widening gap between income and consumption. But at the time when the absolute income theory reigned, economists doubted that the interest rate would fall enough, and that investment was sufficiently responsive to a fall in interest rates.

Despite its initial enthusiastic acceptance, by the late 1940s this absolute income theory was in deep trouble. Although real income was now substantially higher than in the 1920s and 1930s, the predicted savings glut was nowhere in sight. Moreover, Simon Kuznets had estimated the savings ratio back into the 1870s, and, despite the immense rise in income since then, these data, too, did not show a rise in the savings ratio over time. This was puzzling. The cross-section data, that is, data on families with different incomes at any one time, clearly showed that the higher the income the higher the savings ratio. And yet, as national income rose, the savings ratio did not rise.

14.1.2   The relative income theory

The first widely accepted solution to this puzzle, the relative income theory of James Duesenberry and of Franco Modigliani assumes, in anticipation of contemporary behavioral economics, that a family's savings ratio depends not only on its income, but also on the incomes of other families, since low-income families feel under greater pressure than do high-income families to match, at least partially, the higher living standards they see around them. Hence, although the higher your income relative to other people's the greater is the proportion of it you save, if other people's incomes rise in step with yours, your savings ratio remains unchanged. And not only does your savings ratio depend on other people's income, as well as on your own, it also depends on your own past income, that is, on the living standard to which you have become accustomed. Hence, as the data confirm, the savings rate is higher when income is at its cyclical peak, and thus above people's accustomed level, than when it is at the cyclical trough.

The relative income theory could thus explain both of the facts that the absolute income theory could explain, that is, the cyclical behavior of the savings ratio, and the positive correlation of the savings ratio and the level of income in the cross-section data. And in addition, it eliminated the seeming contradiction between the cross-section data and the time-series data. And since there was nothing that the absolute income theory could explain and the relative income theory could not, the latter, though somewhat more complex, was the better theory.

All the same, the relative income theory did not satisfy economists fully. It introduced a sociological factor, the dependence of a person's savings ratio on the incomes of other people. Despite the rise of behavioral economics in recent years, some economists still consider the introduction of explicitly sociological factors as something of a faux pas, and in the 1950s a much greater proportion probably thought that way. And this was not entirely a matter of academic snobbery and turf protection. Economists try to develop a consistent theory of economic behavior on the assumption that people rationally maximize their own utility, and do not pay much attention to other people's utility. If we use this theory, and do so with considerable success, in explaining the demand for potatoes, computer programs, and iTunes, shouldn't we also use it to explain the demand for net wealth, that is, the demand for the accumulated sum of saving, and hence the amount saved each year? Wouldn't such a theory of saving be more insightful than the relative income theory? What makes this question compelling is that Irving Fisher, one of the greatest American economists ever, had already in 1907 published such a rational utility-maximizing theory. Why ignore it?

A second problem was that using in the time series version of the relative income theory only current income and the previous peak income seems clumsy. Why take just one year's income as representing the effects of previously acquired living standards? And why assume that it is only past income and not also the income anticipated in future years that affects this year's savings ratio?

14.1.3 The permanent income theory and the lifecycle hypothesis

In the mid-1950s, two future Nobel laureates, Milton Friedman and Franco Modigliani (the latter with co-author Richard Brumberg), presented a theory that avoided these problems.[2] They did this, by explicitly addressing the problem of "intertemporal utility maximization," that is, the problem of applying the theory of utility maximization to the case of choosing, not between two goods at one particular time, but to the difficulty of how much of one's resources to consume at different times. Modigliani and Brumberg, in what came to be known as the "lifecycle hypothesis," focused on the formal theory, while Friedman in his "permanent income theory" focused on empirical testing. All in all, their theories are very similar, and since this chapter is intended to illustrate empirical testing I will focus on Friedman's work. But first, a quick look at the theory.

Allocating consumption efficiently over time

Let's see what a theory of saving for a rational utility maximizer would look like. To simplify matters start with the following assumptions: (1) people know with certainty what their life-time incomes will be; (2) they can borrow and lend as much as they want, but with the constraint that before they die they must have repaid all their debts and consumed all their wealth; (3) the utility they derive from any given level of consumption is the same at all times; (4) the interest rate is zero. Finally, to turn a rule about what they should do into a rule about what they *will* do, so that one can predict what will happen, assume that they have sufficient self-control to act rationally.

Given these assumptions, you should consume the same amount every year. To see why assume that you consume more in year X than in year Y. Since the marginal utility of consumption declines as you consume more, the utility you obtain from the last dollar you spend in year X is less than that from the last dollar spend in year Y, so it makes sense to shift some of your expenditures from year X to year Y, until you spend the same amount in each of the two years. How about saving? Since saving is defined as income minus consumption, if your consumption is constant you save each year the difference between your income, which is likely to differ from year to year, and this constant consumption. That is, in a year in which your actual income or "measured income" as economists call it, is equal to your average income, or "permanent income," you saved nothing, in a year in which your measured income exceeds your permanent income, you save the difference, called "transitory income," and, in a year in which your measured income is less than your permanent income, you dissave the difference.

Does it matter for your savings ratio whether your permanent income is high or low? No, it doesn't. Since the same consumption-smoothing rule applies regardless of your income there is no reason to assume that those with high permanent incomes save a larger proportion of their permanent incomes than do those with low permanent incomes. However, those whose measured incomes are high only because their transitory incomes are positive, will have a higher savings ratio than those whose transitory incomes are negative.

Nobody would be silly enough to believe that all the assumptions made to obtain these results hold exactly. But since they do simplify the analysis, let's see whether they hold approximately enough for the permanent income theory and lifecycle hypothesis to be useful tools for analysis and prediction. Only the empirical evidence can answer that question.

The empirical evidence

When Friedman wanted to test his theory that consumption is a function of permanent income he faced the problem that he had no data on people's permanent incomes. The only direct way he could test the theory was to approximate his theoretical term "permanent income" by taking an average of the current year's income and the incomes of many previous years, with each year's income receiving a weight that declines the further back you go. Making this approximation, he could then regress consumption on this measure of permanent income and see whether his theory obtained a higher R^2 than either the absolute and relative income theories do. What he found was that the relative income theory had a slightly higher R^2 than his permanent income theory. However, he dismissed this result as possibly just the product of a statistical bias: since the relative income theory allocates more weight to the current year's income than does the permanent income theory, it is more subject to reverse causation bias, that is, to some of the high R^2 being due to income causing consumption, and not to consumption causing income.

Friedman, therefore, had to rely on indirect tests. For example, he asked what we should find if we separate people into two groups, one group within which much of the difference in measured incomes among income recipients is due to differences in transitory incomes, and the other, within which much of the difference in measured income is due to differences in permanent incomes. If, as the permanent income theory predicts, people consume all or most of their permanent incomes, but save their positive transitory incomes, and dissave their negative transitory incomes, then we should find that in a group in which transitory income differences account for much of the differences in measured incomes, the savings ratio rises much more steeply as we go up the income scale than it does in another group in which the differences in measured incomes are due mainly to differences in permanent incomes.

The permanent income theory can also explain why, within any one income class, black families have a higher average savings ratio than do white families. Take any measured income class below the mean income. Since, on average, white families have a higher permanent income than do black families, a typical white family that is in this low-income class in any one year is more likely to have a higher permanent income – and hence negative transitory income that year – than does the typical black family in that class. It is, therefore, likely to save little or even to dissave, thus dragging down the mean savings ratio of white families in this class. The opposite occurs in a high-income class. Here the black families are more likely to have positive transitory income than do the white families, and hence to save more.

Middle-aged families have a higher savings ratio than either young or old families. The permanent income theory can explain that too. For the typical family, measured income peaks in middle age, and with their transitory income thus being high, these families have a high savings ratio, while young and old families save relatively little because their transitory incomes are negative.

Friedman provides many other examples in which the permanent income theory can account for what the data show. However, his evidence is subject to two qualifications. One is that the relative income theory can also account for several of his examples. The second is that a theory that is intermediate, perhaps roughly half way, between the relative income theory and the permanent income theory can account for all of the valid evidence that Friedman cites.[3] Such a theory accepts the permanent income theory's claim that families save a larger proportion of their permanent incomes than of their transitory incomes, and hence also of their measured incomes, but does not claim that this explains all of the observed difference between the savings ratios of families with high and with low measured incomes. Some of this difference can be attributed to the emulation effect on which the relative income theory relies. Such an intermediate theory also agrees with the permanent income theory that families make their consumption decisions on the basis not just of their current year's incomes, but it gives more weight to current incomes than Friedman does.

In the late 1950s and 1960s many other economists provided numerous further tests and analyses of the permanent income theory. The most important development was Robert Hall's new version of the theory, a version that has become very popular. In this formulation expected future income plays a more explicit role than it does in the older versions of the permanent income theory. Hall developed it as part of the then ongoing reformulation of economics in a way that pays much more attention to people's expectations (which is based on their rationally taking into account all the information they have available), and it is, therefore, called the "rational expectations consumption function."

If the permanent income theory and the rational-expectations consumption function are correct and people consume all or most of their permanent income, and none of their transitory income, then we should be able to use consumption as an indicator of permanent income. And there is a simple way to test whether this works: regress consumption in the current year on consumption in the previous year and on the current year's income. Since last year's consumption is a more accurate measure of permanent income than is this year's measured income, the regression coefficient of last year's consumption should be large and significant, and the regression coefficient of this year's income should be small and insignificant. If these conditions do not hold, that means either that people consume significantly out of their transitory incomes, or else that they change their estimates of their permanent incomes so much from one year to the next that permanent income is not a useful concept.

What is the result of all this testing? There is still some disagreement, but there is a broad consensus that the permanent income theory, the lifecycle hypotheses, and the rational-expectations consumption function have made a fundamental contribution to our understanding of consumption and saving. While I suspect that most, or at least a majority of, economists believe that people do consume some of their transitory income as they receive it, and do not fully maintain their consumption when their transitory income becomes negative, they also believe that people are much more prone to save transitory income than permanent income. Moreover, while a majority of economists probably believe that those with a high permanent income have a higher savings ratio than those with a lower permanent income, it is now generally accepted that the strong positive relation between measured income and the savings rate substantially overstates the correlation between permanent income and the saving rate.

What accounts for the imperfect fit of the theory to the data? It is that its assumptions are not realistic enough, or put differently, that the version of the theory I described is too simple. Particularly suspect, is the assumption that, when their transitory incomes are negative, families are able to maintain the level of consumption appropriate to their permanent incomes by running down their assets or by borrowing. Moreover, if, contrary to the assumption made above, families do not know their permanent incomes with certainty, a sense of caution should induce them to consume less than is appropriate for their permanent income levels. And, more fundamentally, a family may not be fully rational, and may be unable to resist the temptation to spend some of its transitory income as it receives it. Moreover, figuring out one's permanent income is time consuming, and some families are, therefore, likely to follow a rule of thumb of spending each year a certain percentage of their measured incomes. In addition, high-income families may feel a stronger inclination to leave bequests than low-income families do. Furthermore, those people who are imbued with the Protestant ethic are likely both to save more and to work harder than others, thus generating a correlation – though not a causal one – between high income and a high savings ratio.

Does that mean that we should not have built a theory on such unrealistic assumptions? Of course not: we would then have lost the great insights of the permanent income theory. It was a much better strategy to build the theory, see that it does not fully fit the data, and then modify it as needed; or if this cannot be done, to treat it as an approximation. Economics needs a lively conversation between theory and data, not a monologue.

The contributions of the permanent income theory and lifecycle hypotheses are not just matters of academic interest. They have important practical implications. They guide our forecasts of consumption and thus of GDP. They also tell us that a sales tax, although it is still regressive when measured with respect to permanent income, is not as regressive as it is when it is measured with respect to measured income. Moreover, they warn us not to expect a large effect from cutting taxes temporarily in a recession if the public expects taxes to be raised again.

14.2   Should You Choose a Large Mutual Fund?

Many investors select their mutual funds primarily by looking at the previous earnings of various funds. However, previous earnings are a useful guide to future earnings only for a few months; after that the previously high earners fare on average no better other mutual funds. By what other guide then should you select a fund for longer-term investment in the stock market? One sensible solution is to select one with a low expense ratio, that is, a low ratio of the fund's management costs (which the shareholders have to pay) to its total assets. But what should you do if you locate several funds with an equally low ratio? The instinct of many investors is to go for the largest, or at least one of the largest, of these funds. Surely everyone has heard the phrase "economies of scale," and a large fund's economies of scale in picking stocks should be reflected in a higher yield to its holders. Besides, a fund can become large only if it earns an unusually high rate of return. So isn't it sensible for investors to move into one of the biggest funds?

No it isn't, says an exceptionally thorough analysis by Joseph Chen, Harrison Hong, Ming Huang, and Jeffrey Kubik.[4] They looked at a sample of 3,439 diversified mutual US stock funds over the 1962 to 1999 period, and found just the opposite: as you go from moderately small funds (in most of their analysis they excluded the smallest 20 percent) to large ones, both gross returns and returns after fees and expenditures, which is what matters to stockholders, decline.

If this is so for individual funds, how about families of funds? Many funds belong to what is called a "family," that is, a group of funds that, though independently managed, are owned by a single company, Vanguard and Fidelity being the largest and best-known examples. Here, an advantage of large scale does show up, a fund performs better the larger are the assets of the other funds in its family. The authors suggest that this is due to large fund families being able to negotiate lower commissions on their trades, and to obtain higher fees when, as funds do, they lend some of their stocks. This combination of diseconomies of scale for individual funds and economies of scale for fund families is puzzling and needs explanation. But before turning to such explanations, let's see how Chen and his co-authors discovered these facts.

Finding the relation between a mutual fund's size and its performance might seem simple: you just rank funds by the size of their assets and look at the average earnings per dollar invested in each size class, or for greater precision run a regression of earnings per dollar invested on a fund's total assets. Yes, that would be simple – and also highly unreliable. One reason is that the size of a fund and the size of the other funds in its family are correlated, so that a simple correlation of a fund's earnings on its size combines the negative direct effects of size on earnings with the positive indirect effect coming from the size of other funds in its family. Moreover, stock mutual funds come in a variety of what can be called "styles." Some specialize in the stocks of large companies ("large cap funds"); others in the stocks of smaller companies ("small cap funds"); some trade frequently, others less frequently; some charge high fees and presumably spend extensively on stock research; while others charge lower fees and presumably do less research. Some are high-risk funds; others more conservative "value" funds. With different funds thus offering different products one would expect their costs and performances to differ. Before comparing the earnings of small and large funds, one should, therefore, adjust their earnings for such differences. Otherwise, suppose, as seems plausible, small funds are more likely to be small cap funds, and large funds large cap funds. Then, a regression of fund earnings on fund size is likely to pick up the difference in earnings that comes from investing in small cap funds rather than in large cap funds. And since small companies, and hence a portfolio of small cap funds, is riskier than a portfolio of large cap funds, if small funds earn more than large funds, some of this extra earnings will just be a payment for taking greater risk.

Accordingly, to compare like with like, the authors use several alternative portfolio models to estimate the effect that different fund styles have on earnings, and then adjust the recorded earnings of funds for these differences. They then regress these adjusted earnings on a measure of fund size and on a number of control variables, such as size of the fund's family, the rate of turnover of its portfolio, its age, and the expense ratio it charges its stockholders.

This regression shows a negative effect of a fund's size on its earnings that is both statistically and substantively significant, with an increase in a fund's size by two standard deviations typically lowering its annual before-expenses earnings by about 0.7–1.0 percentage points, depending on the particular adjustment for fund style that is used, and lowering earnings after expenses by only slightly less. However, the size of a fund's family turns out to have a statistically positive effect on a fund's earnings.

The authors then consider three ways of explaining their results. One is what they call the "liquidity hypothesis": when a large fund buys or sells stocks, its trading volume is often large enough for its trades to turn prices against it, so that its trades are less profitable than those of a small fund. The second, the "clientele hypothesis," is that a large fund can attract many customers through its adverting volume, and can, therefore, get away with offering a relatively poor return, whereas a small fund has to offer a superior return to stay in business. The third hypothesis is that when a fund starts out and is still small it has to scurry and take risks to establish a strong record. (If its risk taking is not successful, it simply goes out of business.) Once it becomes large, it can play it safe and take much less risk, even if this means earning less. The authors are skeptical of the last two of these hypotheses, because they imply that fund managers are not maximizing their profits. They take the liquidity hypothesis more seriously, and conclude that "liquidity plays an important role in eroding performance" as funds grow.[5]

But they then add another hypothesis, one that can account not only for the negative relation between a fund's size and its earnings, but also for their finding that being a member of a family of large funds raises a fund's earnings. They resolve this seeming paradox by pointing out that, within a family of funds, the managers of the individual funds make their investment decisions essentially independently of each other, so that if there is some particular factor that makes a large fund less efficient than a small fund, it will not make a family of large funds less efficient than a family of small funds. And this factor is an organizational one. Imagine you are the sole manager and stock picker of a small fund. There is much information you can acquire about firms whose stock you are considering. Some of it comes from quarterly reports, balance sheets, or SEC filings, and is objective and hard information, such as a firm's earnings and growth of sales. Some of it is vague and impressionistic, for example, the gossip you hear, or the impression you obtain from talking to a firm's CEO. When other things are equal, objective and precise information is better than subjective and vague information – but not always when other things are not equal. On many important issues, such as the ability of the firm's CEO and the morale of its employees, vague and subjective information is all that is available. You, as sole manager of the small fund, can readily take such information into account, and allow your gut feelings a significant role in picking stocks. Assuming that you are competent (if you are not, you are not likely to have become a fund manager) your gut feelings, vague as they are, will improve your decisions.

Now, assume instead that you are one of, say, seven managers at a large fund. To induce your fund to buy a stock you have to convince at least three other managers that you are right. And while they will listen as you rattle off earnings data and other objective facts, they are less likely to pay attention to your subjective impressions and gut feelings. A large fund will, therefore, miss out on some valuable information that a small fund can use to evaluate stocks. As supporting evidence, the authors show that small funds hold a higher proportion of their assets than large firms do in stocks of local companies, and it is highly likely that, for local companies, soft information is more readily available than for more distant companies. Further evidence is that small funds get better returns from investing in local companies than large funds do. And when the authors distinguished among small funds by the number of managers they have, they find that those with a single manager invest significantly more in local companies. The data also suggest that they do better with their local investments than those small funds that have several managers.

14.3   The Slave Trade and African Economic Development

Although in recent decades economic growth in many less developed countries has accelerated dramatically, the growth rates of many African countries have been dreadful. Despite some improvement in the last few years, in some of these countries per capita income is now lower than it was a few decades ago. What is it that makes most of sub-Saharan Africa so resistant to growth? A natural place to look for an explanation is in the unusual history of Africa. Two events stand out in Africa's history: the slave trade and colonialism. It is not that slavery was unique to Africa, and perhaps it did not even exist in non-Islamic Africa prior to European contact, while it did exist on a massive scale in ancient Greece and Rome. When the Mongols conquered China in the thirteenth century they initially planned to kill all the inhabitants, but then they decided it would be more profitable to enslave them instead. And medieval Europe exported Caucasian slaves to northern Africa. What was special about African slavery was its extent. In addition to the well-known transportation of slaves to the New World, there were also lesser transportations to North Africa and India. One source estimates that by 1850 the slave trade had reduced the African population to one-half of what it otherwise would have been. Moreover, the African slave trade had an unusual feature: people of the same or similar ethnicity enslaved each other.

It is tempting to argue that this dreadful experience is the cause of Africa's underdevelopment. But is there any evidence that these two factors are directly related, with the export of slaves being the causal factor? Yes there is: as stated in a paper by Nathan Nunn,[6] who has traced the low present-day economic development of sub-Saharan Africa (which I will just refer to as Africa) to both population losses, and to the social and political disruptions caused by the slave trade.[7] To do that, he had to show that the occurrences of the slave trade and of subsequent unsatisfactory economic development is more than a mere coincidence. Simply to say that Africa suffered both massive slave exports and low current development is to base the entire argument on a single observation.

To avoid that, Nunn argues that if the export of slaves is a major cause of low development, then we should find a negative correlation between a country's current GDP and the proportion of its population that it lost to the slave trade. That required painstaking research into the historical record to estimate the number of slaves exported through various ports. And since some of the slaves sold at a particular port could have originated in the interior and not in the country where the port is located, these data on the export of slaves had to be adjusted by estimating the ethnicity of the slaves sold at various ports.

Nunn's next step was to use these adjusted data to regress a country's current per capita income on its population losses due to the slave trade (relative to the size of its territory), as well as on control variables – 13 of them in some regressions – that are also likely to affect economic development, such as its distance from the equator, the length of its coastline, average rainfall, humidity, oil production, gold production, percentage of the population that is Islamic, and the identity of the former colonizers. The resulting coefficient for slave exports is statistically significant and remains so in the robustness tests that Nunn presents. It is also substantively significant: a one standard deviation in estimated slave exports is associated with 0.36 to 0.62 standard deviations in a country's income, depending on the control variables used. Assuming that causality runs entirely from slave exports to income, this implies that a one standard deviation increase in slave exports lowered per capita income in the year 2000 for a country that was at the mean per capita income level ($1,249) by about 50 percent ($615).

But does causation run from slave exports to income, and not at all in the reverse direction? In principle, it could have run from low development to high slave exports, since it is possible that slave traders focused on the less developed African areas because these were less able to defend themselves. And if the factors that inhibited development at that time, say limited rainfall or high humidity, also reduce current incomes, this could be the explanation for the negative correlation between slave exports and current incomes. But Nunn cites the work of several historians to show that this is not what happened. Just the opposite. Initially, since a large part of European–African trade was in commodities and not in slaves, European traders focused on the more developed areas, because these had more resources to trade. And later, when slaves came to predominate, traders focused on the more densely settled areas, and these were likely to have been the more developed ones. (This implies that the regression coefficient for slave exports is likely to understate the effect of slave exports.) Moreover, the less developed areas may well have been the most violent ones, and hence the ones able to offer the fiercest resistance to slavers.

An alternative way in which causality could have run from a low level of income to a greater slave trade is that slave traders tended to concentrate on areas where slavery already existed, and these were more likely to be the less developed areas of Africa. But as Nunn points out, that is not plausible, because it is far from clear that in the non-Islamic parts of Africa slavery existed prior to the appearance of European slave traders.[b]

But even well-established correlations combined with favorable evidence on the direction of causation do not make a conclusive case for a hypothesis if there seems to be no plausible mechanism by which the purported cause can generate the claimed effect. Nunn, therefore, asks just how slave exports more than a hundred years ago could affect current income. His answer, which he calls "preliminary and exploratory," was that economic development requires a government that is effective, so that it can enforce the rule of law over a significant area, curb violence, etc. And the slave trade inhibited the development of such states. Since slaves were often acquired by villages or small kingdoms raiding each other, such slave raids made it more difficult for them to coalesce into larger units. It is, therefore, not surprising that the data show a positive correlation between the slave trade and ethnic fractionalization. This is important because the data also show that ethnic fractionalization has a strong effect on ethnic cohesion, the provision of public goods, such as roads, schools, clean water, etc., and the quality of government – factors that,

---

[b]   Another way Nunn dealt with the causality problem was to use "instrumental variables." This means that instead of regressing y on x, essentially, you regress it on a component of x, a component which you are sure cannot be caused by y. For example, in trying to measure the effect of government expenditures on GDP you run into the problem that not only do government expenditures affect GDP, but changes in GDP also affect government expenditures. One solution is to use only government defense expenditures on the reasonable assumption that these are caused by exogenous defense needs and not by changes in GDP. The instruments that Nathan employs, instead of slave exports, are measures of the distance between the source of slaves and the markets where they were ultimately sold. (Presumably, the closer the market is to a source of slaves, the more slaves are taken from there.) Here, causation is not a problem: for example, slaves were used extensively in the West Indies because the climate favored sugar plantations, and not because they are relatively close to Africa.

in turn, are important for economic development. Moreover, some slaves were acquired within a village or kingdom by accusing innocent people of crimes, so that they could then be sold into slavery as punishment. This, too, inhibited the development of cohesive and efficient states.

Is it plausible that these effects lingered on until the present day? As Nunn points out, there is a negative correlation between slave exports and the extent to which African states had developed politically in the nineteenth century. And other data show that the history of a state's political development is an important factor in its current economic development. Moreover, that the long-ago slave trade still exerts an influence on economic development is not all that surprising, because the political development of states was put on hold while they were colonies. And Nunn shows that the positive income gap between those states that exported many slaves, and those that exported fewer, grew in the post-colonial period, when it mattered more than in the colonial period how African states function on their own.

14.4   The Effect of Tax Changes on Real GDP

In 2001, President George W. Bush asked Congress for a substantial tax cut. As one of the major reasons, he cited the then ongoing recession, and thus the need to stimulate the economy. There are four potential problems with such a policy. One is that it may prove a great deal easier to cut taxes in a recession when a deficit is appropriate, than to raise them again later on when rising demand makes a balanced budget or a surplus appropriate. The second is that changing tax rates is a slow process, and by the time the tax cut has its major effect on the economy the recession may already be over, and excess demand, not inadequate demand, may now be the danger. The third is that our forecasts, both of the future course of the economy and of the effects of a tax cut, may not be reliable enough for a policy that tries to fine-tune aggregate demand. Finally, there is the basic question of whether even a substantial change in taxes has much effect on aggregate demand.

It might seem that the last of these questions is easy to answer: just regress changes in GDP on changes in tax revenues and see if the regression coefficient is both statistically and substantively significant. But that won't work. One reason is the problem of reverse causation – the computer combines into a single hodgepodge those cases where GDP rose because tax rates and hence tax receipts fell, thus leaving the public with more money to spend, and cases where tax revenue fell because GDP fell. Well, how about regressing changes in GDP on changes in tax *rates* rather than on tax *revenues*?

This gets rid of some of the reverse causation (tax receipts falling, although tax rates are constant, because GDP is falling), but it does not get rid of all reverse causation. It may have been a fall, or fear of a fall, in the growth rate of real GDP that caused Congress and the administration to cut tax rates, so that again causation runs from GDP to tax rates. What needs to done is to separate out those cases where tax rates were changed, not because of an actual or anticipated change in GDP, but for some other reason, and then use only these cases.

In a recent paper Christina and David Romer do just that.[8] Their first step was to plough through various sources that describe the reasons why tax rates were changed, such as the *Economic Report of the President*, the *Annual Report of the Secretary of the Treasury*, reports of the Congressional Budget Office, etc. They then selected for their main econometric analysis only those cases in which these sources listed reasons other than cyclical changes in GDP, thus hoping to end up only with cases in which the tax change was exogenous.

It is, of course, possible that these sources are not entirely forthright. For example, it seems likely that President Bush would have pushed for his signature tax cut even if there had not been a recession, and that he used the argument that a recession calls for a tax cut – an argument previously made by many liberals and old-fashioned Keynesians, and rejected by conservatives – merely as a rationalization. If such rationalizations caused Romer and Romer to classify some tax changes that were actually exogenous (that is, independent of fluctuations of GDP) as endogenous, that reduced the size of their sample, but did not bias their results. In addition, Romer and Romer also eliminated all tax changes that were motivated by changes in federal spending, because a change in expenditure has an effect on GDP that should not be intermingled with the effect of the associated tax change.

They then regressed the quarterly growth rate of real GDP on the exogenous tax changes in the current and the previous 12 quarters and on other variables. The resulting regression coefficients for the current and first 10 quarters have a negative sign, as they should, since a tax increase reduces real GDP. For lags 3 through 9 these coefficients are substantively significant, and some are also statistically significant, suggesting that it takes about 3 calendar quarters for the effect of a tax change on income to build up, and that it then becomes smaller after 9 quarters. For all the regression coefficients taken jointly, the t value is -3.5, thus making it highly implausible that they differ from zero only due to sampling error. The regression coefficient of their main regression (they ran several regressions) suggests that when it reaches its maximum the effect of an exogenous tax cut that is equal to 1 percent of real GDP is to raise real GDP by about 3 percent.

R^2 is low, very low, 0.09, but that is not surprising. One would hardly expect the 65 exogenous tax changes that occurred in the sample period, 1950 first quarter to 2006 second quarter, to explain a large proportion of the total change in real income over this period. Neither is it surprising that so few of the coefficients are statistically significant, because with the total effects of a tax change being spread over thirteen quarters, the effect in any single quarter taken in isolation is low relative to its standard error. This illustrates that to evaluate the success of a regression one should look at its R^2 and t values not in a mechanical way, but in a common-sense way that makes allowance for its particular circumstances.

After presenting these results, Romer and Romer tested them for robustness. One test was whether, due to the small size of their sample, perhaps just a single outlier can account for their entire results. They, therefore, ran their regressions four more times, each time excluding one of the four largest tax changes. Their overall results survived these tests. In another test, they included the lagged GDP growth rate as a control variable. Real GDP growth has considerable momentum. If it is high in one quarter, it is also likely to be high in the next quarter. Including the GDP growth rate of previous quarters in the regression is, therefore, useful to avoid the danger that this momentum effect is polluting the coefficient of the tax variable. But the inclusion of lagged GDP leaves Romer and Romer's results virtually unchanged.

Since monetary policy, too, has an important effect on real GDP, Romer and Romer included as another control variable two measures of shifts in Federal Reserve policy that were not themselves induced by the Fed's reaction to changes in tax rates, such as the Fed tightening monetary policy to offset some of the effect of excessive fiscal easing. This inclusion of a variable for changes in monetary policy reduces the coefficient of tax changes by about 20 percent, but still leaves it substantial. If changes in taxes are correlated with changes in government spending, that, too, could bias the coefficient for tax changes. Accordingly, Romer and Romer introduced a control variable for government spending, but it has little effect on the coefficient of tax changes. The final control variable that Romer and Romer considered is the change in oil prices. Because of the importance of oil prices and their erratic behavior, this is frequently done in macroeconomic regressions. But here this variable has only a trivial effect on the coefficient for tax increases. All in all, none of these control variables change Romer and Romer's previous finding of a substantively significant effect of tax increases on GDP.

Romer and Romer's result that a tax change equal to about 1 percent of GDP results, depending upon the particular regression used, in something like a 2 or 3 percent change in real GDP, could, in principle, be due either to a supply-side effect, that is, to a decline in incentives to work and save, or to a decline in aggregate demand. To see which it is, one can look at inflation and unemployment. If it is a supply-side effect one would not expect the unemployment rate to rise as taxes rise, people would simply work fewer hours or leave the labor force. And there is also little reason to expect a change in the inflation rate. But if the effect of a tax increase on real GDP comes about from the demand side, one would expect unemployment to increase since aggregate demand is falling, and for this increased unemployment to hold down wages, and thus reduce the inflation rate. And when Romer and Romer regressed unemployment on their tax variable they found that a tax increase raises unemployment. Moreover, it also reduces inflation, so that the demand-side explanation wins out. However, this does not necessarily mean that the level of taxation does not also have additional effects on incentives and hence on real GDP.

Romer and Romer also ask whether the effect of exogenous tax changes have varied over time. To do that they split their sample at the end of 1980 and fit separate regressions for these two periods. While not conclusive, these regressions suggest that the effect of tax changes has become weaker. Finally, Romer and Romer looked at the various components of aggregate demand and found that, when expressed in percentage terms, the effect on investment is much greater than the effect on consumption – a result I found surprising. They suggest that this may be due to firms reducing investment in response to changing economic conditions.

Although Romer and Romer thus show that tax policy can be used to change real GDP, this does not necessarily mean that it should be used to try to reduce cyclical unemployment. While I have no data, I suspect that the majority of economists believe it should not be, for the reasons mentioned above: the greater readiness to cut taxes during a recession than to raise them again during an expansion, the length of time it usually takes to change taxes, and the limited reliability of our forecasts. Indeed, in one important way Romer and Romer's results reinforce the case against using tax policy counter-cyclically by showing that it takes a long time for tax changes to have their major impact on GDP. In most of their regressions, it takes more than two years for the maximum effect to occur. By then, economic conditions are likely to have changed substantially.

NOTES

1   J. M. Keynes, *The General Theory of Employment, Interest and Money*, New York, Harcourt Brace, 1936.

2   Milton Friedman, *A Theory of the Consumption Function*, Princeton, Princeton University Press, 1957; Franco Modigliani and Richard Brumberg, "Utility and the Consumption Function: An Interpretation of Cross-section Data," in Kenneth Kurihara (ed.), *Post-Keynesian Economics*, London, George Allen and Unwin, 1955, pp. 388–436.

3   See Thomas Mayer, *Permanent Income, Wealth and Consumption*, Berkeley, University of California Press, 1972.

4   Joseph Chen, Harrison Hong, Ming Huang, and Jeffrey D. Kubik, "Does Fund Size Erode Mutual Fund Performance? The Role of Liquidity and Organization," *American Economic Review*, December 2004, pp. 1276–1302.

5   Ibid., p. 1290.

6   Nathan Nunn, "The Long-term Effects of Africa's Slave Trades," *Quarterly Journal of Economics*, forthcoming.

7   Ibid.

8   Christina and David Romer, "The Macroeconomic Effects of Tax Changes: Estimates Based on a New Measure of Fiscal Shocks," Department of Economics, University of California, Berkeley, unpublished working paper, 2007.

Epilogue

This book has presented several themes. A basic theme (see part I) is that economics does have much of value to add to discussions of economic and political issues, though its role is circumscribed by the need to bring in value judgments from the outside, as well as judgments about political and administrative feasibility. A second theme (part II) is that the emotive and careless language which is so often used in popular discussions of economics should be replaced by the more dispassionate and precise language employed by economists. A third theme (part III) is that a market economy is not a planless chaos, but despite some serious shortcomings, is a *relatively* efficient way – though a far from faultless one – of coordinating the actions of producers with the wishes of consumers. It also shows, through the use of many examples, that economics can elucidate many longer-run and indirect effects of various policies and proposed policies. The theme of the final section is the need for skepticism when presented with statistical results. Throughout all these strands, there runs an overall guiding theme: caveat lector.

I hope the book has persuaded you that in analyzing economic issues you can get quite far without much technical apparatus, just by systematically thinking about a problem in a common-sensical way. I also hope that you will want to go beyond this book. If so, here is an excellent way to learn economics: be your own teacher. As you read statements and arguments just ask yourself: "is this really so"? or "under what conditions is it true?," or else, "what indirect or longer-run effects would the proposed policy have?" Another way to train your economic intuition is to try to explain something which you observe in the ordinary course of living.

Here are two examples: right after Christmas many stores sell Christmas cards at half price. Why is that? Surely the cost of holding the cards in inventory until next Christmas cannot be all that great. A likely answer is that at the start of the Christmas season a store does not know which cards will appeal to its customers. At the end of the season it does know which cards are less valuable, and prices them accordingly. Here is a more difficult example: when you buy a flashlight you usually get two batteries with it, but these batteries are of low quality and soon run down. Why aren't they as good as the replacement batteries you can buy? One possible explanation is that the makers of flashlights try to save money and believe that their customers will not realize that they are getting low-quality batteries. But are customers really that ignorant? A better explanation, better because it does not require the implausible assumption that consumers are so ignorant they refuse to learn from experience, is that while some customers use their flashlights frequently and, therefore, require long-lasting batteries, others use them only infrequently. Their batteries may well become useless before they are drained of all their power as the battery acid starts to leak. For these people, it is efficient to buy cheap batteries that do not last long. Such people are also likely to buy replacement batteries less frequently than other people do. It is, therefore, efficient for the batteries that come with a flashlight to be of lower quality than are replacement batteries. Robert Frank's *The Economic Naturalist* (New York, Basic Books, 2007) has many other such examples, as has Charles Wheelan's *Naked Economics* (New York, W. W. Norton, 2002). But try to find your own examples, because thinking is often more fun, and is a better way of learning than reading.

However, reading does help: so here is a list of books and other sources. These books should convince you that the "dismal science" is not so dismal after all, and that there are many counter-examples to the generalization that "economists can't write." I offer this list with trepidation. There are surely many books that should be included that I have not read or have failed to appreciate. Moreover, any such list will soon be outdated. And besides, different people enjoy different books. But anyway here in alphabetical order are a few suggestions in addition to the two books just mentioned.

Alan Blinder in *Hard Heads and Soft Hearts* (Reading, MA, Addison-Wesley, 1987) makes a well-argued case for liberal policies, focusing on macroeconomics. It is clearly written and to the point.

If you think that economics is all rational-behavior models read Diane Coyle's *The Soulful Science* (Princeton, Princeton University Press, 2007). It will introduce you to the new world of modern economics that takes account of cognitive errors and biases.

Robert Frank has written many excellent books on economics for the general reader. Several are powerful criticisms of our "winner-take-all" regime, starting with his *Choosing the Right Pond* (New York, Oxford University Press, 1885).

David Friedman's, *The Hidden Order* (New York, Harper, 1996) and Steven Landsburg's *The Armchair Economist* (New York, Free Press, 1993) provide cogent reasons for the efficacy of the price mechanism, with Friedman's book being a bit more technical. In a subsequent book, *More Sex is Safer Sex* (Landsburg, Free Press, 2007) throws an economist's spotlight on many topics.

Steven Levitt and Stephen Dubner's *Freakonomics* (New York, William Morrow, 2005) is that rarity of rarities, a deserved bestseller on economics which is other than a textbook. For a serious economics book, its success has been phenomenal. It is full of fascinating stories that illustrate the hidden workings of rational utility maximization within a seemingly disorganized world.

Melvin Reder has produced a somewhat more technical book, *Economics, the Culture of a Controversial Science* (Chicago, University of Chicago Press, 1999) which is particularly good at showing the progress that certain sub-fields of economics, such as finance, have achieved, and at standing back to look at the methodology of economics.

This book has been sympathetic to free markets. For a well-argued opposite point of view, see Tom Slee's *No One Makes You Shop at Wal-Mart* (Toronto, Between the Lines, 2006). It brings out some sociological and ethical issues that lurk between the scenes of a market economy.

Thomas Sowell has written many books on economics that are insightful and enjoyable: for example, his *Applied Economics* (New York, Basic Books, 2004), which like many of his other books, contains essays on individual topics rather than a systematic exposition. This is useful for those who lack the time to read the entire book. A more recent book of his is *Economic Facts and Fallacies* (New York, Basic Books, 2008). His *Vision of the Anointed* (New York, Basic Books, 1995) is a powerful indictment of the political attitude of "right-thinking" people, while his *A Conflict of Visions* (New York, Basic Books, 2007) grounds many disagreements on current economics and political issues in a fundamental distinction between an unconstrained and constrained vision of humans and human-reasoning capacity.

There are also several excellent books that help you to avoid the perils of bogus statistics. If you don't believe that a book dealing with statistics can be a wonderful read look at Darrel Huff's *How to Lie with Statistics* (New York, W. W. Norton, 1954). Three others well worth reading are: Joel Best, *Damned Lies and Statistics* (Berkeley, University of California Press, 2001); Robert Hooke, *How to Tell Liars from Statisticians* (New York, Marcel Dekker,

1983); and David Murray, Joel Schwartz and Robert Lichter, *It Ain't Neces-sarily So* (New York, Bowman and Littlefield, 2001). Two books that are not explicitly on statistics, but should give you much insight into statistics – and into correct investment decisions – besides being excellent reads (with many caustic comments on financial "experts" and economists), are Nassim Taleb's *Fooled by Randomness* (New York, Random House, 2004) and his *The Black Swan* (New York, Random House, 2007). Several Federal Reserve Banks have informative (and free) reviews largely intended for the non-economist, available on the web as well as in print. Among them are *Current Issues* of the Federal Reserve Bank of New York, the *Business Review* of the Federal Reserve Bank of Philadelphia, the *Review* of the Federal Reserve Bank of St. Louis, the *Economic Letter* of the Federal Reserve Bank of Dallas and the weekly *Economic Letter* of the Federal Reserve Bank of San Francisco. These banks, as well as the Federal Reserve Board of Governors, also make their working papers available. The Federal Reserve Bank of St. Louis provides access to its large data base.

Economists have numerous professional journals. Most of their papers are accessible only to those with graduate training in economics, and frequently only to those in the same subfield. But the *Journal of Economic Perspectives* published by the American Economic Association carries many non-technical, yet authoritative, articles, often in the form of symposia on topics such as African economic development, organ transplants, and anti-trust policy. The *Journal of Economic Literature* and the *Journal of Economic Surveys* carry survey articles that summarize much previous research. The former is also the profession's leading source for book reviews.

Strange as it may seem, in economics there is often a lag of several years between the time a paper is written and its publication. Economists, therefore, rely on access to unpublished working papers. Many can be obtained for a small fee from the National Bureau of Economic Research (www.nber.org/publications).

Aaron Schiff's website, "Economics Blogs Ranking," provides an updated listing on the most popular economics blogs. To that list I would like to add Ecobrowser.

A great deal of information on economics ranging from the latest GDP statistics to jokes about economists is available at the American Economic Association's website, "Resources for Economists."

Index